Sarah Levinson

TORN FROM MY HEART

TORN FROM MY HEART

The True Story of a Mother's Desperate
Search for Her Stolen Children

PATSY HEYMANS WITH
WILLIAM AND MARILYN HOFFER

WARNER BOOKS

A Time Warner Company

First published in 1995 in Paris, France, by Éditions Lafont-Fixot

Warner Books, Inc., 1271 Avenue of the Americas, New York, NY 10020

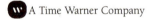 A Time Warner Company

Printed in the United States of America
First U.S. Printing: June 1996
10 9 8 7 6 5 4 3 2 1

Library of Congress Cataloging-in-Publication Data

Heymans, Patsy.
    [Kidnappes!   English]
    Torn from my heart : the true story of a mother's desperate search
for her stolen children / Patsy Heymans with William and Marilyn Hoffer.
        p.   cm.
    ISBN 0-446-52006-3
    1. Heymans, Patsy.   2. Kidnapping, Parental—Belgium—Case
studies.   I. Hoffer, William. II. Hoffer, Marilyn Mona.
III. Title.
HV6604.B42H49413   1996
362.82'97'092—dc20
    [B]   95-50997
                                                                  CIP

Book design: H. Roberts

I dedicate this book to all others who can relate to my story.

Introduction

In 1986, when I brought my daughter Mathob home at last, I knew next to nothing about the abduction of children by their own parents. I assumed my own case was unique. I had no inkling that "Not without My Daughter!"—the words I had cried out to my husband in my agony—had been uttered by many other women before me.

Patsy Heymans is one of those women.

She was young, confident, and in love. She adored Israel, the adopted country to which her husband, Chaim Edwar, had brought her. Then suddenly everything went horribly wrong. Her lover became her torturer. Israel turned into a prison for Patsy Heymans, as her freedom of thought and action dwindled to nothing.

Eventually the lives of Chaim and Patsy were transformed into a relentless, cruel confrontation. Their existence became a death struggle between two antagonists, one of whom was determined to crush and enslave the other.

When the slave rose up against her paranoid tormentor and tried to rescue her children, her husband stalked, harassed, and threatened her. Finally he wreaked the only vengeance he knew to be absolute, unanswerable. He snatched away the couple's three children and vanished with them. There was nothing fatherly about this act, nor was there any serious intent on Chaim's part to raise his family himself. Marina, Simon, and Moriah were sacrificed upon the altar of his vengeance.

But Patsy Heymans refused to yield. A fragile young mother bereft of her children, she withstood unspeakable mental anguish. Her suffering ground on, day after day, month after month; she weathered six years with only the vaguest indication as to what had become of her children. It was not until her husband's arrest that she gained the certainty that they were still alive, somewhere in the world, in the care of people unknown to her.

In reality Patsy's children had been abducted not only by their father but also by a religious sect based in the United States, which gave him financial and logistical support. Operating outside the law, this sect appropriated Patsy's children, claiming it was protecting them from "corruption" by the outside world. Thereafter the Heymans children were brainwashed with suffocating, alienating doctrines. They forfeited all contact with their natural family.

On December 11, 1985, when Patsy Heymans's children were kidnapped, their ages were six, four, and three. From that day on, Patsy scoured the world to find them, crossing the Atlantic scores of times, following up every clue, and enduring every conceivable form of blackmail, moral torture, and psychological pressure.

She never broke.

I saw with my own eyes that Patsy's maternal instinct was strong enough to move mountains. She earned the deep admiration of all of us with whom she came into contact. Her own family stood solidly behind her, and there can be no question that without the financial help of her relatives, she might never had been able to transcend laws and frontiers, or convince the FBI to do battle on her behalf against the powerful forces conspiring to imprison Marina, Simon and Moriah.

I am also lost in admiration for the sheer toughness of Patsy's three children and the way they survived their hideous ordeal. Will they ever forget the moment when Patsy timidly opened the door of the FBI office in New York and said: "I am your mother"? I doubt it. For Patsy is much more than a mother. She is their lost childhood. She embodies a love which never lost hope, which refused to abandon them. Yet when she held out her arms that day, they still dared not go to her.

Many people around the world, in the name of religion and who knows what else, deliberately set out to turn the very young into mindless fanatics. Marina, Simon, and Moriah, had it not been for the love and loyalty of their relatives, stood no chance of escaping this fate. Yet in abduction cases like theirs, religion is never more than a pretext. The fact is that sects offer support and a way out. In the name of religion, they persuade parents that they really are acting for the "good" of their offspring.

After her six years of struggle, Patsy Heymans had to teach her children how to live normal lives. They learned to go to ordinary schools; they learned again how to talk, to think, and to show affection without fear or constraint.

During their long confinement, people had tried—without success—to convince the Heymans children that their mother was dead. This extreme psychological cruelty was the doing of their father, who never imagined that a woman like Patsy would rather die than abandon her children to a world empty of her love.

Today, the story of Patsy, Marina, Simon, and Moriah, is a symbol of hope for parents who, against all odds, continue to fight against child abduction.

—Betty Mahmoody
Michigan, July 1995

This is a true story.

The characters are authentic, the events real. But the names and identifying characteristics of a few individuals have been disguised in order to protect them and their families against the possibility of retribution. These characters are: Samuel Katz, my father's friend in Tel Aviv; Rachel, my friend in Israel; "the Duchess"; the Browns; the undercover agent Nechemiah; Sarah, the Hasidic woman in Brooklyn whose nine children were taken from her; the informants called Abraham, Judas, Source, Echo, and Samaritan.

From time to time, throughout the course of the events described in these pages, I have been accused of anti-Semitism. Nothing could be further from the truth. As it happened, I found myself in physical, mental, and emotional conflict with one Jewish man and a few of his allies. My battle was only with them, and it had nothing to do with religion or race. For my antagonists to charge me with anti-Semitism is merely a convenient—and false—defense of their own illegal acts. I am quite willing to let God be my judge.

TORN FROM MY HEART

Prologue

At 1:00 A.M. on a misty autumn night in 1977, the shadowy figure of a nineteen-year-old man appeared on the sidewalk directly across the street from my family's spacious three-story house, located on Avenue des Fleurs in the exclusive Woluwe Saint Pierre community on the southeast side of Brussels, Belgium. His strong-featured face was clean-shaven and his dark hair was clipped short. He held the stub of a Camel cigarette against his lips, but its soft orange glow was insufficient to illuminate his olive complexion. The pack of Camels rested in the palm of his left hand along with a disposable plastic lighter. He wore a tight elastic bandage on his right elbow.

The young man's penetrating brown eyes stared past the bank of manicured shrubs, flanked by three heavy, white iron gates that guarded our yard. He studied the house. He must have been impressed with the comforts of our lives, so much in contrast to those available at his own parents' home in the dusty, desertlike countryside east of Tel Aviv. A home like this was something to which he aspired.

His gaze rose to the wide-open window on the second floor. He assumed it was an attic window, but, in fact, it was the bedroom where, amid restless dreams, his image had begun to fade from my sixteen-year-old fantasies. Deep inside I knew that I still loved him, but many months had passed since his last letter, and I was convinced that he had forgotten all about me. How different it would have been if he had.

Two of his own pronouncements best characterize this mysterious Israeli. When I had first met him in Jerusalem—more than a year before this night—he had proclaimed brazenly, "I'm the best." The statement covered any and every form of human endeavor, and he truly believed it. For a very long time, so did I.

Six years and much pain would pass before he would utter the second statement, the one that proved far more truthful. We would be together in the living room of this same house on Avenue des Fleurs. Our three small children would be upstairs, under the watchful eyes of my mother. My father would be in the kitchen—banished from this discussion at my request, but ready to leap to my defense, should I call out.

By then, Chaim Edwar would have changed his name to Chaim Yarden. The brown eyes would be just as intense but the voice deeply sinister, as he promised: "Whatever it takes . . . I will destroy your life."

Over the ensuing decade he would prove that, at the task of destroying my life, he was, indeed, the very best.

1

Père Edgard slid a second helping of crispy-brown *frites* onto his plate. With a practiced right-hand grip he sliced into his steak. Wielding his fork left-handed, the tines inverted, he popped the meat into his mouth and, as he chewed, considered my mother's request.

My fifteen-year-old heart pounded in anticipation.

For as long as I could remember, the jovial Roman Catholic priest had joined us at our dinner table every Wednesday evening. He was like a member of the family, sharing Christmas and other celebrations with us. In general, I did not care much for the strict, humorless nuns who dominated my school life, or the parish priests I had known, but the open-minded and enlightened Père Edgard was different. He ran a halfway house for troubled teenagers and had a natural and relaxed ability to relate to my generation. When he heard a joke or a story that he thought was funny, he quickly wrote it down in a small notebook so that he could remember and retell it. To me, he seemed more of a grandfather than he did a priest. My parents enjoyed the twinkle in his eyes and his lively sense of humor, and my devoutly Catholic mother admired the sacrifices of his life. My parents trusted him implicitly, and when he had first mentioned that he was planning an Easter-week trip to the Holy Land, they saw an opportunity to lift me from my depression. They had, perhaps, already discussed this matter with him and had now decided to address it in my presence. As Papa refilled Père Edgard's glass with wine, Maman asked, "Would it be possible for Patsy to go with you?"

The priest was aware that this was not an idle request. He knew that my parents were troubled by the combination of my physical complaints and my severe tendency toward teenage rebellion. During the past two years, changing hormones had created a litany of health problems for me. My period came erratically and, when it did, the cramping was so severe that I could barely walk. Sometimes I came home from school doubled over in pain. A doctor prescribed medication but, instead of helping, it caused rapid weight gain. I was a small girl, only five foot two, but I ballooned to one hundred and forty pounds. My three brothers teased me without mercy, calling me "fat boat" or "huge truck" and making oinking sounds. I felt, as we say in Belgium, "very bad in my skin."

The rapid weight gain caused me to suffer heart and kidney problems. Another physician placed me on a strict diet and ordered me to sleep for at least nine hours every night. I experienced extreme mood swings and cried hysterically. For a time, I took as many as sixteen medications daily. My physical problems were clearly associated with my female chemistry, and that gave rise to a particular fear that I would never be able to have children. Nightmares plagued me. Periodically I rebounded, but always the problems returned.

I was also, by nature, a headstrong, stubborn girl who knew how to exploit her position as the only daughter in the family. Maman has said: "Since you were three years old, when you wanted something, you fought until you got it." I argued constantly with my brothers and parents, especially Papa; we both shared a strong-willed determination to have things our way. I never used drugs or abused alcohol—I did not even smoke cigarettes—but my parents and I clashed on almost every subject, notably, religion and education. I refused to accompany them to mass, and I was once expelled from school for losing my temper and telling a nun to go to hell. I chose the easiest possible courses of study, and I did not apply myself.

Like Belgium itself, I am an amalgam of different cultures. French-speaking Belgians tend to be romantics; Dutch-speaking Belgians are realists, known for their serious, Teutonic-style devotion to duty. My father, Jacques Heymans, does not quite fit into either category. He was raised in the Dutch-speaking portion of Belgium and studied in Dutch-language schools, but at home the family spoke French. Throughout his career, he was a prominent businessman, involved in the export of military technology to various world governments. He has a deep, raspy, and resonant voice even in the calmest of circumstances. When he is angry, it is a voice that can shake the walls. But in general he is a gregarious and generous man with an easy, frequent, infectious laugh. His passion is the hunt.

My mother is a French-Belgian woman of extremely high energy. She wears her emotions close to the surface and cries when she is happy as well as sad. Her name is Hélène, but everyone calls her Mizou—a childhood nickname of forgotten origin. A gracious and accomplished hostess, she is happiest when she is surrounded by family and friends. She is also quite beautiful. Blond hair highlights her fine features, and her tall, thin frame moves with vitality and grace.

The combination of my father's business contacts and my mother's flair for entertaining made our home a magnet for people from all over the world. The immense concrete complex between the center of Brussels and the airport, which houses the NATO headquarters, brings the country a steady stream of international military personnel and defense contractors. Americans, Britishers, Canadians, Pakistanis, Indians, Egyptians, and various other nationals appeared regularly at our dinner table.

For some reason that I could never clearly explain, Israeli visitors held a special appeal for me. My father developed business relationships with a number of Israelis, and I found them to be particularly intelligent and charming. And beneath the surface, they radiated a strong sense of character and purpose. One of the happiest times of my youth had occurred the previous year when we took a family holiday to Israel. The moment the jetliner landed at Tel Aviv's Ben Gurion Airport, I felt that I was *home*. While my parents and brothers viewed the tourist sites, I studied the young people. In Europe, teenagers were exhibiting their rebellious natures by flaunting long hair and wearing outrageously sloppy clothes. But the Israeli youth were clean-cut and mature, dutiful sons and daughters of the bold, brave pioneers who were determined to carve out an existence amid hostile neighbors. I was very impressed with them.

From that time on, my pocket money disappeared in exchange for any newspaper or book that could tell me more about Israel. I was lackadaisical in school unless I managed to devise a study project associated with the Holy Land. In the evenings I could often be found lounging on the floor of my bedroom, ignoring the schoolbooks that were strewn about and, instead, devouring yet another story concerning Israel. It was a fascination that was, perhaps, the only passion of my early teen years.

I longed to visit Israel again. My parents had agreed that if I earned half the air fare, they would pay the rest. The strength of my resolve motivated me to accept every available baby-sitting job; once a week I cleaned windows at the home of a German woman. My savings grew steadily until I had, indeed, earned half the cost of my ticket. My parents were willing to fulfill the bargain, yet they could not send a young girl off to Israel alone. Now, Père Edgard's Holy Week holiday appeared to be a godsend. The priest was an adult whom I liked and respected; my parents considered him the ideal chaperone.

Maman's dinner-table question, "Would it be possible for Patsy to go with you?" hung in the air for several moments as Père Edgard pondered his decision. He leaned forward to grasp his wineglass and took a sip, weighing the alternatives. Would he prefer the luxury of a quiet pilgrimage? Or was it his duty to God and our family to help yet another troubled teenager? His fingers scratched at his close-cropped, snow-white hair.

Finally he leaned back in his chair, a grin spreading across his face. His blue eyes sparkled. "Yes, of course," he said. "Patsy would be welcome."

2

During the first few days in Israel, I felt ill and weak. Then, during Good Friday services at a Roman Catholic church in Jerusalem's Old City, I grew faint and nauseous. Père Edgard sent me back to our hotel.

The next morning I was still uncomfortable and not up to an outing. We planned to visit sites in both the Old City and Bethlehem this day, but I could see from Père Edgard's expression that he was resolved to attend to his responsibility as chaperone. He said he would spend the day in his adjoining room, so that he could look in on me from time to time.

"No, no," I protested. "I just need rest." The idea that I was disrupting his long-planned holiday made me feel even worse. "You go ahead," I insisted. I told him that if I felt better I would meet him at 2:00 P.M. at a designated spot in the Old City; from there we would visit Bethlehem together.

Satisfied with this plan, Père Edgard set off on his own.

Feeling much improved after a nap, I decided to keep the afternoon appointment. I pulled on my faded denim jeans and a baggy white shirt, caught my shoulder-length, dark-blond hair into a ponytail, and slipped my feet into wooden sandals.

In the lobby I asked the concierge how I could catch a bus to the Old City. He directed me to a bus stop a short distance from the hotel. I waited for quite some time in the shade of a small shelter, but no bus came. By now, I knew that I would be late for my meeting with Père Edgard, but I hoped that he would wait for me. More minutes passed. Still, there was no bus. Suddenly I remembered that it was Shabbat—the Sabbath—the period of time between sundown on Friday and sundown on Saturday that religious Jews observe with quiet reverence. Of course there were no buses.

I returned to the hotel and explained the problem to the concierge. He was embarrassed that he too had forgotten it was Shabbat, and he arranged for me to take a hotel shuttle bus into the Old City. The driver let me off at the spot where I was to meet Père Edgard.

The priest was nowhere to be seen. I checked my watch. It was already well past two o'clock. As time passed, I realized he must have concluded that I was still too ill to join him. Apparently he had already left for Bethlehem.

Aimlessly I made my way through narrow streets lined with high-walled courtyards that sheltered clusters of houses. I walked through the shouk, the sprawling area of markets and tourist shops. Just past the Porat Josef Synagogue I came to the famous Wailing Wall, part of the retaining wall on the southwest side of the remains of Solomon's Temple. More than one hundred and fifty feet long and nearly sixty-five feet high, the massive structure dwarfed me. Despite my spiritual apathy, the sight filled me with awe. This is the holiest place on earth for Jews, and it is also revered by two other religions. It was here that the baby Jesus was presented in the temple; it was here that He cast out the money changers and was tempted by Satan. And the area above and beyond the wall, after Mecca and Medina, may be the most important shrine of Islam.

I wandered about the Old Temple precinct. Dutifully I removed my sandals and entered the silver-domed al-Aqsa Mosque and the elaborate, gold-emblazoned Dome of the Rock Mosque; both are twelve centuries old. Inside the Dome of the Rock, I saw the visible portion of the large boulder that gives the mosque its name. Although Mohammed never traveled to Jerusalem, the faithful believe it was from here that he ascended to heaven on a white horse.

It was not until I stepped back outside that I began to think about my predicament. How would I get back to the hotel? On Shabbat, Jerusalem closes down almost completely. Only a few taxis were available—most of them driven by Arabs—but I did not have a single Israeli pound in my purse anyway. Where and when would Père Edgard return? I could not understand Hebrew. If I was able to find one of the scarce taxis that worked on Shabbat, could I persuade the driver that the hotel concierge would pay the fare?

My confusion must have been obvious.

Suddenly, from behind my back, I heard a man's voice ask in English, "Do you need help?"

My English skills were limited, but I knew the meaning of the word *help*. At first I tried to ignore the questions of a stranger, but he persisted. "Do you need help? Do you need help?" The tone was warm and friendly, the volume low.

I turned and studied the source of the voice. He was a slim but muscular young man who stood more than six inches taller than me. He wore the dull-green uniform of the Israeli military and had a sharply handsome face, with a smooth olive complexion. He was the image of the strong, capable soldier in what was, perhaps, the world's most respected army. Cigarette smoke curled into his dark brown eyes, causing him to blink.

There were people all around us, so I did not feel threatened. The young man's military uniform was also reassuring. The fact was, I did need help, so I decided to respond to this soldier's friendly initiative. I tried to speak with him in French, but he did not understand. So, in halting English and with great difficulty, I explained, "Yes, well, I need to go back to my hotel."

He listened patiently and politely. He introduced himself as Chaim Edwar. Although communication was difficult, since English was a second language to us both, he was able to explain that he was a paratrooper in the Israeli Army. We talked a bit about how I had found my way here alone and what I had seen. He was glad to be of assistance, he said, and if I wished, he would show me other parts of the city and then escort me safely back to my hotel.

This seemed like the best of my limited alternatives, so I agreed.

We strolled off through the Old City. His English was better than mine, so I let him chatter as I nodded; I understood only about one word in ten. I glanced down at my jeans and baggy shirt. I could not believe that I was worthy of his attention. I saw myself as an overweight and rather unattractive, pimply-faced teenager, yet here I was, alone in an exotic city, strolling with this handsome young soldier. If I had sat down to sketch the ideal man, this dashing paratrooper's image would have appeared.

Still in the Arabic section of the Old City, we stopped briefly at a café. Chaim had coffee; I sipped a glass of juice. I learned that he was eighteen, more than three years older than me, and he seemed far more sophisticated.

"You have been to Israel before?" he asked.

As best I could, I told him of our family's earlier trip, how much I enjoyed it, and a little bit about how I was able to return. "Your family travels a lot?" he asked with interest.

"Yes," I said, and told him of some of the other places where we had vacationed in the past—Spain, Scotland, Yugoslavia, and France. Chaim asked many questions about these trips and seemed impressed that we had the means to travel so extensively.

We walked together through narrow streets sandwiched between high stone buildings, many with connecting archways overhead, until we reached the King David Hotel, where we caught a shuttle bus back to my own hotel. The driver let us off on the main roadway at the bottom of a hill, and we walked up the winding path that approached the hotel from the rear, past a grotto carved out of the hillside, and around to the tree-lined courtyard that guarded the hotel's entrance. A perfect gentleman, Chaim bade me a gracious good-day.

As I entered the hotel, I turned to watch him leave. The afternoon had turned into a magical interlude, and I wondered if I would ever see him again.

Père Edgard had already returned to the hotel and was worried by my absence. I told him how, after realizing that I had missed our rendezvous, I had walked about the Old City by myself and ended my tale by explaining vaguely that "somebody had brought me back." To avoid too many questions, I purposely left out details.

The next morning, as I prepared to attend Easter service with Père Edgard, the concierge called my room and said, "There is someone here to see you." With a mixture of confusion and anticipation, I hurried downstairs. It really was Chaim! and he invited me to go for another walk with him. I desperately wanted to say yes, but I knew that Père Edgard would disapprove of a private excursion with an Israeli soldier. I thought: What worked yesterday might work today. I asked Chaim to wait for me on the winding road at the rear of the hotel, and I hurried back to my room.

"I'm still not feeling very well," I lied to the priest. "I'm afraid that I might get ill again in church."

Père Edgard agreed that I should continue to rest.

"I might take a walk," I said. "Fresh air might help."

Père Edgard went off to Easter mass, unsuspecting.

Once freed from the watchful eyes of my chaperone, I rushed to meet Chaim. We walked south on Rav Uziel Street to the suburb of Bayit VeGan until we came to the grounds of the Holyland Hotel. "I have something to show you," Chaim said.

There, in an area encompassing about two and a half acres, was a replica of Jerusalem as it appeared in the time of the Second Temple, soon after the reign of Herod the Great: the time of Christ. It was fashioned of sandy-colored stone, marble, and metal, making a protective roof unnecessary. The vista stretched from the high point of the Tower of Psephimus to the lowland Kidron Valley. The model was properly oriented to the compass points, accentuating the effects of sunlight and shade. I felt swept back in time. I wondered: Why couldn't the nuns at school make history come alive like this?

For the next few days the illness alibi served me well. Each morning after Père Edgard went about his holiday activities, I met Chaim behind the hotel. I was so smitten with the handsome young soldier that it did not matter where we went or what we did. We walked together through the wide streets, past three- and four-story apartment buildings. When Chaim explained that the ground floor often served as a bomb shelter, I was even more impressed with the spirit of the Israeli people. Most of the buildings featured small but exquisite flower gardens. In the parks, gnarled olive trees and dark-green cypress flourished. We occasionally stopped for an ice cream or a cool drink.

Chaim chattered on and on in an easy, self-assured manner, endlessly repeating his points for emphasis. From what I could understand, he seemed to talk a lot about the army. He was proud of his status as a paratrooper and said, over and over again, "I'm the best." I missed much of the meaning of his conversations, but it did not matter. His energy and enthusiasm were contagious. He asked questions about my family and our lifestyle, and I told him about my father's passion for the hunt and the country house that we owned in Nassogne, in the Ardennes, not far from Bastogne. He listened intently, and I felt very proud and flattered.

This is my first real boyfriend, I said to myself. Although I saw him only for brief periods of time, his image was constantly in my mind. I felt: *La vie en rose* (life is rosy).

One day we walked downhill from the hotel to a military cemetery with graves marked by the Star of David. Chaim pointed to a series of low-rise buildings in the distance and suggested that we walk over to his friend's apartment, "to see how the Israelis live."

"Sure," I said.

As we passed a large expanse of vacant lots, I suddenly felt wary. Is this the right thing to do? I wondered. What would Père Edgard think? But I told myself that I was being overly suspicious. There was no chance that we would be alone together in the apartment. If Chaim's friend was not home, how could we get inside?

After a brisk fifteen-minute hike we reached the apartments. Chaim led me upstairs, located the proper flat, and pulled a key from his pocket. With a grin on his face, he explained that his friend allowed him to stay in the apartment whenever he was in Jerusalem.

It was too late to turn back, and if I protested I would feel embarrassed. I told myself that everything was okay, that Chaim's intentions were honorable. He slid the key into the door, opened it, and we entered. Chaim's friend glanced up from the sofa and greeted us.

Chaim appeared to be surprised—and disappointed—that his friend was at home. He showed me around the unremarkable apartment, composed of just a few small rooms with a low trundle-bed sofa in the living room. We drank a cup of tea. After staying barely ten minutes, we left.

After several days of such clandestine excursions, Père Edgard grew suspicious. Perhaps someone at the hotel told him about the dark Israeli paratrooper who was hanging about, or perhaps he caught a glimpse himself. In any event, he had spent his life working with teenagers, and he knew the ways of quiet rebellion. In a soft but insistent manner, he suggested that I introduce him to my new friend. And so, I was forced to present Chaim formally to my chaperone. Père Edgard extended the hand of friendship and said simply, "Nice to meet you."

"Nice to meet you," Chaim replied.

"He seems nice. He's very polite," Père Edgard said to me after the brief meeting. The expression in the old priest's eyes conveyed a combination of amusement and a bit of apprehension.

The day before our departure, late in the afternoon, Chaim again met me on the winding access road behind the hotel. We walked the short distance to the cavelike area in the side of the hill. There, in our small, private world, we solemnly promised to write to one another. We exchanged addresses on scraps of paper. Chaim tucked my address into the breast pocket of his uniform shirt. I stood with my back to the wall of the grotto as he moved slowly toward me, bent low, and kissed me for a precious few seconds. Then he gave me a small military patch from his uniform, "to remember me." I clipped it to the strap of my purse.

I walked back to the hotel, alone and despondent; it was only a short distance, but it seemed like a million miles. Suddenly, life was no longer rosy. *Broyer du noir* (I felt as though my world had ended).

3

At home in Belgium, I waited by the mailbox like a lovesick puppy. Very quickly I was rewarded with my first letter from Chaim, penned in bold, handprinted strokes. I dashed up to my room with it and opened my English/French dictionary. The effort of translating the words allowed me to savor them. "I miss you. I love you. I miss you. *I miss you*," Chaim wrote. Some of the phrases were underlined so heavily that the imprint could be seen pages later.

I wrote back immediately, and we settled into a frequent correspondence. The letters usually arrived on Wednesday, and I anxiously counted the days of the week. When a letter came, I raced to my room with it. As I cuddled with my brown, long-haired midget dachshund, Princesse, I read and reread the letters. Chaim's words were predictably sweet and passionate, containing little news but many simple professions of his affection, repeated at length.

Maman noticed the letters, of course, and she had undoubtedly been briefed by Père Edgard as well. "What does he write?" she asked. I supplied a vague answer, and she did not intrude further. Our family is very respectful of privacy. She assumed that I was in the throes of a fleeting crush that would soon run its course.

One day a small package arrived, addressed in Chaim's distinctive handwriting. It was secured with layer upon layer of tape. Maman watched as I sat at the long wooden table in the kitchen, impatiently trying to pull at the tape. I finally resorted to scissors. Inside the package I found a small note. When I saw the words "I love you" and realized that Maman was looking over my shoulder, I quickly covered up the message. Beneath the note was a triangular plastic pendant bearing Chaim's zodiac sign: Scorpio. I immediately fastened it to my purse strap, next to the precious military patch.

My feelings for Chaim increased my passion for Israel. I badgered my parents until they agreed to enroll me in twice-weekly Hebrew lessons.

I continued to write to Chaim faithfully, but gradually the intervals between his return letters grew longer and longer. When he stopped writing completely, I was heartbroken.

My sixteenth birthday came and went. Easter approached and I tried, in vain, not to think about my lost love in Israel. Month after dreary month passed.

In September my parents enrolled me in private school for secretarial training. I was overwhelmed by the pace of the study and lacked the discipline and maturity necessary to succeed. I was bored, frustrated, lonely, and filled with self-doubt.

Such was my mood when Chaim, unannounced and unexpected, arrived in Brussels. Only later did I learn that he spent that first night pacing the sidewalk and surveying our home on Avenue des Fleurs.

As I came down the stairs from the second-floor classroom of the secretarial school, I was startled to see Maman standing on the landing. Something must be terribly wrong, I thought. Then, with a mischievous look in her eyes and a hint of mystery in her voice, she announced, "Look who came." She stepped aside to reveal Chaim standing behind her, smiling broadly. He was dressed casually, in jeans and a long-sleeved shirt. His left hand held the ever-present pack of Camels and a lighter. Earlier in the day he had simply appeared on our doorstep.

I was excited and flattered that he had traveled so far to see me, but I was also taken by surprise and quite angry at him for not answering my letters. I murmured a shy hello. We sat together in the backseat of the car. Chaim's hand inched toward mine, until he clasped it. Glancing into the rearview mirror, Maman saw this display of affection, and I knew by the expression on her face that she was a bit uncomfortable. So was I. The three of us rode in silence.

When we arrived at home, Chaim explained that he had been unable to write to me because he had injured his arm during military maneuvers. He showed me the elastic bandage he wore on his right elbow and displayed scars that testified to a soldier's bravery. Even now, he said with pride, he had to receive extraordinary permission to travel from Israel to visit me. That news made me feel very special. I thought: He came all this way just to see me!

The constant parade of guests through our home made it second nature for my parents to extend an invitation for Chaim to move out of his hotel and stay with us during the remainder of his visit to Belgium. Maman prepared a bedroom on the second floor.

Over the years my mother had been careful not to serve pork to those dinner guests who followed the Jewish dietary laws. But she knew other Jews who ate pork—and she wondered about Chaim. "Does he keep kosher?" she asked.

"No," I replied.

That evening at the dinner table, as Chaim reached for a second portion, my mother smiled and remarked, "I'm glad you like the pork."

Chaim almost choked. "Don't say that it is pork," he said sharply.

Maman was very confused and taken aback by his tone of voice. She said, somewhat defensively, "But it is pork."

"No," Chaim commanded, "you may not say it's pork." The

expression on his face made it clear that he was very serious, and the scolding tone of his voice left us all uncomfortable. An uneasy silence clouded the room. Finally, Chaim announced his solution. "You must call it 'the meat I like.' "

Maman's tight lips and raised eyebrows expressed her disgust, but she agreed. " 'The meat I like,' " she repeated.

"Yes." Chaim grinned, but he declined to eat any more pork that night.

The following day, while I was in school, Chaim asked my brother Eric to take him hunting in nearby Gentinnes, where hunting platforms had been built up in the trees. After a few hours they returned and the expression on Eric's face prompted my mother to ask him if something had gone wrong.

"This guy is no paratrooper," Eric said derisively.

"What do you mean?" my mother asked.

"He is afraid of heights," Eric said. "When I showed him one of the platforms, he made excuses about his hands being too cold to climb. But the truth was obvious."

The possible deception worried my mother, but at the time she said nothing.

In the afternoons and evenings, Chaim and I spent hours reacquainting ourselves during long walks. He carried a small camera with him and several times asked me to pose in front of our house. He claimed that he wanted to show off his European girlfriend to his army buddies, but I had a fleeting suspicion that our lovely house was really the centerpiece of the pictures.

Nevertheless, his attention and affection quickly rekindled my infatuation. But I could sense that my parents and my three brothers were not as enamored of him as I was. Although they were never rude, occasional small comments or facial expressions conveyed their opinions. I was not even sure that Princesse liked Chaim. But the general disapproval only served to draw me closer to the handsome young Israeli.

On the weekend, my parents took us to our country house in Nassogne, about an hour's drive south of Brussels. As a young girl, some of my happiest moments were spent in a small trailer that Papa had situated here. More recently, my parents had bought a larger home on the other side of the woods from the trailer. I liked it, although I sometimes returned to the trailer alone, just to breathe in the fresh, clean air.

The one-story country house had a warm, rustic ambiance and served as a monument to Papa's success at the hunt. The paneled walls were covered with plaques displaying the small antlers of roe deer that he had stalked and conquered. A stone wall at the side of the living room was home to an almost-always burning fireplace. One of Maman's dogs was usually nestled close to it, enjoying the warmth. The furniture was plain, comfortable, and arranged to encourage conversation. The small coffee table in the center of the room overflowed with nuts, pretzels, wineglasses, candles, and whatever flowers were blooming in Maman's well-kept gardens. In winter, boughs of evergreens festooned the heavy oak mantel.

Off to one side was an elongated table that easily seated twelve. It was plain and sturdy, like the farm tables of old, with a line of stout oak chairs flanking its length.

Here, in this rustic setting, Maman entertained with style. Candles and flowers always found their way to the center of the long wooden table. Tableware, quite properly arranged, surrounded each place setting. Wineglasses and water goblets stood in their time-honored positions. Beef, lamb, venison, and "the meat I like" were always cooked and served to perfection.

Chaim took in this bucolic opulence with both his eyes and his camera lens. And he found a way to fit in. When it came to handling tasks around the house, my father freely admitted, "I have two left hands and ten thumbs." Chaim, by contrast, was an excellent handyman, and he was happy and proud to tackle various chores. Whether the task involved carpentry, plumbing, or electrical work, Chaim's skills were obvious. As Chaim worked to repair a latch on the bathroom door, my father chuckled and said, "We shall call you 'Golden Fingers.'"

Chaim looked up, grinned at the compliment, and proclaimed, "I'm the best."

* * *

Back in Brussels, I introduced Chaim to my best friend, Didier Mulders. Chaim quietly observed the tall, squarely built young man with the brownish hair, blue eyes, and easy laugh. Then, after the encounter, he cross-examined me about this "best friend." I explained that my family had been friends with the Mulderses for as long as I could remember. Didier was like a brother to me. When my temper flared, he was often the only person who could placate me. Chaim seemed to file this information in the back of his mind.

Near the end of his visit, Chaim startled me by asking, without preamble, "Are you a virgin?"

I did not understand. "What do you mean?" I asked.

"Are you a virgin?" he repeated. "Have you made love with anyone?"

"No, of course not!" I answered, embarrassed and confused by the exchange.

My reply must have satisfied him because, after he returned to Israel, his letters frequently referred to me affectionately as "my virgin girl."

Before long, Chaim wrote to say that he was coming back to Brussels. He would arrive when my parents were away on a brief holiday in Spain, but they were confident that my older brothers, Eric and Géry, would supervise properly. I had just turned seventeen, and I was more infatuated with the young Israeli than ever. My family wondered why the young "paratrooper" had so much free time, but I dismissed their concerns.

Soon after he arrived, Chaim began initiating conversations about sex. He asked a question or two on the general subject, and repeated his inquiry as to whether I had ever been with a boy. Each time I reacted with embarrassment. I answered him quietly, quickly, and honestly: "No, I never have." My virginity seemed to be vitally important to him, but my word was not good enough; he wanted proof. How could I prove such a thing?

Chaim declared that the only solution was for me to sleep

with him so that he could determine for himself whether I was a virgin. "It will be better for you, your first time, if you are with someone who has some experience," he said proudly.

"What if I get pregnant?" I asked in a voice filled with worry.

He was aware of the medications I was taking and some of my health problems. "No, no," he assured me, "for you it's impossible."

Chaim was the first person I had ever encountered who was more persuasive and stubborn than I was. He had a determined manner, a practiced, unrelenting way of getting what he wanted. He explained and analyzed, re-explained and re-analyzed everything he said, always bringing the discussion back to the point that he wished to make, as if he were pounding away with a hammer until the nail disappeared into the wood. But, in truth, even without the badgering, in the throes of my first romance, I would probably have walked through fire for him.

My resolve weakened. "Maybe we should use—some kind of birth control," I suggested.

His face tightened and he shook his head. "You don't need it," he said with a shrug. "With all of your problems, you are sterile. But," he added, "if you are worried, just wash yourself with water afterward."

Finally, perhaps inevitably, I surrendered to his insistent pressure. We waited one night until we were certain that my brothers were asleep upstairs and we were alone in the living room.

I did not know what to expect from my first sexual encounter. The reality was very quick—five minutes at the most—and unremarkable, but I took pleasure in the fact that I was pleasing him.

Chaim said proudly, "See how good I am?"

I thought: Is that it? Is that the big experience?

The aftermath was strange indeed. "How come you didn't scream?" he asked. "If you are virgin, it is supposed to hurt." He also claimed that my physical reactions indicated experience. In an all-knowing tone, he declared that I had not been a virgin only moments before.

"Yes, yes," I insisted.

Then he asked the impossible: *now*, he wanted me to prove that I had been a virgin when I gave myself to him. The conversational hammer-pounding began once more.

His refusal to believe me was shattering. Once I had given myself to him, I was more committed to him than ever. My Catholic upbringing would not allow me to take the matter lightly. After a few days of Chaim's nagging, I decided to phone my gynecologist. Feeling hesitant and ashamed, I picked up the phone at least ten times but could not bring myself to place the call. Chaim continued his inquisition. He pushed and pushed until I gave in and called. Sheepishly I asked the doctor, "Do you remember, when I first came to visit you? When you examined me, was I a virgin?"

The doctor was a bit surprised by the question. He stammered, "Well, so far as I can remember, yes."

"Can you put that on a piece of paper for me?" I asked.

He was reluctant to do so, and he asked why I would need such a document. When I explained, he advised, "If a man does not want to take your word that you were a virgin, he is not a good man. Leave him."

Rebellious as always, I resisted this advice. My mind chose to filter out the negatives. I was in love.

Even though Chaim continued to question my virginity, he also demonstrated that he cared about me. He convinced me to wean myself, gradually, from my daily supply of prescription medications. My health improved remarkably, and I came to believe that the "cures" had been worse than my various maladies.

We held extended conversations about the future. He listened with empathy to my litany of complaints: I was unhappy and restless at home. I was doing poorly in my secretarial studies and my life seemed to have no direction. There were constant altercations between my brothers and me. Papa's temper, and mine, continued to flare. The thought of Chaim's return to Israel and the consequent void in my life was thoroughly depressing.

"If you are so unhappy, you could come to Israel with me," he suggested. He promised long walks through the countryside and enticed me with tales of exciting things to do.

I needed little persuading. After he returned home, he wrote frequently, insistently repeating his invitation. His professed love for me gave me the opportunity—or the excuse—that I needed to break away from home.

When I announced my intention to visit Chaim, my parents and I argued loudly. "It's crazy," Papa said, his deep, gravelly voice rising in volume. "What about your education? Visiting Israel now means giving up your studies!"

Maman tried a different approach, asking quietly, "Patsy, are you sure this is the right boy for you?"

Refusing to listen to my long-suffering parents, I declared, "That's it. Take it or leave it. I'm going to Israel to visit Chaim."

"For how long?" they asked.

"I don't know exactly. We're going to make a hiking trip through Israel. I don't know how long it will take—two weeks, maybe three."

My parents knew that if they objected too forcefully, they might alienate me completely. Reluctantly they agreed to add to my savings so that I could buy a round-trip ticket. We left the return flight open.

Chaim was eager to show me what his country was really like. We took a bus from Tel Aviv to Jerusalem and slept in a trailer at a new settlement on the Arabic side of the city.

After breakfast the next morning, we strapped on backpacks and set off across the desert to the northeast. Our destination was the famed ancient city of Jericho, about twelve miles distant. We were now in the occupied territory known as the West Bank of the Jordan, captured by the Israelis during the Six Day War of June 1967.

Chaim strode ahead of me at a brisk pace. The desert floor

was composed, not of sand, but of small stones that chafed at my sandal-clad feet. We followed a winding path used primarily by Arab goatherds. Despite my discomfort, I was thrilled to be exploring the country I loved with the man I loved. I felt happier than I had ever been in my life.

During the course of the afternoon, huge blisters erupted on my feet. Each step among the hard pebbles produced increasing pain. Tears of exhaustion began to trickle from my eyes. Chaim heard me sniffle, turned, and regarded my agony. He helped me sit and offered encouragement: "We've almost reached Jericho. Look, the path is easier ahead."

After a few minutes of rest, I tried to walk farther. The path led upward on a steep slope. My feet throbbed. My body was weak. I moaned, "I cannot. I think I will die on this spot."

Chaim urged me on. "We have to get up there, just a little farther," he said.

I struggled for several more minutes, until we reached the top of the rise. "We will stay," Chaim announced. "We will camp here for the night."

By morning, I was sore but rested and ready to try again. Slowly we hiked the remaining distance to Jericho, passing a United Nations refugee camp, consisting of row after row of small, low, earthen houses that sheltered Palestinian Arabs. At the edge of Jericho we found a small grocery where we stocked up on supplies of canned corned beef and assorted vegetables.

Jericho was like a dream, an oasis in the desert, lush with giant hibiscus flowers. The people were very friendly, and the air was a fresh, clear contrast to that of the nearby wastelands. We found a shop and bought a supply of gauze for my battered feet. We visited two-thousand-year-old Roman ruins that filled me with awe.

Our original plan was to turn toward the northwest, cross the width of the West Bank, and continue on to Mishmarot, a kibbutz located midway between Tel Aviv and Haifa, where Chaim's eldest brother, Mordekhai, lived. But Chaim examined my blisters—some of them nearly an inch across—and took pity. He knew that I could not make the sixty-mile trek without proper footwear. Before heading to the kibbutz we would divert west, back to Tel Aviv, where I could buy hiking boots. We rode buses for small portions of the trip, but mostly we walked. We ate picnic lunches in groves, picking fruit from the trees. The scent of fresh lemons, limes, oranges, and grapefruit was heady, almost intoxicating. We slept under the stars. Everything I did, everything I saw, was wondrous.

Chaim urged me forward; he seemed to understand my limits and was always careful to stop before I collapsed. In a strange way, the physical pain was part of the high I was experiencing. For a change, I felt good about myself. It meant that I was pushing my limits and accomplishing something.

In Tel Aviv I bought a pair of military-style boots that eased my discomfort considerably.

We moved north along the Mediterranean shore, working our way past towns and villages with names that evoked ancient and romantic images: Herzliya, Shefayyim, Netanya, Avihail, Hadera.

My affection for Israel grew ever stronger as we trudged along. So did my affection for Chaim. This was so romantic! Who needed posh hotels and room service when you could sleep under the stars? Who needed fancy restaurants and cafés when you could build a campfire and eat from tin cans? Who needed indoor plumbing when you could shower under the irrigation sprays in a fragrant grove?

Finally we arrived in Pardes Hanna. Chaim said that the name meant "Hanna's Grove." Indeed, there were lush citrus trees all about. From here, we took a bus to a side road that led to Mishmarot. The road to the kibbutz was only about a third of a mile long, but I was suddenly exhausted and I pestered Chaim, asking continually, "How much farther?" He humored me, and I could tell that he was proud of the endurance I had shown.

Mordekhai Edwar, who lived at Mishmarot with his wife, Gila, and their two young daughters, was very gracious to me. He was the most educated member of the Edwar family, and he worked in some technical capacity in the kibbutz's small factory. This was my first opportunity to study the communal lifestyle, and I found much to commend it. Everyone worked for the common good. Each morning the men went to their jobs in the fruit groves or at the factory. Some women worked in the factory also, but others divided their time among traditional female duties: cooking, laundry, gardening, child care, schooling. Periodically they rotated to different tasks. The houses were small and sparsely furnished. Meals were taken in a large common hall. My one criticism was the lack of privacy.

We remained in Mishmarot for two days. By the time we returned to Tel Aviv, my feet—despite the boots—were nearly destroyed. The blisters had broken and were infected. Nevertheless, I was more in love than ever, with Israel and with Chaim.

When Maman answered the telephone, I came straight to the point. "I am not coming back," I said. "I'm going to stay in Israel with Chaim." Her arguments fell on deaf, stubborn ears. The brief conversation ended with Maman informing me that she and Papa would be on the next plane to Tel Aviv.

Chaim and I were summoned to the Hilton Hotel, where my parents tried desperately to convince me to return home.

It was a tense encounter. Here in Israel, away from my parents' home, Chaim was more aggressive and confrontational. As my parents tried to persuade me to come home, he changed the subject abruptly and complained that I had not been a virgin when I gave myself to him. Listening to this ridiculous contention, delivered in such a challenging and embarrassing manner, Maman's face displayed a mixture of anger and disbelief.

Never before had Chaim treated my parents with such disrespect. It was, as Maman would say later, "the beginning of many upsetting days."

I had made up my mind. What were my parents to do? They did not approve of Chaim or of my decision, but they knew that if they opposed the idea too strongly, they risked losing contact with me altogether. If and when I finally came to my senses, they did not want me to be afraid to come back to them. They took some small comfort in the knowledge that I still had my open-flight return ticket. And so they reverted to a typical strategy. If they had to give in to me, they wanted me, somehow, to gain from the situation. Papa paced the room, his stocky, muscular body tense and nervous. "Okay, you may stay," he said finally, "but the condition is that you continue to learn Hebrew. You go to school. You take lessons."

I agreed quickly.

I was not quite eighteen years old.

4

I woke early but remained very quiet, lest I disturb Chaim's sleep. In the quiet hours of morning, I surveyed my new home. It was a tiny concrete structure in the backyard of Chaim's parents' house, situated east of Tel Aviv, between the small towns of Ramat Gan and Petakh-Tikva.

Our living quarters consisted of one main room, a minuscule kitchen, and a shower stall. In the winter, heat was supplied by a freestanding kerosene unit. As in many Israeli homes, we used the sun to heat our water. To me, this shack could have been the Taj Mahal. A grand house would have been comfortable, but a spartan existence was new and romantic to me. I felt like a pioneer.

Chaim slept soundly until nearly 1:00 P.M. When he woke, he showered, then dressed carefully in a business suit and tie. Here, in the heat of Israel, people commonly worked in shorts and casual shirts, but Chaim believed that it was important to present the appearance of a successful young businessman. He was out of the army now, and he had plenty of time to begin building his—our—financial future. He had grand plans to become an entrepreneur, perhaps heading up his own export-import firm. For now, prior to starting his own business, he was selling encyclopedias door-to-door. Sometimes I saw him in the company of another well-dressed young man, whom Chaim said was also in the encyclopedia business.

Once Chaim had left for the day, I set about my duties. I switched on the radio and tuned to Kol ha Shalom (The Voice of Peace), a station that broadcast from a ship sitting outside of Israel's territorial limits. Chaim told me it was illegal—since it was not state-owned. Its soft music, in both Hebrew and English, seemed to promote a message of peace and love.

The background music helped pass the time as I swept and dusted the tiny home. Then I set about the more difficult task of doing the laundry by hand. I stripped the sheets off the bed, scrubbed them by hand, and hung them outside. In the hot sun they dried in thirty minutes.

There was a little time left in my afternoon to visit Chaim's aunt, who was married to a Frenchman named Henri. They lived close by, and I found it relaxing to speak my own language with Uncle Henri.

Slowly I was developing a routine for my new life.

Even though my mother was an accomplished cook, I had never bothered to learn my way around a kitchen, so we took most of our meals with Chaim's family. This pleased Chaim because he did not have to spend money on food, but I often found these encounters unsettling.

The home of Shlomo and Leah Edwar consisted of one central living area, surrounded by three smaller, multipurpose rooms. Each room had a couch for sleeping; blankets were stacked in an armoire. There was a kitchen and one small bathroom. As time had passed and the house had settled, the roof line had separated in places from the walls, allowing sunlight, and occasionally rain, to seep through.

Chaim's father, Shlomo, was a thin, wiry man who sported a pointed white beard and short *peiyot*—the traditional side curls that denote a religious Jew—which extended to just beneath his earlobes. Atop his gray hair he wore a dome-shaped, camel-colored hat. He moved about slowly. I was surprised to see him constantly grasping at the walls with his thin, bony fingers, until I realized that he was almost always drunk.

Shlomo's attitude, rather than his words, made it clear from the beginning that he would never accept me. I was a Christian, and to this Yemen-born, religious Jew, that was anathema, a liability that could never be overcome. Shlomo worked on an assembly line, producing cloth. He arrived home about 4:00 P.M. and spent his evenings poking through cupboards and drawers in search of hidden supplies of vodka. In his pocket he always carried a shot glass. Sometimes he drank so heavily that he passed out on the floor.

During dinner one evening, Shlomo rose abruptly from the table, muttering in my direction. Angry Hebrew phrases flew about, too quickly for me to understand. It was evident that I had done something wrong, but I did not know what. It was just as obvious that Chaim had come to my defense. Everyone felt very uncomfortable. Later, when I asked Chaim what had happened, he told me that his father thought I had poured milk onto the plate with my chicken. He had complained that he could not eat at a table with someone who did not keep kosher. "It was mayonnaise, not milk," I pointed out. Obviously Shlomo was so drunk that he could not tell the difference.

Over time, from Chaim and others I learned that the original reason for the kosher dietary laws was a concern for hygiene. One may not eat the meat of carnivorous animals. Hogs, considered scavengers, were unclean, as were all the various forms of seafood without scales. Some of this made sense to me, but it seemed that, over centuries, the laws had been compounded with minutiae. The incident that caused Shlomo's flare-up was based on the rule that one must wait several hours between consuming meats and dairy products. Why? I did not know, nor could I make sense of it. All I knew was that dinnertime was routinely disruptive.

In contrast to Shlomo, Chaim's mother, Leah, a short, solidly built woman who wore long dresses with loose slacks underneath, accepted me warmly. She was also from Yemen and had been married to Chaim's father before she had even experienced her first period; after her first or second menstrual cycle, she had become pregnant. Leah's culture taught her that she was the property of her husband; she was also a dutiful subject to the sons she had produced. She spent her days as an aide in a school for abused and abandoned children. In the evenings she scurried about the house, waiting on her husband and sons. Despite her difficult station in life, she had a warmth about her and I liked her very much. She made a clear attempt to accept me into the family.

The triumph of Leah's life was that she had borne five children and all of them were boys. One son, Zvi, had died of a kidney ailment when he was a teenager. The eldest, Mordekhai, was married and living at the kibbutz. Asher was a nice young man with a surprisingly enlightened attitude toward women and children. Eight-year-old Goory was the baby, much younger than Chaim; but Chaim was clearly his mother's favorite. In her eyes, he was simply stating an acknowledged truth with his oft-repeated pronouncement, "I'm the best." To Leah, he was the son who could do no wrong.

As a young teenager, Chaim had been charged with delinquency, but Leah explained to me that whatever difficulties he had experienced were someone else's fault. With pride, she told me about the time that Chaim was wounded in action. There had been some sort of skirmish, and Chaim was hit in the elbow. He had come home that night with blood all over his uniform. She searched through a cardboard box to show me the torn, stained shirt.

"Why didn't you wash it?" I asked. "It's dirty."

"Oh, Chaim wants to keep it as a souvenir," Leah explained. I realized that, as far as Leah was concerned, what Chaim wants, God wants.

Chaim grumbled at this story, complaining that the army had never provided him with proper medical care.

Almost all Israeli army veterans—until they reach retirement age—must return to duty for at least one month each year and are always placed on alert during times of crisis. I wondered why Chaim, an elite paratrooper, was not required to perform any reserve duties. He explained that this was due to his elbow injury.

Honoring the promise to my parents, I enrolled in Hebrew class, but the sessions turned into tedious political discussions. Egyptian President Anwar Sadat had recently made an unprecedented visit to Jerusalem to address the Knesset, the Israeli parliament. Never in decades had there been such optimism that Israel could find peace with its Arab neighbors. I wanted peace, of course, but I hated politics. I certainly backed Israel's position in its historic disagreements with the Palestinians, but I also observed that most Palestinians were not terrorists; they were ordinary people trying, like everyone else, to make their way through life. Languages come easily to me—and I already had taken some classroom instruction in Hebrew back in Belgium—so I soon quit the class, deciding that I could learn conversational Hebrew faster by interacting with Chaim's brother Goory. Children have a natural affinity for languages, and, simply by spending time with them, one learns quickly. Goory loved having me as a playmate. He taught me Hebrew songs. And, as we chatted, he was quick to correct my grammatical mistakes. My conversations with Leah also helped. We held long discussions about cooking Yemenstyle, cleaning, and taking care of the men.

In bits of conversation, as we struggled to understand one another, Leah told me some of the family history. She said that the Edwars had quite a lot of money before they moved here from Yemen, but they had fallen victim to thieves and con men. This was a typical story for the Yemenite Jews, most of whom had migrated to the Promised Land shortly after World War II. They were herded into ramshackle camps and housed in sheds constructed of corrugated metal; in the heat of summer, the living conditions were unbearable.

Leah told me horrible stories of European Jews, childless, who victimized Yemenite Jews. A European woman, pointing to the deplorable living conditions, might say to a Yemenite, "Oh, what a beautiful child. May I bring him to my home and take care of him for a while?" With this seductive approach, they took children and never returned them.

I was surprised by Leah's description of the castelike hierarchy among Jews in Israel. Those with roots in Europe and America ranked highest on the social scale. Moroccan and Tunisian Jews ranked lowest. Yemenite Jews, like the Edwars, were on the lower-middle end of the scale and thought to be lacking in sophistication. They were considered rude and clannish, and more Arab than Israeli in their family habits. The first generations of Yemenite immigrants were a comparatively uneducated people who maintained their own cultural peculiarities, which kept them somewhat separate from other Israeli subcultures. Thus, Leah concluded, they were victims of oppression, and many of them lived in poverty.

I performed my daily chores with care, for Chaim inspected carefully the moment he returned home and was quick to point out anything that did not meet his standards. One day after he examined the bed, he declared, "You are a bad woman. It has been three weeks, one month, and you have not washed the sheets."

"No," I said. "I wash them twice a week, just as you said. You just don't see it. I wash them and hang them outside. In this sun, it only takes a half hour for them to dry. You just don't see them."

Chaim appeared skeptical. From that time on I learned to leave the sheets outside on the clothesline until he returned.

At times I was supremely happy. At other times I was beset by a sense of malaise. I was in love with Chaim, but running off to Israel had not solved all my problems. I still did not know who I was or what I wanted to do with my life.

One morning there was an insistent pounding at the door. Peering outside, I saw Chaim's fellow encyclopedia salesman standing on the small porch. Chaim opened the door and stepped outside to speak with him. A loud argument ensued. I could not speak Hebrew well enough to understand what it was about, but both men were clearly agitated. After a few moments the other man took a pistol out of his jacket pocket. He did not point it at Chaim, but the threat was clear. Chaim grew visibly nervous.

I thought: People who sell books don't come to your house with guns. This is not my business. I don't want to be involved in this kind of thing. "Excuse me," I said. I pushed my way through the door, rushed past the two men, and went to visit Chaim's uncle Henri.

When I returned about a half hour later, the other man was gone. Chaim was enraged. To my surprise and horror, I realized that he was angry with *me!* He spoke in an intense, menacing tone that cut through me like a knife, lecturing: "You should be alongside me always." His voice reached an unnaturally high pitch as he raged, "Your duty is to be next to me and even protect me when it's needed." But he would not tell me why the man had threatened him.

The events of that day clashed with my idealistic picture of Chaim as the young man I loved and wanted to remain with for the rest of my life. I tried to suppress the negative thoughts in my mind—new images of Chaim: first, as a coward and, second, as someone who might be involved in questionable or even illegal activities.

But Chaim would not let me forget. For several days he refused to speak to me and he decreed that, as punishment for my betrayal, I was not allowed to speak to anyone without his permission. During meals with his family, he acted as if nothing were wrong, but the moment we returned to our backyard shanty, the silent treatment resumed. I could discuss my predicament only with myself, and two Patsys argued within my head. One was furious over the injustices of Chaim's treatment, but the other lectured: Patsy, you are immature and uneducated, and you must learn to obey the man you love. The submissive Patsy acquiesced. By the time Chaim lifted his silent treatment, I slipped gratefully back into his world, but I was changed.

Overcome by depression, I wanted to sleep away my days. I

lost all interest in food and dropped twelve pounds. I worried that all my old health problems were returning. One day, in conversation with Leah, I uttered vague comments about my unhappiness. Concerned, Leah discussed my problems with her son. To his mother, Chaim expressed empathy and promised to try to help me. But in private he was furious with me and claimed that I had humiliated him by suggesting to his mother that he was not able to keep me happy. Once again he forbade me to speak to anyone without his permission.

Left alone in our small shack, I decided to hard-boil some eggs. I placed a small saucepan on top of the kerosene stove and waited for the water to boil. But apparently there was a fuel leak and flames suddenly shot up from the stove. Instinctively I ran to the door and yelled for help. Asher responded and quickly took the heater outside and quashed the flames. That fire was out, but later, when Chaim found out about the incident, it was his temper that flared. He was furious that I had disobeyed him by speaking to Asher. I tried to defend myself. "There was a fire! It was an emergency!" I said.

"I told you, no matter what happens, you may not speak," he decreed. "Now you may not even go out of the house."

The resumption of the silent treatment only compounded my distress. Again, two Patsys fought within me and, for a time, the angry, defiant Patsy took over.

One afternoon while Chaim was out, I decided that I had reached the limits of my endurance. But I did not know where to turn. I still did not understand Hebrew very well. I had no money; I had no friends. I was dependent upon Chaim for everything. The thought of calling upon my parents for help filled me with despair, for I had rejected their advice and declared my independence. In desperation, I decided to seek help from Samuel Katz, a friend of my father who lived in Tel Aviv. He was a successful businessman and a reasonable, helpful person. I knew that he would offer me temporary shelter and would be able to act as an effective intermediary between my parents and me.

In panic, I packed a small suitcase and set out on foot to

make my way to Mr. Katz's home. But somewhere along the way I lost contact with reality. Disoriented, I took refuge under a grove of orange trees. Before long, I was fast asleep.

The grove happened to be on the grounds of a mental-health facility. I do not know how long I laid there before an attendant approached and noticed, with alarm, that I clutched a small razor in my hand. I had no memory of bringing it with me, nor did I know what I intended to do with it. The attendant spoke to me gently and determined that I was not a threat to myself or to others. He offered to escort me home and, meekly, I accepted.

It was the passive Patsy who returned to face Chaim's rage. I had defied him by going out on my own and had further sinned by speaking to someone. Worst of all, the stranger who brought me home was a man. This fact alone enraged Chaim. His anger was palpable and he expressed it in a fierce, verbal tirade. Hours passed as he yelled and screamed at me. And then, the silent treatment resumed.

All Israel buzzed with the news of the signing of the Camp David Peace Accord between Egyptian President Sadat and Israeli Prime Minister Menachem Begin. But I had more personal concerns. I had lost more weight. Fatigue numbed me. When I finally visited a clinic, a doctor informed me, "You've been pregnant for three months."

I must have known instinctively. For weeks I had been idly sketching profiles of pregnant women. The news brought a sudden, euphoric sense of energy, determination, and purpose. My medical history and Chaim's persuasive arguments had convinced me that motherhood was impossible for me. But my body had decided otherwise and, now, all other considerations receded from my thoughts. I said to myself: This is a fresh start. We will have this baby and everything will be wonderful.

Chaim received the news with surprising calm. He did not express joy, and he did not choose to recall his past pronouncement that I was sterile. None of this really concerned him, for, in his world, children were a women's issue.

I visited a woman gynecologist who confirmed the news. She asked, "What do you want to do now? What's your decision?"

I realized that she was raising the issue of abortion. In Israel, abortion was not legal, but it was easily available. My response was swift and sure. "I'm keeping it," I declared.

Concerned about vaginal bleeding, my obstetrician ordered me to bed for a week. Chaim was very sweet and protective, hovering, catering to my whims.

My parents sent airline tickets so that Chaim and I could return to Belgium for a brief holiday. Even though they knew that we had been living together, my parents decreed that Chaim and I would sleep in separate bedrooms during our stay.

I wore loose-fitting dresses to hide my expanding waistline, but Hélène, the cleaning lady who had been with the family since my mother was born, and who was like a surrogate grandmother to me, noticed. "Patsy," she said, "I remember what it's like to be young. You can talk to me." But I refused.

Maman chose not to see the obvious.

One afternoon I visited an obstetrician in Brussels for a sonogram; I wanted to make sure the baby was healthy, but I chose not to learn the sex. The test was covered under Belgium's national health service, so I assumed that no one would ever know.

Within days, however, an invoice arrived at my parents' home addressed to Mme. Heymans. My mother, assuming the letter was intended for her, opened the envelope and was surprised to learn that Mme. Heymans was four months' pregnant. She thought: I am definitely not pregnant; there must be some mistake. Then she realized that there was another Mme. Heymans in the house.

Patsy! she thought.

Maman found me in the bathroom, combing my hair. Without a word, she handed me the invoice. I studied it and confessed to the truth.

Outwardly, Maman took the news calmly, if not joyfully.

What was done was done, and she was determined to make the best of a less-than-perfect situation. That very afternoon she took me shopping for maternity clothes, and she chose her moment carefully. As we looked through racks of dresses, she asked, "Well, what do you plan to do now?" I shrugged and, for the moment, she let the matter drop.

But the pressure mounted over the next several days. My parents lectured, quietly but firmly, that, in choosing to live with Chaim, I had declared I was an adult. Now I had to confront the consequences in an adult manner. To them, that meant I would have to do the responsible thing, which was to marry Chaim and legitimize the baby.

Marriage was not on my agenda. In fact, it was the farthest thing from my mind. A marriage license was never important to me. For me, the real commitment came from inside; muttering vows to a mayor's assistant or a priest meant nothing. As far as I was concerned, I could live with someone and feel exactly as if I were married. But Chaim seemed to like the idea of marrying me, and my parents' insistence wore me down. I finally agreed.

Maman immediately began making plans for a small civil ceremony.

My friend Didier pleaded with my parents not to insist upon the wedding. Standing in the kitchen, he declared, "It's stupid. It's crazy. Don't do it."

Maman replied, "If there is one chance in a million that it will work, we have to do it. She's pregnant and Catholic. She has to get married."

They argued sharply for some time, but my parents would not change their minds.

My maternal grandfather, having taken an instant dislike to my prospective husband, insisted that I sign an agreement promising to keep my assets separate from Chaim's. I resisted, and Chaim too was against the idea, but my grandfather was adamant. "Patsy," he warned, "if you don't do as I ask, I will see to it that when I die, your mother will not inherit. Because I don't want one dime to get to Chaim in the end."

That night Chaim and I argued bitterly. He complained, "I'm going to be part of the family, and they are rejecting me by this."

Caught in the middle, I did not know what to do. It was very difficult for me to resist Chaim's pressure, to side with my parents against him, but finally I said, "We have to do it. We have to do it for my mother."

Chaim stormed off to his room. In the morning he refused to speak to me. He found some business in the city and went off for the day. When he returned, he continued to ignore me, and the silent treatment lasted five days. When he finally began to speak once more, I was contrite and docile.

Finally, we found ourselves in a notary's office to sign the papers for the agreement. The notary asked, "Chaim, do you agree to this?"

The air in the office was tense. Chaim's features were dark and heavy. All the color seemed to drain from his face as he muttered yes.

July 20, 1979. I dressed in a roomy, dull-brown shirt and a beige maternity jumper. My grandmother presented me with a lovely diamond brooch—a valuable family heirloom—that I pinned to the center of the jumper.

Chaim appeared calm and cool in light-colored slacks, a blazer, and tie.

As we stood before the mayor in the town hall in Brussels, I was at his side, surrounded by my family and a small group of friends. Père Edgard stood next to me as my witness. The service was very short. I heard Chaim answer yes to the mayor's question.

Then it was my turn. I felt as though someone had punched me in the face. I hesitated. A kaleidoscope of images flashed through my mind: Chaim's face contorted in irrational anger; his mother's submissive posture; his father searching for a hidden bottle of vodka; the echoes of silence when Chaim refused to talk to me. A small voice inside of me wanted to scream no and run out of the room. But I could not speak.

I glanced quickly over my shoulder at the expectant faces

behind me: Maman, Papa, Eric, Géry, and Michel. I thought: Oh, my God, I can't do this to my parents. They have prepared all this. All the food at the reception is waiting. They sent us the tickets to come home. Chaim would be humiliated. The baby. I cannot say no.

"Yes," I murmured.

5

Maman bought two new twin beds and a fresh supply of linens and blankets and, on our wedding night, finally allowed Chaim to move into my bedroom.

Now that our intimacy was acknowledged, she came to me with a quiet, embarrassed request. "Patsy, can you ask Chaim to take off his underpants before he goes into the shower?" she asked. "Every day I find his shorts in the shower, on the floor, sopping wet."

This was curious behavior, and when I spoke with Chaim about it, he reminded me that in his society nakedness was taboo; therefore, he showered with his boxer shorts on and only removed them when he was ready to cover himself with a robe or towel. I knew this was true: I was carrying his child, yet I had never seen him naked; whenever we made love, he always insisted that we remain under the covers. "But, okay," he said with a shrug, "I'll put them in the laundry."

From then on, again to her displeasure, my mother found Chaim's drenched shorts thrown in with our laundry.

Following much discussion, we decided that we would remain in Belgium until I gave birth.

Papa made the logical suggestion that Chaim try to find a job. But Chaim did not wish to work for anyone; he would be his own boss. He began to use my father's office, which was located in the room adjacent to our bedroom. He spent hours on the telephone, placing calls to various contacts scattered about the world, trying to concoct import and export deals in various commodities, ranging from petrol to cigarettes. At the dinner table he regaled us with stories of the windfall profits that we would soon reap. He was not talking about thousands of dollars but millions. "Such a deal," he said, "that I would never have to work again in my whole life." Sometimes he rose in the middle of the night to place calls to far-flung time zones. Often he woke me also, so that I could type a lengthy telex for him.

He found a business associate, a petite, dark-skinned, brown-haired woman who lived at the Hotel Metropole, located in Place de Brouckere, close to la Bourse (the stock exchange) in the center of Brussels. Chaim spoke with her frequently by phone and went to see her almost every day. They conversed in English, so I concluded that she was neither Belgian nor Israeli, but I knew little else about her.

My days were long and dull. If I did not have office tasks to perform for Chaim, I helped Maman with the laundry. Sometimes we went shopping for the baby. Most of my time was spent waiting.

Chaim's possessiveness was once flattering, but, as time passed, he became increasingly jealous of everything and everybody that received my slightest attention. "You love that dog more than you love me," he whined. "What do you need her for?"

"Princesse? That's crazy," I countered. "And it's not true that I love her more than you."

"It is true," he argued.

The subject of Princesse became another of Chaim's long, grinding campaigns. He never said outright that I should get rid of her, but that was clearly his message.

It was much easier to acquiesce to Chaim's petty requests than to argue. I had seen flashes of a dangerous temper lurking just below the surface. I refused to part with Princesse, and yet Chaim won the point, for I consciously began to ignore and neglect the little dachshund. Before long, she died, leaving me feeling extremely guilty.

The next target was my best friend. "Tell me about Didier," Chaim said, with a hint of accusation in his voice. "Was he ever your boyfriend?"

I laughed at this and admitted, "We talked about dating once, but we didn't want to spoil our friendship."

Chaim sulked at this news. Some days later he grumbled, "You spend too much time with Didier. I want you to cut off the friendship."

And so, as I had learned to ignore Princesse, I also began to distance myself from Didier.

Yet I was forbidden to voice suspicions of my own. Chaim spent more and more time working with his attractive young associate in her room at the Hotel Metropole. Often he prevailed upon Maman to drive him to the hotel first thing in the morning. It was, quite obviously, a pleasant working environment. The hotel is both old-fashioned and luxurious, with high-ceilinged suites, ornate, palatial decorations, and a fawning service staff. Chaim sometimes did not return, via taxi, until 4:00 A.M.

"How come you need to spend so much time with her?" I asked one day. "You go to expensive restaurants with her. The only places you ever take me are to Quick's or McDonald's."

"It's business. It's only business," Chaim reassured me. "If you want me to succeed, you have to let me work the way I work."

I felt properly chastised. How could I criticize my husband for attempting to provide for his expanding family?

We still had not decided on potential names for the baby, and Chaim could not be bothered to discuss them. But the baby, whoever he or she might be, was ready to enter our lives. In mid-October, more than one month early, I experienced mild contractions.

During a regular checkup, my obstetrician informed me that I had already dilated three or four centimeters. "Go home but stay calm," he advised. "Read a book. Stay off your feet." Maman did her best to care for me.

A few days later, on October 18, the contractions grew more regular. As an eighteen-year-old first-time mother, I was unprepared and panicky. My body was ready to give birth, but my mind was not.

By the time Chaim and I arrived at the hospital, I was in a tremendous amount of pain and my terror had grown. In the labor room, a nurse instructed me sternly, "Calm down, take my arm." My response was to grab her arm and bite into it, drawing blood. The animal-like reaction calmed me, but the poor woman refused to come into my room after that.

As the labor progressed, my throat became extremely dry. When I was in the final stages of labor and almost fully dilated, what I wanted most was a sip of water. But the obstetrician was reluctant to give me anything to drink in case a Caesarean delivery became necessary. When the doctor left the room, between contractions I begged Chaim for ice chips or even a damp cloth to suck on, but he too refused. Finally, when I was once again alone with the nurse, she took pity on me and agreed to get me a sip of water. But as she went to get the water, I panicked. What if Chaim finds out? I thought. He wouldn't allow me any water. What will he do if I disobey him? My mind spun with the possible consequences.

Before the nurse returned with the water, I felt a tremendous need to push. I screamed out, and I was whisked away into the delivery room.

I gave birth to a tiny, five-pound baby girl with shiny black hair and huge bright eyes. I was suddenly overcome with the awesome reality of the new life I had created and the responsibilities that came with it. The instant I saw her I was filled with unconditional love.

"You are Marina," I said. The name just came to me; Marina was a young girl for whom I used to baby-sit. I thought the name had a soft, lyrical quality. Nurses allowed me to hold her for only a few seconds before they wrapped her in protective silver paper and took her away.

Marina suffered from a calcium deficiency and her blood sugar and body temperature were too low. Although she did not require an incubator, she had to remain in a special room where the temperature was kept at ninety-two degrees Fahrenheit. A feeding tube was inserted into her tiny nose. I was allowed to nurse her two times a day, but I had to wear a mask, gloves, and sterile boots in order to hold my baby. I was told that if she had been born one week earlier, she would have been in very serious condition.

The three other new mothers in my ward all had their babies with them, while mine was isolated in a separate room. As they nursed their full-term infants, I submitted to the indignity of a breast pump. Despondent, I cried my way through a severe case of postpartum blues. Chaim was supportive. "She will be fine," he assured me.

Five days after the birth I was discharged from the hospital, but Marina had to remain. Her condition improved steadily, but I worried constantly. One evening at ten o'clock, I said suddenly, "I've got to see Marina."

"But you may not see her this late," Chaim reminded me. "It is against the rules."

"I may not go in to hold her. But I can stand in the hall and see her through the glass."

Chaim understood. He drove me across Brussels to the hospital, just so that I could stare at our marvelous creation. Despite her small size, Marina was a perfectly formed baby, and even strangers commented on her beauty. I was very proud.

I thought: Patsy, you are made for kids.

Finally, after about ten days, I was able to bring Marina home.

Chaim repaired and repainted all the windows on the house on Avenue des Fleurs. In payment, my parents bought us a used Ford Escort. It provided Chaim with mobility, and he began spending more and more time away from the house. He never told me where he was going or how long he would be away, and he did not bother to report to me when he returned, other than to boast of progress on his business deals.

But there was no income for heavy expenses. Chaim spent so much time on the telephone that Papa's clients could not get through to him. When my father traveled he could not call us, for the phone was always busy. Papa's business suffered. One telephone bill amounted to more than eleven thousand dollars. Whenever my parents tried to speak with Chaim about this, he always seemed to have something else that required his attention.

As time passed and nothing came of Chaim's business schemes, Papa's considerable patience wore thin. "You are not going to use my telephone anymore," he declared. Chaim complied, but the next biweekly telex bill showed charges of two thousand dollars.

Everyone's nerves were on edge. Now, whenever Chaim declared, "I'm the best," my parents shared knowing glances.

Despite a history packed with internal squabbles, the Heymanses had always closed ranks tenaciously against outsiders. We might fight among ourselves, slamming doors, yelling and crying, but no outsider dared to criticize or cause trouble. I now surprised myself by reverting to this position. Chaim waited until my parents were out one day, then complained to me about my father's treatment of him. We fought bitterly. It seemed that I could not defend my own position in his life, but when he dared to attack Papa—or any member of my family—I fought back. Chaim realized this very quickly and stormed off in anger.

Furious, I locked all the windows and doors. When Chaim reappeared, I yelled at him through the door, "You went out, you can stay out! This is my parents' home. I have the right to stay here. You just fly away!"

He was immediately contrite. "Oh, I'm so sorry," he said. "I won't start again. I don't know why I behave that way." I softened and unlocked the door, to let him back in before my parents could witness his humiliation at the hands of a woman.

* * *

"Where is your wedding ring?" Chaim asked. Through narrowed eyes he glanced pointedly at my left hand. The expression on his face warned of a rising temper.

I looked down and was surprised to realize that the ring was missing. "Oh," I said, "I took it off when I helped Maman with dinner. I think I put it on the windowsill."

It was New Year's Eve. We were at the country home in Nassogne. Following tradition, Maman had busied herself preparing a special plate of seafood appetizers—oysters and smoked salmon—to be followed by a venison roast. Now, dinner was almost ready.

I hurried into the kitchen to retrieve my ring, but it was gone. Returning to Chaim, I reported, "I don't know where it is. I'm sure I left it on the windowsill." I was concerned that Chaim might react with the disproportionate anger I had seen him exhibit in the past. Struggling to hide my anxiety, I tried to affect a casual manner as I explained, "I lost it, temporarily, you know, until I find it." I wished that my parents were in the room, for their presence would keep him civil.

Suddenly Chaim poked me sharply in the shoulder, hard enough to throw me off balance. His hands clamped around my wrists and he shook me roughly, insisting that I find the missing ring immediately. I ran off to look, but I felt very guilty and I was too upset to search systematically. Maman saw me frantically pulling open cupboard doors and tugging at drawers, and she asked, "Patsy, what's wrong? What are you doing?"

"I must find my ring," I answered.

She joined in the search. We sped through the house, moving cushions aside and peering under furniture.

"Did you find it? Did you find it?" Chaim asked insistently. Maman grew as nervous as I. Back in the kitchen, we emptied out the contents of the cupboards. There was no sign of the ring.

Chaim lay down on our bed with the door open. As Maman and I checked every nook and cranny of the house, he calmly smoked a cigarette. With a self-satisfied smirk on his face, he goaded: "It's a pity you can't find your ring, because that means that you are not my wife anymore."

With tears streaming down our faces, near total panic, we continued to search. But it was in vain. The ring had disappeared. Dinner was ruined. I cried periodically throughout the meal, and my sobs brought empathic tears from Maman. Papa did his best to make casual conversation, but the holiday was ruined.

For the next two weeks Chaim kept me in a state of misery, chiding me for my carelessness.

Then one day he came to me, displaying the ring. I was overjoyed. But my relief turned to disgust when he disclosed that he had found it in the kitchen on New Year's Eve. It was on the windowsill where I remembered leaving it. He had hidden it in the back of a radio where he was sure that no one would find it. "Good joke I made for everybody," he declared with a sarcastic laugh.

I was appalled by his malicious stunt. He had delighted in our misery.

When I told Maman the story, I could not look into her eyes. She was as shocked as I was, but neither of us could admit what this episode told us about Chaim's character.

Put it aside, Patsy, I commanded myself.

Close yourself.

Hold it in.

Now that I was tied to him as his wife and the mother of his child, Chaim exhibited a roving eye. I tried not to notice.

A French girl, a pleasant-looking teenager with a lovely complexion and light-brown hair that fell to her shoulders, came to live with one of the neighborhood families. I spoke with her a few times, but we both seemed to realize intuitively that we were incompatible personalities. I found her to be a bit snobbish. But Chaim apparently liked her. She contracted a bad cold or flu and was confined to bed for an extended period. From the window of my bedroom I saw Chaim cross the street to visit her, once or twice every day. From his demeanor—and the guilty look in his eyes—I knew what was on his mind, and I finally asked him,

"Why do you go all the time to see her? Why do you need to go to her?"

He asked a sarcastic question in response: "What's bad about having friends? You had a friend—Didier—and nothing was wrong with that?"

My younger cousin Cathy, a very beautiful girl of half-Spanish descent, came to visit us in Brussels, staying with my grandmother at her house next door to ours. One day she sought me out to talk. I happened to be alone in my bathroom. With embarrassment, Cathy told me that Chaim had written her a note, asking for a date. She explained that she had written him a curt letter in return, telling him what a low opinion she had of him.

Choosing not to acknowledge what she was telling me, I snapped, "Oh, you are wrong. You misunderstood."

Cathy turned and walked away, having said what she had to say.

Chaim's grand business deals never came to fruition. In February he decided that we should return to Israel; he assured me that things would be different in his homeland. My parents helped us purchase living-room and bedroom furniture, and we packed it all into one twelve-foot shipping crate. I stuffed boxes of disposable diapers into every available space, for they were very expensive in Israel. I packed my hopes and dreams also. I was confident that Chaim and I would be more at ease with one another in his homeland. We would manage to overcome our troubles and build a happy life for our new family. We shipped our possessions, including our old Ford Escort, by sea.

My mother promised to visit us in Israel and also to pay for us to come back to Belgium for occasional holidays.

My father, in yet another display of generosity, loaned Chaim $8,500 to help him get started.

We left on the day that Marina turned four months old.

6

When our flight arrived in Israel, Chaim filled out my entry papers in Hebrew and instructed: "Sign there." He explained that the papers qualified me as a new immigrant, entitled to receive direct government financial aid as well as housing benefits. He counseled me, "You have to pretend to be a Jew in this country if you want to be accepted." I signed.

We rented a house in the town of Hod Hasharon, a few miles from his parents' house. It was only a tiny, two-bedroom house, laid out in a simple rectangle, but it was our first real home.

Huge banks of red and pink impatiens decorated the front and sides of our yard. Across the front of the street were four lemon trees, and I developed a taste for the fruit, picking it fresh and eating it like an orange. The house was situated next to a kindergarten, and I delighted in watching the children at play, daydreaming about the time when Marina would become a happy schoolgirl.

Once our furniture arrived, I decorated the modest home as best I could. I arranged chairs in the living room so that we could see out the window, past the covered terrace, to the impatiens and the lemon trees.

As Chaim searched for work, I spent my days caring for

Marina, marketing, and keeping house. Chaim resumed his practice of inspecting the home carefully whenever he returned, demanding that it be spotless. But he treated me with such love and respect that I began to believe that, here in Israel, our marriage would flourish.

Marina was a sweet, docile baby who seldom cried, and slept easily through the night. She spoiled me into believing that all babies were this easy. It was a subject that interested me, because I was certain that I was pregnant again.

Chaim did not bother with the expense of registering our car. In fact, he did not even have a driver's license, and it did not trouble him to continue to drive with Belgian plates.

He made frequent trips to various banks, always insisting that Marina and I accompany him. He obviously did not want me to know anything about his financial dealings because he ordered us to remain in the car. He changed his accounts around frequently and seemed to be welcomed readily by a variety of bank employees.

Times were difficult in Israel, but Chaim was confident that he could turn our borrowed $8,500 into a fortune. A wild run of inflation eroded the Israeli pound, but Chaim was smart enough to keep our money in Belgian francs.

He secured several jobs—or at least he told me that he did—but none of them proved satisfactory. He quit or was fired from each of them almost immediately. Finally he was accepted as general manager of a small company, but within three weeks he came home and decreed, "That's it for me, this job." He complained that the company was run by fools and he could not abide them.

Chaim's lack of success in the job market ate steadily into our bank balance. Our $8,500 dwindled to $1,400. Then a strange event occurred, which Chaim regarded as the key to our future fortune. As part of his routine financial manipulations, he deposited our $1,400 into a new account at Bank Leumi in Hod Hasharon. But when the statement arrived, Chaim discovered a clerical error. Someone had added an extra zero, crediting our account with 400,000 Belgian francs. Chaim was too ecstatic to be able to keep this news to himself.

At the time, my mother happened to be visiting from Brussels. During a call home, she mentioned the incident. Papa advised, "Listen, the bank made a mistake. They will find out someday and want their money back. The most he can do is put it in a one-month account, which will give him interest. Then, when they want it back, he can give it back and keep the interest. The bank will not bitch too much about it."

Maman reported this advice to Chaim, and he said he would think about it. But, instead, believing himself to be smarter than my father, Chaim withdrew the money and purchased high-risk stock options. He told me wondrous stories of all the money he would make.

A few of the initial investments went bad. Chaim acknowledged that he had suffered some losses, but he was confident that the market would soon turn in his favor. But it did not. Within weeks, all the money was gone.

We returned to Belgium for a brief holiday, paid for by my parents. One evening, as I attended to Marina, Chaim left the room. A few minutes later I heard him speaking to someone in Hebrew. Curious, I stepped out onto the balcony between our second-floor bedroom and the first-floor foyer, where the phone was located. It took me several minutes to understand the thrust of the conversation. I realized that he was speaking to the woman he referred to as his aunt. In reality, she was his brother Mordekhai's mother-in-law, a modernized Jew whom Chaim liked and respected. When I heard Chaim use the word *hapala*, I realized that he was asking, "How can we get an abortion?" Chaim wanted to know if the procedure would be safe midway through a pregnancy.

I was shocked that he could consider destroying our unborn child. As soon as he was off the phone I went on the attack. "Why do you speak about an abortion?" I demanded.

"It's too soon after the first baby," he said. "The child might not be normal. We cannot afford a second one. It's crazy."

"I won't do it," I declared.

I tried to swallow. The burning lump in my throat gave way to tears as I fled to the bedroom. I wanted to disappear. I stood beside the window and wrapped the curtain tightly around me, rocking back and forth, crying. I don't know how much time passed before my mother entered the room.

"Patsy, Patsy, what's wrong, what's happened?" she asked. She was reluctant to intrude, but my sobs, she said, were coming from my heart. Near hysteria, I blurted out Chaim's wish to abort our child. Her reaction was maternally predictable. She stormed from the room to confront Chaim.

Standing on the mezzanine above him, she told him that abortion was out of the question and berated him for even suggesting such a thing. He countered with protestations that it was too soon after Marina's birth and that we could not afford another child.

"If it's money that is the problem, I will support the child!" she declared. "Medical bills, food, clothing, it doesn't matter, I will do it!"

Chaim reverted to a steely silence, shrugged his shoulders, and turned away.

Day after day he tried to raise the issue. I was unable to resist his will on many things, but this was one point where I could make a firm stand. Eventually the matter was dropped.

The price for my victory was Chaim's renewed attempt to assert his authority in other ways. Maman watched in sad silence one day as I pulled a pair of his blue jeans from the washing machine. Chaim said, "I want to wear those. Iron them."

"They are still wet," I pointed out.

"Iron them until they are dry," he ordered. He stood over me, supervising as I pushed the heavy iron back and forth. I dared not look at Maman, afraid of the message I might read in her eyes. When the blue jeans were finally dry, Chaim cast them aside. "I think I'll wear a different pair," he said.

Back in Israel, as my pregnancy progressed, I found myself overcome with lethargy. I neglected the housework, and Chaim sometimes helped out by washing the dishes or picking up after himself. At other, more frequent times, he pointed out my lapses, inspecting carefully and screaming whenever he found a real or imagined speck of dust. It was as if, having successfully defied him on the abortion issue, I had to be reinstructed as to who was in control.

I slept as many as sixteen hours in the course of the day, rising only when Marina needed care or when I knew that Chaim would be home soon. I must have been depressed, unwilling to face reality, but I was not aware of this at the time. Once, when I had spent the entire day in bed, Chaim came home and exclaimed, "Wow! the house is really clean."

I laughed in his face. "I didn't touch it!" I said, feeling a clear sense of victory.

He grinned sheepishly and shrugged. Determined to have the final word, he said, "Well, it's not clean but it looks clean."

I said to myself: Patsy, just shut up. Don't get into a fight over this.

Yom Kippur, 1980. Chaim did not bother to attend synagogue services, but he followed the custom of fasting on this Day of Atonement, as penance for his sins of the previous year. He was supposed to spend the day in prayer. He was supposed to be on his best behavior. But, instead, complaining of a headache, he grew bored and irritable. Usually he paid no attention to Marina, but he suddenly decreed that he was taking over the process of her education.

The baby was not yet one year old, but she was beginning to test her legs, learning to pull herself up, grasping at the cloth upholstery of a hassock, until she reached a standing position. From a chair in the far corner of the living room, Chaim watched her do this a few times and saw me help her gently back to the floor.

"If she's able to stand up, she must be able to sit down," Chaim declared.

Marina once more pulled herself up. She clung to the hassock and looked to me for approval and praise. "Bravo!" I said, clapping my hands together. She grinned proudly. Then her eyes showed a twinge of uncertainty and begged for me to help her sit. I moved toward her, but Chaim growled, "No!" He lectured Marina, as if she could understand, that she had to let herself down. She whimpered in response. Her lower lip quivered and her face took on an expression of fear.

Once more I moved to help her, but Chaim rushed across the room, grabbed me by the arm, pulled me through the kitchen, and shoved me out the front door. He slammed the door behind me and locked it. I rushed to the terrace window and watched in anguish as he forced my baby to remain standing. Her frail legs trembled. Chaim ignored her and sat in the chair next to her, calmly reading a book. Marina's cries grew louder. Her entire body quivered in fear. Unconcerned, Chaim rested his feet on the hassock. Marina turned her tiny head and spotted me peering in through the window. The volume of her sobs increased. Watching from the outside, helpless, I thought I would lose my mind. Crying and shivering, I wrapped my arms around my belly, as if to protect the six-month-old fetus in my womb.

Many minutes passed and Marina's terrified tears intensified. I could watch no more and I collapsed onto the porch, pulling my knees up to my chin. With my fingers I tried to plug my ears, but my baby's cries pierced through my brain. I wanted to die.

The nightmare continued for about ninety minutes before Marina's legs gave way and she fell to the floor. She was still sobbing as she drifted into a troubled sleep. Only then did Chaim unlock the door and allow me back into the house.

"Okay," he said, "she learned."

I cradled her in my arms and tried to make her feel safe, but I too was afraid. I could not bring myself to confront Chaim about his cruel behavior.

My doctor in Israel calculated that the new baby would arrive around Christmastime. Once more we returned to Belgium for the birth.

Because we could not predict the baby's arrival with certainty, we celebrated Christmas early. In honor of the holiday, as well as my twenty-first birthday and the impending birth, Maman had the diamonds removed from one of her brooches and commissioned a jeweler to create a beautiful ring for me. Mounted in white gold, the ring featured two one-karat stones, placed on the diagonal, and flanked by two smaller rectangular diamonds. It was a magnificent piece and I loved it the moment I saw it, but unfortunately it was too tight on my finger, which was swollen from pregnancy. Maman took it back to the jeweler to have it properly sized.

My mother's generous gift wounded Chaim's pride. He immediately went off on his own and, for two hundred dollars, bought me a ring with a small sapphire.

We awaited the onset of labor, but days passed and nothing happened. Christmas Day felt strange, since we had already celebrated.

Okay, we decided, we will have to celebrate New Year's early, since the baby will certainly arrive by then. We journeyed to the country house at Nassogne for a New Year's party. Everyone was careful not to mention the previous year, when Chaim spoiled the evening by forcing us to search for my wedding ring. Still, tension filled the air.

Back in Brussels, more days passed with no signs of labor. My obstetrician wondered if the Israeli doctor had miscalculated. Finally, after we had gone to bed the night of January 1, contractions came on strong and very suddenly. I woke Chaim but he refused to get out of bed. "Just wait, just wait," he ordered in a sleepy voice, pushing me aside.

I lay in silence, waiting as Chaim had commanded, but the time between the contractions steadily decreased. I repeatedly tried to rouse my husband, and when my mother, awakened in the adjacent bedroom by my movements, joined in, we finally convinced him to rush me to the hospital. I was already feeling the need to push.

We were almost too late. In the maternity ward, an examining nurse determined that the baby's head had already crowned. She immediately called for the obstetrician. With a clump of gauze in her hand, she forcibly held back the baby's head.

The doctor arrived quickly, and she was very angry that I had waited so long to come to the hospital. Then, as she guided the baby's head through the birth canal, she realized that the umbilical cord was wrapped tightly around the neck—twice. Had I given in to the urge to push while we were driving to the hospital, the baby surely would have suffocated.

Amid a flurry of activity, our son was born.

Someone asked us what name to write onto the baby's wristband. "Rony," I said, mentioning the first name that came to mind. This was not official. We had five days to visit town hall and certify the baby's actual name.

Chaim was extremely proud of producing a son and he immediately phoned his parents in Israel. Then, apparently exhausted by the experience of my giving birth, he returned to my parents' house and crawled into bed.

Both Chaim and my parents visited the next afternoon. But, after that, Chaim did not return to the hospital for twenty-four hours. When he finally arrived, it was obvious that he had been drinking. "Where have you been?" I asked. "Why haven't you come to see us?" Chaim brushed away my questions with the excuse that he had been exercising his right to celebrate the birth of his son. I wondered with whom he had been celebrating. Chaim had few acquaintances in Brussels.

He had not bothered with the trivial detail of naming our daughter, but now, without consulting me, Chaim visited town hall, filled out the necessary papers, returned to the hospital, and announced, "His name is Simon."

Chaim left Marina in my mother's care, for that was women's work. Meanwhile, he had unspecified business in the city. "Can you pick me up downtown this afternoon?" he asked.

"It might be difficult," Maman replied. She had her hands full with Marina, and she wanted to visit Simon and me later in the day. She did not need the added burden of functioning as Chaim's taxi service. Nevertheless, she wanted to do what she could to build a better relationship with her son-in-law. So she agreed.

Chaim nodded. "Okay," he said, "I will call you by two o'clock if I need a ride."

Two o'clock came and went with no call from Chaim, so Maman proceeded with her plans to bring my grandmother and a family friend to visit me. I was miserable and lonely but unwilling, or unable, to explain why. When she returned home later that afternoon, Maman found Chaim waiting angrily; he was also drunk. He railed at her for failing to pick him up: "You let me wait on the sidewalk! You told me you would come!"

"But you said you would call and you didn't," Maman protested.

Chaim stormed about the house, shouting and berating my mother for her shabby treatment of him. Finally he went into the bedroom to sulk.

"Patsy was so miserable when I visited her today," Maman confided to Papa. "Chaim should be with her. At least he could call. He's mad at me for not picking him up, but why does he have to ignore Patsy?"

Papa simply shook his head in bewilderment.

That evening, I called home and asked to speak to Chaim, but he refused to take the phone. My parents and my brothers begged him to speak to me, but he would not. Everyone was upset.

The next morning, as my parents and brothers sat around the breakfast table and Chaim languished in bed, Papa reached the limits of his patience. "I'm going to go in and chew his ass out," he declared. The entire family agreed that it was time to teach Chaim a lesson.

Papa rapped sharply on the bedroom door and then entered without invitation. Chaim was still asleep, but my father awakened him and demanded his attention. Calling Chaim lazy, insensitive, and cruel, Papa raged at him for ignoring his wife and new son. He finally vent his past frustrations, pointing out that

Chaim's big business talk never resulted in any visible success. He ordered Chaim to get up, get dressed, and visit me.

My father's wrath caught Chaim off guard. His manhood was attacked on the twin fronts of family and business. He probably wanted to lash out, but instead he adopted the characteristic posture of the coward when confronted by force. Sullenly he dragged himself out of bed, his mind whirring, devising a plan to punish my father by turning his wrath upon me.

He arrived at the hospital in a full rage, complaining bitterly in a low, menacing tone about my father's unfounded accusations. His revenge was typical; he would impose the silent treatment and force me to join him. He demanded that I no longer speak to either of my parents.

How could this be? How could he expect me to refuse to speak to my own mother and father? We were living in their house! I felt ill. What was I to do? Must I obey my husband and thereby dishonor my parents? I tried to get him to change his mind, but he was firm. I tried to resist, but his manner was threatening. I could not believe the horror of this latest development.

In the loneliness of my hospital bed, when I should have been overjoyed by the presence of a new life at my breast, the old life beat me down. I was too weak, too defeated, too much under Chaim's control to fight back. One by one the support systems of my life had been torn away. Former friends had drifted off. Didier had reacted predictably to my seeming indifference and no longer called. Even Princesse, in reaction to my neglect, was gone. Now Maman and Papa were to be shut out too, and my isolation would be complete.

Later that day, I left my room to wander through the first-floor shops. As I entered the elevator to return to the maternity floor, I saw my mother. She greeted me cheerfully but I turned my head, refusing to answer. We rode upward in silence. At the first opportunity, I got off the elevator, leaving my mother alone and bewildered. It was at that moment that she realized the extent of Chaim's hold over me.

When I returned to my room I found a note waiting on the

pillow. It read: "Patsy, if you need me and Papa, we are always there for you."

I spent hours alone, crying, focusing on my inner terror, feeling alienated and vulnerable.

The obstetrician engaged me in a quiet, careful discussion. "Don't you think it would be better if you go to another place—just you and the baby—and have time to think things over?" she said. She offered to transfer me to another hospital and, for a time, to keep Chaim away from me.

"What if he finds me?" I asked, imagining the terrifying consequences.

The obstetrician's eyes were filled with compassion. She tried to explain that there were laws to protect me and the baby.

"I'll think about it," I promised. "But I don't think I would do it."

And I did not. I was too afraid that Chaim would track me down.

A few days after we were discharged from the hospital, Chaim drove us to the house of a religious Jew, a kosher caterer who also specialized in performing circumcisions. Chaim explained that he wanted our son to undergo the procedure—not commonly performed in Belgium—for hygienic reasons; he had absolutely no regard for the Jewish spiritual dictates. In fact, the man who performed the procedure was neither a physician nor a rabbi. He did not so much as mumble a prayer. But he did his work swiftly and cleanly, right on his dining-room table. Simon did not even cry.

We remained as guests in my parents' home, but I obeyed my husband. Each morning, Maman quietly placed clean laundry in front of our bedroom door. Without comment, she cared for Marina. She prepared the meals that we ate together—even as Chaim and I maintained our cold, cruel silence. My family made the painful decision to tolerate this absurd situation only to prevent me from getting into further trouble with my husband. Chaim had effectively woven an impenetrable circle. My family

realized that confronting him only created more misery for me—
and, by extension, them.

Chaim chose this stress-filled time to decree that Marina,
only fifteen months old, would be toilet trained. He worked at the
task day and night, forcing her to sit on the potty seat for hours
at a time. He allowed me to speak with her and read to her to try
to get her to relax, but I was forbidden to remove her from the
potty seat. Her whimpers brought anguish. Maman and I communicated this to one another with our eyes, but we dared not
speak.

My mother picked up my diamond ring from the jeweler,
but she did not give it back to me. Once more we communicated
silently. Her eyes said: Patsy, I am not doing this to hurt you, only
to keep it away from Chaim.

Simon was a high-strung and fussy infant. He seldom slept
for more than forty-five minutes at a time and seemed to cry constantly. Tending to him night and day left me sleep-deprived, irritable, and unable to concentrate.

On the spur of the moment, Chaim decreed that we would
return to Israel. Abruptly at 6:00 A.M. one morning, when Simon
was two weeks old, we left. My family watched us go in silence. I
was filled with sadness but dared not say good-bye.

7

We moved from the small house in Hod Hasharon to an apartment in Tel Aviv, and, for a time, I was able to bury my grief over the loss of contact with my family.

The young city of Tel Aviv is adjacent to the historic seaport of Jaffa, which, according to tradition, was founded by Noah's son Japheth after the flood. Tradition also holds that here, Jonah embarked upon his fateful voyage. Today, the legendary town combines with its twin to show both the ancient and modern faces of Israel. To some, Tel Aviv is a lively metropolis; to others, it is noisy and unattractive. I hated it. To me, it was a city of unimaginative concrete. Traffic was horrible. The humidity was always high. I never went to the center of the city, but people said there was so much air pollution that neither flies nor mosquitoes could survive there.

The unrelenting sun over Tel Aviv beat down upon me. So did Chaim. He was like a coin. One side of him was a charming, charismatic little boy. The other side was an unreasonable, violent bully. There was always a cloud of uncertainty over my life. When would the coin flip, turning the gentle, fun-loving Chaim into an unreasonable tyrant? I never knew what would set him off. Often the smallest aggravation created the greatest fury.

Whenever he arrived home, I had to guess at his mood. But even this was futile, for the mood could change dramatically within five minutes.

I do not remember the first time that Chaim actually hit me. Perhaps it began with shoving, and simply grew out of control.

Several times we went out to dinner, but I was not allowed to hire a baby-sitter for the children. We always waited until Marina and Simon were sound asleep before we left. I knew that it was wrong, and dangerous, to leave two small children home alone, but I dared not raise strong objections against any of Chaim's wishes. Fortunately, nothing happened during our absences.

Prime Minister Begin's government, beset by an ailing economy, instituted drastic measures. Israelis tightened their belts, and Chaim grew desperate for money. One night when he invited me out to dinner, he told me to dress nicely and to wear the beautiful diamond brooch that my grandmother had given to me as a wedding present. As soon as we arrived, I felt very much out of place. This was a modest, casual restaurant, and I was overdressed, as if I had worn an evening gown to go to the market. We were joined at our table by a man whom I did not know, and Chaim immediately drew attention to my brooch. The man regarded it carefully, as if he were appraising it. "It's not too bad," he said, "but the diamonds are not very big. And the quality—I don't know." His comments made me feel very uncomfortable.

Later that evening, after we had returned home, Chaim told me to give him the brooch for safekeeping. It was the last time I ever saw it.

On business matters, as with everything else, I deferred to Chaim completely. One day he shoved a blank piece of paper in front of me and said, "Sign this at the bottom."

"But there's nothing there," I protested. "What am I signing?"

"It's nothing. Just a form for tax receipts that I will have to fill out. It's easier if I don't have to come back to have it signed."

I shrugged and did as he asked, affixing my signature to the bottom of the page.

"In case I make a mistake," he added, "do the same to these."

He shoved several more blank pages in front of me and I obediently scrawled my signature on them.

Chaim began a systematic campaign to destroy anything that had come to me through my family. Many times, after an argument, he would rummage through my closet, pull out a piece of clothing that my parents had bought for me, and slash it into tatters with scissors. I did not want him to have the satisfaction of knowing that this juvenile behavior bothered me, so, after one of these tantrums, I took additional pieces of clothing from the closet and handed them to him. "Here, you want to cut?" I said. "Then cut some more. Take these." He grabbed a dress and cut it up, but his anger had dissipated; I had taken the fun out of the game.

There were other small victories.

Once, Chaim suddenly ordered me to take the children outside. I did as he said and then he came out after us, locked the door behind him, and drove away. I had no idea what I had done to deserve this punishment, but there I was, banished and defenseless, with Marina at my side and Simon in my arms. I worried about what I would do when Simon began wailing for his bottle.

A strange battle of wills surfaced. As I waited, I became determined not to let Chaim win this particular skirmish. When he eventually returned, I said brightly, "Oh, what a good idea you had! We had such fun. We made a pretend picnic and played in the fresh air. We made bracelets with the grass and really enjoyed ourselves."

But the ruse backfired on me. Instead of locking us out of the apartment, Chaim began to shut us in. For days at a time we were locked away, forbidden to speak to anyone, with no money and very little food. Several times, when Chaim did not bother to go to the market and there was no milk, I had to concoct a mixture of flour and water for Simon's bottle. I had no choice.

Chaim's punishment of choice continued to be a maddening silence, which fostered extreme loneliness and isolation. The only way to get back into his good graces was to sit at his feet, crying in submission and begging for forgiveness. As I babbled, he occasionally glanced down at me as if I were an irritating puppy. Then he would return to the book he was reading or light a cigarette, and deny my existence until he felt that I was sufficiently contrite. The humiliations chipped away at my already fragile self-esteem. I felt as though I were disappearing.

Chaim appeared very worried as he prepared to discuss a serious problem with me. And he did so only because I was an essential part of the solution. The previous year, when Bank Leumi in Hod Hasharon had erroneously inflated our account from $1,400 to $14,000 Chaim had lost the entire small fortune by dabbling in the stock-futures market. Now, as Papa had predicted, the bank had discovered its error and demanded that Chaim return the money.

I hid my anger. Diplomatically I pointed out that the bank would have trouble collecting $12,000 from someone who had no money. This was an uncomfortable situation, but was it disaster?

Chaim had difficulty telling me the rest of the story, but it finally came out. On October 19, 1978, a criminal court in Nazareth had convicted him of breaking and entering and had imposed a one-year jail term and three years of probation; the jail sentence was suspended but, if at any time during the probationary period he got into additional trouble, he would have to serve the prison sentence. Thus, if Bank Leumi filed new charges, Chaim's probation would be revoked. If he did not reimburse the bank—quickly—he would go to prison.

The awful realization that I was married to a common thief was quickly replaced by concern for my children. What would become of Marina and Simon if their father went off to jail? My mind was too clouded to reason properly. Chaim may have been a poor provider, but he was the only provider we had. What were we to do?

To Chaim, the solution was simple though distasteful. My parents were the only people he knew who could supply the necessary amount of money. He ordered me to call them, explain the situation, and offer a deal: If they paid the money to keep him out of prison, then he would allow me to resume my relationship with them.

My mind reeled at this repulsive suggestion. Chaim was holding the children and me hostage! What's more, he demanded that I handle the negotiations.

But I could not disobey my husband. Swallowing every ounce of my self-respect, I phoned my parents in Brussels. They were, of course, thrilled to hear from me and full of questions about the children. At the same time, they were deeply concerned over my tears. As best I could, I sobbed out the story. Papa asked for details, and I tried to provide them in a way that portrayed Chaim in the most favorable light, but it was impossible. Chaim had a prior conviction for burglary. He had swindled the bank. Now, he would allow me to speak with my parents in return for a hefty cash payment.

After lengthy discussions and tense negotiations with Chaim, they agreed. But, of course, they acted out of simple love and concern for Marina, Simon, and me. Mother immediately flew to Israel to bring us the money. As she handed the check to Chaim, she vowed, "This will be the last time you ever get money from us." Before this incident, my parents held few illusions about Chaim's character; now they had none. From this moment on, they remained alert for any way to help me get away from this destructive man.

For me, a deep emotional retreat was necessary. I could not cope with the reality of what I had done. My only alternative was to black out the memory. For years afterward, I would insist—quite sincerely—that it was Chaim, not I, who called my parents and demanded the ransom money.

The bank-fraud case was so well reported in the Israeli press that Chaim's very name was now a liability. As Chaim Edwar, he could not hope to land a respectable job. But in Israel it is easy for anyone to change his legal name; this is for the convenience of immigrants who wish to be identified by a Hebrew surname. My husband filed the necessary papers to become Chaim Yarden and, with the stroke of a pen, the children and I also became Yardens.

Chaim felt emasculated because once again he had been forced to accept help from my parents. Day after day his mood darkened. The moment he woke, he found some reason to argue. Whenever he left the house, he snapped out orders. Whenever he returned, he found something wrong with my behavior. I felt as if the walls had a thousand eyes that monitored everything I said or did—or even thought.

I was no match for him physically, so I engaged in mental warfare. I tried to keep him off balance, downplaying actions that really hurt me, never giving him the satisfaction of knowing that he had succeeded. Instead, I feigned anguish and disappointment over trivial episodes that did not bother me.

But when he really wanted to demonstrate his anger, nothing helped. Once or twice I stood on tiptoe and attempted to swing back at him, but he was much larger and much more powerful. In the end, my resistance only increased his wrath. Usually the beatings were administered in such a way that the bruises would not show. He struck me on the back, kicked me in the stomach, or yanked out fistfuls of my hair, leaving no visible evidence for the outside world to see. The physical assaults were sporadic; the emotional terrorism was constant.

Over time, Chaim's beatings grew more frequent and more violent. I learned to expect them on a regular basis and was almost numbed to their effect. During these horrible, seemingly endless episodes, my desperate goal was to deny him the satisfaction of my tears. I learned to numb myself by silently counting numbers or reciting the alphabet until the pounding stopped. My natural tendency to bury my feelings was deepened by Chaim's abuse.

Occasionally his aim was flawed. One day, after we had a bitter argument, I put Marina and Simon into a stroller and walked to the government office where I picked up the voucher for my regular payment for being an Israeli immigrant. Normally I took the voucher directly home to Chaim. But on this day I was so furious that I went to a bank, cashed the voucher, and spent all the money on clothes and toys for the children and a bit of makeup for myself.

Back in the apartment, when Chaim realized what I had done, he lashed out violently. His hand crashed into my face with such force that I was certain my nose had broken into a thousand painful pieces. It bled profusely and I had difficulty breathing.

The next day I walked to a clinic. "I want to check to see if my nose is broken," I said to the doctor. "Is there any medication you can give me, because I cannot breathe."

The doctor regarded me carefully. "How did this happen?" he asked.

"I got up in the middle of the night and crashed into a door."

The doctor rolled his eyes as if to say: We both know what has happened to you. His examination determined that my nose was not broken. He clearly wanted to know more about this episode, but all he could do was prescribe medication to reduce the swelling—and send me back home to my husband.

After each beating I could expect one of two responses. Chaim might suddenly turn into the contrite husband, wailing, "Oh, I'm so sorry! I will never do it again." But more often he lectured me, contending that my own misbehavior had forced him to punish me. Sometimes he kept me awake until 4:00 A.M. with his catalog of my supposed sins. I learned to doze off with my eyes open, mumbling an occasional, acquiescent yes.

The only people whom he allowed me to visit without restriction were a few friends whose family lives were like our own: the husbands made the rules and the wives obeyed—or risked a beating. Chaim seemed to need their examples to justify his own behavior. Slowly, I forgot that there were other ways of life—I even forgot the example of Maman and Papa's marriage. I slipped into a state of submissiveness and came to believe that this was a wife's lot, that my marriage was the norm.

It was as if I lived in a cloud.

Despite the abuse, it was my duty to be willing and ready whenever Chaim wanted sex, which was several times a week and always performed in what is known in Israel as "Yemenite style," which simply means that it was over very quickly. Afterward, I felt emotionally raped.

I sat in our small dining room, feeding Marina and Simon. To simplify the process, I fed them both from one dish. The same spoon went first to one and then to the other. When Chaim saw what I was doing, he growled, "Such a mother! So lazy and so stupid. How can you do such a thing?"

"It's easier this way," I said, "and the kids certainly don't mind. Why should you?"

My response made him angrier. "You're treating them like dogs," he complained.

That night, as I tried to sleep, Chaim brought up the subject once more and yelled at me for what he saw as my repeated failures. "I cannot sleep with such a woman," he decreed. "Go and sleep in the living room."

The prospect of sleeping alone was fine with me. I picked up a blanket and settled in on the living-room couch. Soon I was fast asleep.

Sometime during the night I wakened, sensing that Chaim was standing over me. "Go back to the bedroom," he ordered. I knew what he had in mind, and I wanted no part of it. I kept my eyes closed, pretending to be fast asleep. Chaim returned to the bedroom quietly.

The next night, on my own initiative, I once more slept on the couch. Chaim's anger simmered for days.

A deep storm brewed, but I could neither stop it from coming nor predict the strength of its fury. My emotions were raw, and my own mood swings were accentuated by altered chemistry: I tired easily, my breasts swelled, my sense of smell was acute—I was beginning to sense the unmistakable signs of early pregnancy.

One day I said, "Chaim, we need milk for Simon's bottle."

He grumbled, "Mix flour and water, like you did before."

"But, Chaim," I said, "he's a growing boy. He needs—"

Chaim pushed me so forcibly that I crashed to the floor. I was stunned and dazed by the suddenness of the attack. The sharp toe of his shoe kicked me in the stomach, forcing the air from my lungs. I doubled over in pain and gasped for breath. His foot pushed at me, rolling me over. His shoe smashed into the small of my back. Sharp pains shot up my spine.

Watching from a corner, Marina screamed in fear. Baby Simon joined in with his own wails. This was the first time that Chaim had dared to attack me in the presence of the children, and their terror hurt worst of all.

Again and again Chaim struck. I tried to roll away from the blows, but his foot found its target repeatedly. Pain rolled over me in waves. I felt the onset of shock.

Through a dimmed consciousness I heard someone bang on the door of our apartment. The concerned voice of a neighbor asked, "What's going on?"

Chaim pushed me aside, went to the door, and opened it slightly, so that I remained out of view. "It's nothing," he said. "I dropped a large ashtray."

For the next two weeks I could barely walk. Only with supreme effort did I manage to care for Marina and Simon's basic needs. I ate my meals standing up. At every available moment I lay in bed, almost motionless, on my stomach. For another month I needed pillows just to be able to sit on my bruised and swollen tailbone.

Chaim decided to take advantage of an Israeli government offer of discounted mortgage rates for young families who agreed to settle in the northern part of the country. I was still recovering from his beating, but he made me go with him to visit the site of a new apartment building in Karmi'el, a town about twenty miles inland from Haifa. We signed a contract to purchase a condominium on the eighth floor, the top level.

To qualify for the mortgage, Chaim needed proof of employment and salary verification. But he had neither employment nor salary, so he once more called upon my father to bail him out of difficulty. He phoned Brussels and asked Papa to provide him with a letter on his company's stationery, verifying his employment and indicating a salary. Implicit in this request was the threat that, if my father refused, the silent treatment would be imposed once again. Feeling cornered, Papa complied.

Immediately we began to prepare for the move. Our apartment was soon littered with crates and boxes.

As time passed, I realized that my body was reacting differently to this new pregnancy. My anxiety escalated. I was increasingly aware of a sense of emptiness, as if nothing were growing inside me. I worried constantly about this but was unable to motivate myself to seek help. Then one night I began to suffer contractions. Blood soaked my clothing. An ambulance rushed me to the hospital as Chaim remained at home to arrange for someone to watch Marina and Simon. In the ambulance, the paramedic instructed me to hold my legs together, as if the force of my will could prevent the inevitable.

Once I arrived at the hospital, despite my pain and fear, I refused to allow the male physician to examine me without my husband's permission. "This is nonsense," the doctor said. "Even the Hasidic people allow a male doctor to examine a woman in an emergency." The Hasidic Jews are the most conservative.

Still, I was more terrified of Chaim's wrath than I was of my physical complications. When he finally arrived, he demanded a woman physician, but none were available. Finally, reluctantly, he agreed to let the male doctor treat me.

After several tests, the doctor concluded that the fetus was dead. He performed a D & C and sent me home the same day. Since he could find no apparent reason for the baby's death, he ordered a series of tests and told me that he would inform me of the results as soon as possible.

My father happened to be in Israel on business and came to visit me the following evening. He found me alone in bed, grieving over the loss of my child. His face registered deep sadness.

That night I was plagued by what would become a horrible, recurring dream, a vision of an infant's limbs being torn from my body and discarded like useless pieces of chicken. I awoke, drenched in sweat and breathing heavily. I dreaded going back to sleep, knowing the vision that awaited me.

Bearing two children so close together, followed by the stillbirth, left me exhausted, weak, and fearful that I would never again be able to carry a baby to full term.

8

The building in Karmi'el was not completed by the time we had to vacate our apartment in Tel Aviv, so we moved in with Chaim's parents for one month. I tended to the house while Leah was at work.

When I returned to the clinic, the doctor informed me that the baby I had lost had been normal in every way. He was unable to determine a cause of death, but he said that the child had died in utero two months before I went into labor.

My mind raced back in time. The baby's death coincided with the beating when Chaim had kicked me so viciously in the back. I was horrified, but I filed the tragic realization in the dark recesses of my mind and never spoke of it. I knew that if I confronted him, Chaim would convince me I was responsible for the tragedy, and that was something I would not be able to bear.

In his own home, Shlomo Edwar declared war. When Leah was around, Chaim's father simply ignored me. But whenever she was gone, he became a beast. He referred to me openly as a "son-of-a-bitch Christian" and as Chaim's "Christian whore." When he was home he followed me about for hours, as if to check on the quality of my housework. When I opened a window, he closed it. When I turned on a light, he switched it off.

Generally I could disregard him, but one day he was particularly obnoxious. When I went out to shop, he followed me into the street, swaying from the effects of too much vodka, yelling obscenities at my back. The spectacle unnerved me, but I did not let my agitation show.

By evening, as Chaim and I sat at the table with the children, eating soft-boiled eggs, I was exhausted. Shlomo wandered in, gestured at the children, and bellowed, "They are dogs of Christians!"

Something in me snapped. I thought: He can call me whatever he wishes, but no one is going to subject my children to this type of abuse. I scooped the eggs from in front of Chaim and my wide-eyed children and hurled them at my tormentor. One splattered against the wall, but another landed squarely atop the old man's cap. I screamed, "As long as you touch me, I don't care! Make me nervous, I don't care! But if you touch the children—" The threat hung suspended in the air.

"Oh, bravo!" Shlomo said with a sarcastic laugh. "Look what you did. Are you proud of yourself?"

Chaim said nothing, but his expression told me that, on this occasion, he sided with me.

Shlomo would not allow Leah to clean the mess from the wall or even from his cap. Weeks later he pointed out the stains to a visitor, asking, "Did you see what the Christian did?"

I said boldly, "Yeah, but did you say why? Did you tell him what you did?"

Shlomo walked away muttering, "Christian!"

During my pregnancies, Chaim had decreed that I was not allowed to take any kind of medication whatsoever, and that included prenatal vitamins. As a result, a vitamin deficiency created such severe dryness in my skin that my fingers blistered and bled. I could not open and shut my hand. When I shampooed my hair, new blisters emerged. If I sliced an onion, the acid ate into my skin. My gums began to recede and swell. My doctor lectured, "Lady, you may not get pregnant for at least six months."

I told Chaim of the doctor's concerns and hoped that he would agree to let me use some form of contraception, but he still would not hear of it.

As I rose from bed one morning in the beginning of September, I immediately realized what had occurred the previous night. There were no symptoms. It was just something that I *knew*. I announced to Chaim, "I'm pregnant."

Despite the tension in my marriage and a tinge of fear over my doctor's warning, I was extremely happy. I thought: I am still worth something. I can still make a baby!

Construction in Karmi'el lagged well behind schedule. Our one-month stay with Chaim's parents dragged on, well past our original intentions.

It was at this time that Chaim finally decided to get a driver's license. To do so, he had to change his military status. He had to undergo a series of tests on his injured elbow, to determine if he was sufficiently recovered, and he had to pass a psychological examination. The process took about a week. When it was over, he displayed his new driver's license for me and explained how difficult it was to get. I was confused. I could understand the need for a physical examination, but I asked, "Why do they have to test your head? It's your elbow."

"Oh, it's just rules." Puffing out his chest with pride, he told me that a military psychiatrist had attempted to trick him. Chaim had mentioned that he often flew to Belgium. The psychiatrist had flapped his arms and asked, "You mean you fly yourself?"

"No, no," Chaim responded quickly. "I'm sitting in an airplane." According to Chaim, this astute response convinced the psychiatrist that he was sane enough to be granted a driver's license.

Chaim's reevaluated military status resulted in his assignment to a low-level army-reserve unit that was occasionally called upon to clean up after official ceremonies. It was comprised mainly of aging veterans; almost no young, able-bodied reservists were given such light duty.

Chaim knew that his mother would not tolerate his physical abuse of me, so he resorted to psychological torture. One night, however, he could not control himself. In the privacy of our bedroom, he pulled me off the bed by grasping my long hair, yanking so violently that I feared he would pull the skin from my scalp. Once he had me on the floor, he kicked, aiming his blows with care. With neither the ability nor the will to resist, I could only lay in a heap, counting silently to myself: *"Un, deux, trois . . ."*

He grabbed a pair of scissors and hacked away at my hair until my scalp was nearly bare.

Leah, the next morning, stared at my head and asked, "What happened?"

I could only shrug and mutter, "It's Chaim."

Leah looked to her son for an explanation. Chaim said, "The uglier I can get her the better."

Simon was barely ten months old. He lay on the bed in our room as I changed his diaper. Marina toddled in and said something to me. I turned briefly in her direction and, in that instant, Simon rolled over and fell to the floor, landing squarely on his back and his head. He was eerily silent. I picked him up carefully and cuddled him as I mumbled an apology that he could not understand. Still he did not cry, and I knew that could be a dangerous sign of a head injury. I watched him closely and became even more concerned when he began to vomit.

Chaim was not at home. But when he returned, about a half hour later, I told him what had happened and begged him to drive us to the hospital.

Chaim glanced at the baby and shrugged. "No," he decreed, "I will not take you to the hospital. It's your punishment. If you cannot take proper care of your children, it's what you deserve."

"But it's not for me," I protested. "It's for Simon."

Still Chaim refused.

All evening I watched Simon for signs of improvement, but he remained lethargic and nauseous.

Finally, the next morning Chaim relented and drove us to the hospital.

After examining Simon, the doctor regarded us carefully. Chaim acted the role of a concerned and responsible father, whereas I was nervous and guilt-ridden. The doctor's voice cut through me like a knife. "Why did you wait so long to bring him in?" he asked. "What are you trying to hide?" He charged that I was an abusive parent and had either beaten, dropped, or shaken the baby so hard that a concussion had occurred. I *never* raised a hand to my children, but there seemed to be nothing I could say in my own defense. I dared not blame Chaim for the delay.

Several specialists were called in to check Simon carefully for any other signs of abuse. Because the hospital was overcrowded, Simon was placed in a small crib in a hallway. I spent the day in a chair next to the bed, keeping vigil. Each time a doctor or nurse came in, I could feel an accusing stare. The baby's condition improved steadily, and when he was able to keep small amounts of liquid in his stomach without vomiting we were allowed to leave.

My maternal confidence was badly shaken. I felt responsible and ashamed. Chaim was right—I was a stupid and inept mother. The doctors had affirmed it. I told myself: You cannot succeed at anything, Patsy. Not even mothering.

Chaim seized upon this insecurity. Whenever we argued he reminded me of the incident and cited it as proof of my failures. But, for his part, Chaim was more concerned with Simon's masculine equipment than with his neurological system. Every day he inspected the baby's genitals to make sure they were developing properly. Once, he thought he detected a difference in size between the two testicles. Extremely worried, he sent us to a pediatrician, who assured us that Simon was perfectly normal.

Living under the same roof with Chaim's parents, I observed the differences in their religious practices. Shlomo did not exhibit fervor in his daily life, but he dutifully observed the Shabbat rules. Leah was not religious, but she generally followed her husband's lead. I occasionally saw her switch on a light during the forbidden hours.

On this subject, Shlomo and Chaim clashed. One Shabbat, the children played quietly outside and I left the door ajar to keep an eye on them. Shlomo apparently considered children's play to be inappropriate Shabbat behavior. On wobbly feet, he walked over to the door and slammed it shut so that he would not have to watch.

With a glare at Shlomo, I opened the door once more.

Shlomo slammed it shut with an extra measure of vigor.

The hostile routine continued until Chaim's temper flared, this time in my defense. His father's hand was on the door frame when Chaim slammed it shut himself, crushing Shlomo's thumb. Shlomo yelped. Leah came running. Shlomo lumbered about, displaying a swollen thumb to all who would look. "Do you see that?" he grumbled. "Do you see what he did to his own father? On Shabbat!" But he did not try to close the door again.

A vast spectrum of ideologies is available to all Jews in Israel, ranging from the totally secular to the devout Hasidim, who are easily identified by their attire—the women in formless dresses with long sleeves and low hemlines over thick, high socks; the men in black suits and the broad-brimmed black hats called *shreimel*. The day a religious woman marries she must shave her head in order to make herself unattractive to other men. From that time forward, when she goes out of the house, she will cover her head with a wig or perhaps a scarf adorned in front with a few false ringlets. Hasidic men grow dangling sideburns known as *peiyot*. The Hasidim regard *loshen kodesk* (ancient Hebrew) as a sacred language to be used only for religious purposes; in normal conversation, they speak Yiddish. Hasidim are excused from military service, but they play an active role in Israeli political life. Considering their relatively small numbers, they have a great deal of influence in political decisions and the formation of governments. As a minority swing vote, they frequently hold the key to power.

In between the extremes of faith are numerous philosophical positions, with labels such as Reformed, Conservative, and Orthodox. Another distinction is whether a person "keeps kosher" or sneaks off to a Christian restaurant for "the meat I like." It is all very confusing, and for convenience many Israelis resort to the term "religious." Describing someone as "religious" generally means that he is at least Orthodox and perhaps even more pious. Calling someone "very religious" probably categorizes him as a Hasidic Jew. Depending upon the orientation of the speaker, the term "religious" can either be high praise or evidence of liberal snobbery.

Chaim and I clearly lived a secular lifestyle, but most of the time we tried to show respect for his parents' principles. If Chaim wanted to smoke on Shabbat, he did so out on the porch or in the garden. We did not flaunt our nonobservance of Shabbat other than to use the car. Almost every weekend we escaped on drives into the countryside, where we would picnic and spend the night camping. Chaim usually brought a small, portable television set and spent most of his time watching it, ignoring the children and me. I enjoyed these times very much, amid the beauty of Israel and away from the belligerent Shlomo, until Chaim stole this pleasure from me also.

During an outing in an area close to the Sea of Galilee, Chaim decided to go fishing, and he deposited Marina, Simon, and me in an arid grove of eucalyptus trees. Then he disappeared. I settled the children and began to gather twigs and leaves to make a cooking fire. I managed to get the fire started, but a strong gust of wind swept in, sprinkling a few sparks and embers onto the dry leaves close by. The fire spread quickly toward the trees. Frantically I gathered the children and hustled them to safety. Then I stomped on the burning leaves. Each time I snuffed out one cluster of flames, the wind spread the fire to another pile of leaves.

When Chaim returned he was furious. How could I be so

careless? How could I be so stupid? He was so angry that he commanded, "You stay here. I'll come back and get you when I want to." Then he drove off, leaving me and his children alone.

It was extremely hot. We huddled beneath a shade tree. Marina was old enough to be worried, and I tried to calm her. "It's just a joke," I said, attempting a light tone. "He'll come back for us soon."

A car appeared on the horizon and the driver stopped and asked, "Do you need help?"

"No, it's okay," I lied, knowing that if I accepted help from a stranger—particularly a man—I would only intensify Chaim's fury.

We waited for three hours, until Chaim decided to return for us. As we scrambled into the car, Chaim ordered me out. "I'm taking the children and leaving you here," he said.

Slowly, he pulled the car a short distance away. I ran after it, but before I could reach the door, he pulled farther ahead. Playing with me like a cat, he kept me running after him for several minutes. When I spotted Marina's terrified face peering out the rear window at me I stopped, so that I would not alarm her further.

Seeing that the game was over, Chaim finally allowed me inside.

I was in the first trimester of my fourth pregnancy and having problems with the circulation in my legs. In the middle of the night, Simon began to wail. Chaim would never interrupt his sleep for a crying baby, so I crawled from the bed to go to him. My leg was fast asleep. It buckled and sent me crashing to the floor. By the next morning, the pain in my leg was so severe that I had to go to the hospital. Because of my pregnancy, the doctor did not want to take X rays. "Just go home and lie down for a while," he said. "If it does not get better in one or two days, come back."

Chaim could not countenance the idea of a bedridden, useless wife—even a pregnant one. Upon returning from the hospital, I faced a pile of unwashed laundry. Chaim expected his dinner. I attended to my household tasks by jumping about on one leg.

That night he woke me at 2:00 A.M., demanding that I cook goulash for him. "No," I said groggily.

"Yes." His tone was sharp, mean.

I yawned and complained, "Goulash takes a long time to cook." I attempted to roll over and go back to sleep, but Chaim dragged me from the bed and pushed me toward the kitchen.

"Make goulash!" he screamed, unconcerned that his parents might hear.

My leg throbbed as I went through the motions of cooking, while Chaim hovered, watching. I found beef in the refrigerator, diced it, and cut up onions and tomatoes. I stewed the mixture slowly, adding paprika and other spices, until the meat was tender. Hearing noise in the kitchen, Leah came in to investigate. She tried to help me, but an angry glare from Chaim stopped her. She watched in silence.

Finally the meal was ready. I prepared a plate of hot goulash, turned, and looked for Chaim, but he was nowhere to be seen. I carried the plate through the house, searching for my husband, until I found him in our bed, fast asleep.

I befriended a young woman from Yemen, or Morocco, I was unsure. Rachel had experienced numerous pregnancies, but only one child had survived. Nearly every day I took Marina and Simon over to Rachel's large, sparsely furnished home to play with her silent, sullen child. My attempts to learn more about Rachel's life were usually cut short by comments such as, "Excuse me, Patsy, but you have to go. I have to prepare chicken for my husband, because he asked me to have chicken tonight." Clearly, Rachel was as afraid of her husband as I was of Chaim. We were paranoid about doing anything that deviated in the least from their desires and commands, and we dared not speak about their behavior.

We would not admit it, but we were terribly lonely and miserable. Neither of us could fully trust the other. What if I said something to Rachel and she spoke to her husband and he spoke to Chaim? Rachel obviously felt the same dread.

Without warning, Chaim asked me one day, "Do you hide anything from me?" The tone of his voice carried such menace that I did not know how to respond.

"No," I said.

"Are you sure?"

"Yes, I'm sure."

9

We were permitted to move into the apartment in Karmi'el when it was near completion. As the last bits of construction were under way, we stored our belongings in one of the empty but finished apartments across the hall, and I spent my days running back and forth, cooking in one place, changing Simon in another. Chaim was seldom at home, leaving us to our own devices.

The view from my new, eighth-floor kitchen window was a vista of desert stones and clumps of greenery, surrounded by mounds of craggy rocks jutting from the earth. Less than three hundred feet away, a blue-topped rectangular tent housed an encampment of bedouins. They shared their living space with sheep, goats, and chickens.

Karmi'el was a rapidly developing area, with new facilities such as our apartment building attracting many young families. Chaim determined that this was a growth opportunity, and he decided to open a shop offering bath fixtures, tiles, faucets, and other supplies catering to the needs of new homeowners. For some unexplained reason, he said that he had decided to register the business in my name, not his.

"Why?" I asked.

"You're too stupid to understand. Sign these papers."

I did as he instructed. I had no interest in business; my days were filled with child care and housework. Once the shop opened, Chaim spent less and less time at home. I did not care what he was doing; I was simply grateful for the peace.

There were occasional signs that Chaim did not devote his full efforts to the business world. Several times I noticed what appeared to be cosmetic or lipstick smears on his shirt. When I questioned him, he dismissed me by mumbling a vague explanation, such as a leaky pen. Often, when I entered the car, I found the passenger seat in a reclined position that was not where I had left it. "Who has been riding with you?" I asked.

"Nobody," he replied.

Once, he was gone for the entire night, not returning until ten o'clock the next morning. When I asked him where he was and why he did not try to contact me, he said that certain business matters had tied up his time; he claimed that he had telephoned one of the construction workers at the apartment complex and asked him to relay the message. Obviously, Chaim said, the man had failed to do so.

I thought: Fine, just leave me alone.

The three apartments across the hall remained vacant. We were the only family living on the top floor, and Chaim attempted to further isolate me. He kept my passport, my ID card, and all of our money. We had no telephone, and the nearest pay phone was a mile away. Any calls I made had to be collect.

My understanding of Hebrew was improving greatly, but I still had a limited vocabulary. While listening to the news on the radio, I occasionally asked Chaim, "What does that word mean?"

"You're too stupid to understand," he would reply. With every question came the same message: Patsy, you are too stupid. You are stupid!

By now, I believed him.

I was allowed to visit the grocery store once or twice a week but given no money. I signed for the groceries and, later, Chaim studied the receipts carefully and demanded an explanation for every bag of rice or piece of chicken that I had purchased. He decreed that chicken wings were the only form of meat or poultry we could afford. The only time I was allowed to carry cash was when I went to the open market, and on those occasions Chaim usually accompanied me.

Although Chaim never seemed to lack the funds to buy himself nice clothes—or whatever else he wanted—there was rarely any money for the children. Almost all of their clothing was sent to them by my parents. I complained to Chaim that Marina and Simon had no toys. I had to create coloring books for them and improvise games. "When we go to the market, let me keep whatever coins we get in change," I suggested. "I will save them and use the money to buy toys for the kids."

Chaim sneered at my request.

"But it will seem as though we are not spending anything," I reasoned.

"All right, all right," he grumbled, "keep the coins."

I was surprised at how quickly the coins piled up. Within a few weeks, I managed to buy a few inexpensive games for the children. Then Chaim changed his mind. "You are getting too many coins. Give them to me," he ordered.

The one time Chaim grudgingly purchased a jacket for Simon, it was several sizes too large. Rather than complain, I decided to alter the garment myself. I shortened the sleeves and hemmed them with elastic bands. I was extremely proud of myself. I thought I was a failure at everything, but now I had accomplished something. "Look what I've done!" I said to Chaim.

"How dare you do such a thing without my permission!" he barked. He launched into a tirade that lasted for hours. Once more he reminded me of how I had let Simon fall off the bed. He relived every real or imagined mistake that he could remember. He frequently punctuated his argument with the words "bad wife" and "bad mother."

"Okay," I said finally, "I will ask your permission for *everything*." He smirked, but his expression changed to a scowl as I followed him about the apartment, whining, "Can I open the door? Can I close it again? Can I turn on the light? Can I sit down?" I knew that I would pay for my insolence, but I could not help myself.

"Shut up or I'll beat you in front of the kids," he threatened.

That was a warning I understood, and it persuaded me to hold my tongue.

Twice a day, morning and afternoon, I saw mothers gathered in the courtyard at the front of the building as their children played in the hot Israeli sun. "I want to take the children down to play," I said.

"They can go, but you may not," Chaim said.

I responded sharply, "I cannot leave two small children alone down there, eight floors below me. I have to go with them."

"You may go," Chaim relented, "but you may not talk to anyone."

He could close my mouth but not my eyes and ears. I saw, all about me, young women who were happy and vital—women with relaxed smiles, women whose children shrieked with pleasure over simple delights, women who had money to spend as they wished, women who were free to go wherever they wanted. Their comments amazed me:

"My house is a mess, but I'll clean it tomorrow."
"Well, I was tired, so Aaron cooked dinner."
"He bought me this necklace . . ."

I had almost forgotten that such lives were possible. I began to realize that, slowly and systematically, Chaim had isolated me from reality. My life—our marriage—was *not* normal.

Even though I was forbidden to speak, I made the first tentative steps toward communication with some of the other women. It was impossible not to talk. At first I simply responded yes or no to their questions. But I found them to be friendly and receptive. One of them was a German-American woman. Over time, our quiet conversations evolved from the predictable observances of our children to the more personal aspects of our lives, but our words remained somewhat guarded.

"The walls are thin," she said quietly one day. The expression on her face told me she was aware that Chaim beat me frequently. She wanted to help but feared my husband's violent temper.

Even with the growing realization that my life with Chaim was abnormal and dangerous, my pride and my natural tendency to keep things bottled inside kept me from calling out for help. I was also paralyzed by my irrational fear that Chaim, somehow, knew about everything I did. A part of me wanted to reach out to my family, to beg for their forgiveness and help, but I simply could not do it.

My sense of isolation was heightened when my grandfather took a cruise to Israel. The ship stopped in Haifa, and Chaim and I went to visit Grandfather. He was cool and standoffish, making no secret of the fact that he still disliked and mistrusted Chaim. His reaction was fresh evidence of how much Chaim had alienated me from my entire family. The experience left me very bitter.

The Israeli military launched Operation Peace for Galilee, a full-scale invasion of Lebanon, in an attempt to destroy numerous bases from where PLO commandos had been launching terrorist attacks across the border. Military traffic flowed past Karmi'el toward Lebanon, clogging the lanes.

My contractions began about 5:00 P.M. on June 6, 1982, the very first day of the war. I monitored their progress and, at 1:00 A.M., decided that it was time to leave for the twenty-five-minute drive to the hospital in Haifa. Once we reached the main road we realized that we should have called for an ambulance. The pavement was jammed with tanks and other armored vehicles. I lay down in the backseat of the car, drawing in deep breaths. The pain was intense, and I scolded myself for not leaving earlier. Several times we were stopped at roadblocks by soldiers who demanded to know who we were and what we were doing. Each time, after a brief explanation from Chaim and a glance into the backseat, they waved us on quickly.

Two and a half hours later, when we finally arrived, we learned that this was one of only a few hospitals accepting maternity patients. Most other hospital space had been commandeered for an expected influx of wounded soldiers. Thus, this facility was extremely crowded. Women in various stages of labor lay on gurneys that were sandwiched in the corridors. I was one of the lucky few to be assigned to a bed in a tiny cubicle. Makeshift curtains separated me from adjacent rooms, where other women moaned and screamed. Chaim left quickly to take Marina and Simon on the long drive to his parents' home near Tel Aviv. I felt a sense of relief that he was gone.

I tried to relax, but the bellowing of hysterical Israeli women assaulted my ears:

"Oh, my God!"
"Oh, my mother!"
"Never . . . never again!"

I found their shrieks more tiring than the contractions. I was used to the more restrained behavior of Belgian women, who do not cry out during labor. I tried to concentrate on my breathing, but the howling made it impossible.

The night passed at an agonizingly slow pace. Doctors gave me oxygen; I lost so much blood that they considered giving me a transfusion.

By mid-morning, as I lay on my side in the small cubicle, unable to move, five doctors surrounded me. A fetal monitor was placed inside of me. It was obvious that something was terribly wrong. Finally, they decided to take the baby by emergency Caesarean section and began surgical preparations. I saw the needle that would put me to sleep, but before a doctor could use it, I yelled, "I have to push! I have to push!"

Within minutes I heard someone announce, "It's a girl."

I glanced up for my first look at the new baby, but all I saw was a blur of dark, bluish black skin being whisked away from me. "She's too dark! She's not normal!" I cried out.

"No, no, they are always that way," a doctor reassured me.

"You can't tell me that, it is my third one," I insisted. But the doctor disappeared, leaving me with new fears and empty arms. I cried silently from exhaustion and fear.

I was taken to a crowded ward and was one of seven new mothers in a room designed for three. All day long and into the evening, I watched the other women cuddle and suckle their newborns as I awaited news of my baby. With the country at war, resources were limited. No one changed the bed linens; food was scarce.

When Chaim visited, he did not ask for details about the birth. Perhaps he was disappointed that the baby was a girl.

"Go and see her," I pleaded. "Tell me how she is. They won't tell me anything."

He disappeared for a few minutes. Soon he returned and announced, "She's all right." Then he was gone.

Evening turned into night, and still no one could or would tell me anything about my baby. Each time I asked about her, a nurse promised to check but never returned. The pain in my body was nothing compared to my emotional anguish. Through the entire terrible night, my imagination ran wild.

Finally, the next morning, a nurse brought my baby to me and announced, "She's fine." Flushed with relief, I held her close. I examined her carefully. She had bluish discolorations on one side of her tiny bottom and on both feet, like little socks. There was another birthmark, a small dark-brown circle, on her chest.

"What is this?" I asked a nurse.

She came to my bedside and looked at the strange markings.

"Oh, it's nothing," she said. "The father is Yemenite, and that frequently occurs. They will fade in time." It was true. Simon had a similar marking on his bottom when he was born, and it had already disappeared.

The baby's little arms were twisted in front of her and her hands curled outward. She was the child of a difficult birth, and I hoped that we could get proper care for her. I realized that in my mind I had named her Moriah, after the mountain where Abraham went to sacrifice his son Isaac.

I was accustomed to the Belgian maternity system, which allows mother and baby a full five days in the hospital. The time is valuable for rest and recuperation. But here in Israel, during wartime, there was to be no such coddling—either from the government or from my husband. Twenty-four hours after the birth, Moriah and I were discharged from the hospital.

In Israel, the government authorizes the mother to receive a sum of money for each birth, and Chaim did not wish to wait for what he regarded as his paternal bonus. The moment we arrived home, he ordered, "Go to the bank and get the money." He would stay home with the baby.

I was exhausted, very weak, and still in a great deal of pain. "I can't, I cannot," I pleaded. I craved sleep and could barely lift my head. But Chaim insisted. I had to stand in a long, slow line, waiting for the money.

As soon as I returned with the precious stipend, Chaim announced that he was leaving to pick up Marina and Simon from his mother. "No, I won't be able to take care of them," I said. "Leave them there for one week." He made it clear that he thought the request was foolish and that I was spoiled. To appease him, I plunged into housework. I had been gone only a day, but Chaim had made a mess of the place. When he saw me attack the sinkful of dirty dishes, he reluctantly agreed to postpone Marina and Simon's return.

The following week, when we retrieved them, Chaim's brother Goory said to me, "I guessed that you had another girl, because Chaim didn't tell us anything."

After Moriah's birth, the fights became louder and more frequent, the beatings more severe, and I knew that the neighbors below us realized what was going on. At times, when Chaim was particularly incensed, he threatened to leave and take the children from me.

I tried to avoid confrontation but, inevitably, after several days of sniping and small arguments, some petty remark or incident would send Chaim into a rage. I would be beaten, his tension spent, and then the whole miserable routine began again.

When I needed a new pair of shoes, Chaim attempted to avoid the expense by bringing me a pair of his mother's. "I cannot wear these," I pointed out. "I have bigger feet than she does. They are two sizes too small."

My lack of appreciation infuriated him. "Such a wife," he spat, shoving me, "so stupid and ungrateful." The shoes were cast aside and I continued to wear my old pair.

I began to feel guilty for having brought three children into this chaotic world. I went through the motions of caring for them, but my ability to nurture, to laugh, and to love had been deadened. I blamed myself and my decisions for the dismal life we shared. I thought: Patsy, what's done is done, and you have to make the best of the situation. At least, I vowed, I would not complicate our lives by bearing yet another child. Chaim remained insistent that I not utilize any means of birth control, but I decided to take care of the matter myself. During my mother's visit prior to Moriah's birth, she had given me some money, and I went to a doctor and secretly obtained an IUD.

I do not know how Chaim found out about this, but he did. To my mind, it was additional evidence that he had spies everywhere. He furiously demanded that I have the IUD removed. "No," I declared firmly, "three children in this kind of situation we have now—the fights and beatings—it's three too much already. I will not."

Chaim was livid at my disobedience. He threw me out of the apartment, locked the door, and remained inside with the children. I could hear him ranting and raving, telling the children, "She's bad, she's a bad mother."

I huddled by the door, listening. Moriah began to cry. Many minutes passed, and the crying continued. The minutes turned into an hour. Moriah was not used to being ignored. Her urine had a high ammonia content. That, combined with the effects of the hot summer sun and cloth diapers, caused a severe rash unless she was changed and cleaned frequently, but Chaim could not be bothered. As Moriah's wails continued, I paced back and forth on the landing like a caged animal, desperate to comfort my child. Then I pounded on the door. Finally I screamed. I was terrified to leave, even for an instant, lest Chaim carry through his threat to take the children from me.

Chaim opened the door. "You're making too much noise," he hissed. He pushed me away roughly and slammed the door shut.

Another hour passed, then a third. Moriah continued to cry. I lay across the threshold, like a dog waiting for its master.

Finally, Chaim opened the door and shouted orders: "Okay, I have to go out. You come back in for two hours. You clean the house, cook, take care of the kids. Then, when I come back, I'm throwing you out again."

The baby had missed one feeding and a bottle. Her bed was soaked, her skin inflamed. She was also dehydrated. I cleaned her, fed her, and cuddled her. Several times I thought she had gone to sleep, but she gasped for breath and sobbed. It took me ninety minutes to get her to drift into an exhausted sleep. Then I ran about frantically, trying to clean and cook at the same time.

Chaim stayed away for many hours. When he finally did return, he did not order me out. In fact, he said nothing and I realized that I was in for another round of the silent treatment.

For six long weeks Chaim tortured me with silence. In front of others, he spoke to me politely and treated me correctly. But in our own home he passed me as if I were not there. His eyes avoided mine. He spent his evenings sitting quietly, reading, ignoring me and the children completely. When I could no longer abide the sense of my own nothingness I sat at his feet and sobbed, "I'm sorry." I confessed to a multitude of imagined sins: "I know I'm a bad wife. I know I'm a bad mother. I'm sorry. I'm sorry. Please forgive me."

I continued like this for hours, until he said calmly, "Okay, I forgive you."

But could I forgive him? I thought: Maybe someday I will leave him. No, no, I cannot.

Despite the consequences, I somehow found a new reservoir of strength that enabled me to confront Chaim's unpredictable temper. Although he constantly berated me for my stupidity, when he once again raised his hand against me, I charged, "You cannot win an argument with me, so you beat me."

Chaim immediately realized the implication of my words: He was stronger, but I was smarter. I had challenged his shop-worn slogan: "I'm the best." He responded to my accusation by slapping me in the face. Once more he banished me from the apartment for hours. Ashamed and afraid that neighbors might see me on the landing, I fled to the roof of the building.

I lived in fear that Chaim would someday turn his violence upon the children, and he sensed this. He also knew that I was particularly terrified when he beat me in front of the children, so he adopted a new, more sinister technique. Softly, slowly, he said to me, "I am going to beat you. Go into that room and wait for me. I've got something to do, but in fifteen minutes I'm coming to beat you. Wait for me. Otherwise, I'm going to do it in front of the kids." Terrified, I did as I was told.

Desperate, but with great fear, I confided to my German-American friend, "You know he beats me like hell. Can you help me?"

"You need witnesses when he beats you," she said, "or the police will not help." Domestic violence was not yet a major issue for the Israeli justice system. Unless a woman was beaten severely enough to require hospitalization—or unless there were wit-nesses to the brutality—the police seemed content to merely lec-ture the offending spouse. "I have a friend on the floor just below you," the woman continued. "The next time Chaim beats you, open the door and scream. She and other neighbors will come. They will witness the violence and help you with the police."

I did not have to wait long. As the back of Chaim's hand re-peatedly found its mark, I tried to gather my courage. Finally, I ran to the door, flung it open, and—feeling very ashamed and embarrassed—screamed for help. On the landings below, timid neighbors poked their noses out of their doors and gaped up-ward. Some climbed the stairs to investigate. But even this did not deter Chaim. He followed me out the door and continued to hit me. When I fell to the floor he kicked me viciously. The neighbors turned and, one by one, went back downstairs and retreated to the safety of their own apartments.

I was humiliated beyond belief.

The next day I visited several of the neighbors and asked, "Please, can you be a witness for me?" But everyone refused.

My friend confessed to me, "We are scared. When we saw what he does to you, we were afraid."

More and more I entertained the thought of leaving Chaim. Sometimes I dismissed the idea immediately. Sometimes I allowed it to linger. But I was too weak, too afraid.

Moriah's development was slow. The difficult birth created a number of physical problems. Her hands were deformed and she could not push herself off the floor like a normal infant. Once a week I took her to a clinic in Haifa, where a physical therapist worked with her. The therapist prescribed exercises that I had to follow at home. With Moriah on her stomach, I rolled her wrists across a large rubber ball, using force, to strengthen and train the muscles. This was painful, and several times a day her shrieks filled the apartment, adding to the already grim, stormy atmosphere.

I was the mother of three children and yet, in many ways, I was a child myself. I needed help, yet I was still too ashamed to call upon my family.

I frequently thought of my father's business associate, Samuel Katz. Papa had said, on numerous occasions, that I could contact him in an emergency. Finally, in February 1983, I decided to call. I did not know what I was going to say, but I had to reach out to someone.

Each morning, Chaim demanded to know my plans for the day, and I was not allowed to change the schedule. So I chose a morning when I was supposed to take the children to the clinic. There was a pay telephone nearby.

After I dressed the children, we walked toward the clinic—and the phone—about one mile from our apartment. But when I was nearly halfway there, I realized my mind was in so much turmoil that I had forgotten to bring the small slip of paper with Katz's telephone number on it. My mind raced. Could I return home to get the number? What if Chaim drove back from the shop and saw us? What would I tell him? I was afraid to turn back and afraid to go forward. I shut my eyes tightly, trying to will Katz's telephone number into my memory. My mind drew a blank but for some reason I forged ahead. When I reached the phone, I inserted a token. The instant I heard the tone the numbers miraculously appeared in my mind. I dialed quickly.

I asked Katz not to tell my parents of our conversation, then I said, "I may need your help one day, because I might leave Chaim." I began to speak in a jumble of words, proclaiming my misery but only hinting about the abuse I endured.

Katz spoke calmly, clearly trying to keep me from getting overly excited. He was too diplomatic to ask me the key question: Why? Perhaps he already knew the answer. He simply said, "Okay, Patsy, I'll be there whenever you need me. Don't hesitate to call me."

By the time I returned home, my head pounded with pain.

What I did not know at the time was that my father had already briefed Katz concerning the problems of my troubled marriage. And he also knew that my parents were due to come to Israel soon, accompanying my uncle Philippe on a business trip. When they checked into their hotel, they found a message from Samuel Katz waiting for them. It read: "See me before you visit Patsy."

Their meeting with Katz verified their suspicions. "There are big problems with this marriage," Katz warned. "There is a lot of physical violence." Hearing this, my mother felt as if she had been punched in the stomach herself. She had witnessed some of Chaim's bizarre behavior but had denied in her mind the possibility that he would beat me.

My parents held a long, painful discussion. How could they help me? What was the best thing to do? My father battled the impulse to simply force the children and me to leave. He was wise enough to know that only I could make such a decision. Together, my parents determined that the best course of action—

perhaps the only one—was to assure me that I was not alone, that they would help me in any possible way. All I had to do was ask.

My mother said, "Okay, Jacques, while you and Philippe take care of your business, I'm going to visit Patsy. If she doesn't confide in me, I'm going to say something. I have to." My father agreed.

During my mother's visit, Chaim ignored her, almost refusing to acknowledge her presence. Most of the time he was not around. We went shopping, and Maman bought us expensive steaks for dinner. Chaim ate with relish but did not bother to thank my mother for this treat. I tried to put on a happy face, laughing and singing as though everything were fine, still unwilling and too ashamed to confide the truth.

Maman had to choose her moment carefully. She waited until I excused myself to use the bathroom, then she followed me. Tapping on the door, she asked, "Patsy, can I come in?" In the privacy of the tiny room, my mother said softly, "Patsy, you don't want to tell me anything, but you have to know that I know everything about you and Chaim. If you need any help you will have all the help you want. But it must be your decision."

I nodded and glanced in Chaim's direction. With my fingers to my lips, I mumbled, "Shhhh."

Upon my parents' return to Brussels, Maman said, "Jacques, she will do it. I don't know how long it will take. Perhaps months, even longer, but she will leave him. I can feel it."

We planned a Passover picnic, the kind of outing that in times past was extremely enjoyable. During the solemn remembrance of the flight from Egypt, Jews traditionally eat crackerlike matzoh, but Chaim preferred the taste of nonkosher pita. This was difficult to find in the stores during Passover. Planning ahead, I bought a supply and froze it.

On the day of our picnic, we drove into the lovely Israeli countryside. What could have been a peaceful, scenic drive was marred by yet another argument. I had made a mistake. I put salt instead of sugar into Moriah's milk. "You are such a bad mother!"

Chaim screamed. He was already in a foul mood when he parked the car near a shady grove of eucalyptus trees. He quickly got out of the car, slammed the door, and turned his back on us. I helped Marina and Simon out of the backseat and then returned for Moriah. With the baby propped on one hip, I hefted the picnic basket and walked toward the stand of trees.

Another family was nearby, enjoying the spring day.

I took a cloth from the basket and spread it on the ground. We settled down to our meal, but when Chaim bit into the pita, he spat it out in disgust and raged, "It's not fresh. You didn't get it into the freezer in time."

If he had just complained once, I might have let it pass. But throughout the afternoon he continued to grumble about the bread.

I thought: So now I am not even smart enough to freeze pita.

I looked at the children. Three-and-a-half-year-old Marina was quiet and withdrawn, afraid of everything; wherever we went, she clutched at my skirts for protection. Simon was hyperactive, with a troublesome tendency to vent rage against inanimate objects; he was more than two years old, but he still awoke in the middle of every night, crying. At ten months of age, Moriah still could not sit without support.

That's it, I decided. I will take no more, Chaim. As we say in French, your carrots are cooked!

Marina was in school. I knew that Chaim would be busy for several hours at the shop. I strapped Moriah into the stroller and, with Simon toddling at my side, walked to the pay phone. I took a deep breath and placed a collect call to my mother in Brussels.

The phone rang several times. When my mother finally answered, I said quickly, "I've decided to leave Chaim."

I thought: There, I said it. I finally said it.

10

My father took control immediately.

He checked with an attorney and discovered two problems. First, since Chaim held my passport, we would have to secure a duplicate without his knowledge. Second—and far more troublesome—was the fact that, under Belgian law, the children of a mixed marriage were considered to be the nationality of the father. Even in Belgium, Marina, Simon, and Moriah were Israelis.

I called Brussels again as soon as I could and found my parents waiting by the phone. My father informed me that he would arrive in Israel on Thursday, April 21. He had booked a hotel room in Tel Aviv, convenient to the Belgian Embassy. I was to call him daily at his hotel, between 10:00 A.M. and noon, or 6:00 P.M. and 8:00 P.M., if I could. In the meantime, I was to continue life as usual. If I had any problems before my father arrived, I was to call Samuel Katz.

I realized quickly that my part of the plan was extremely difficult. "Life as usual" in this household was demeaning and dangerous. I dared not give the children the slightest indication that we might be going to visit their grandparents, lest they make an inadvertent comment that would alert Chaim. When he picked a fight with me, I did not wish to provoke another beating; but neither could I shrug it off as if—since all of this would soon be over—I did not care. I knew that I had one, and only one, chance to leave. If Chaim realized what I was trying to do, he would surely take the children away from me.

Once he arrived in Tel Aviv, my father discovered that officials at the Belgian Embassy did not want to get involved in what appeared to be a domestic squabble. They would issue a new passport for me if I supplied the proper photograph, but they would not add the children's names to the document. This was critical because, without it, I would need Chaim's written permission to take the children out of the country. My father pleaded, "Just let me get them into the embassy, and then we can protect them." The answer was no.

Enraged, my father called upon an attorney who had contacts in the Foreign Office in Brussels. A high-level official there agreed to send a coded telex to the Belgian Embassy in Tel Aviv, ordering that the children's names be placed on my new passport. During our daily call on Monday, April 25, Papa told me that we would have to wait a few days until the telex arrived, but he assured me, "You'll be able to leave Chaim on Thursday. I will have the papers ready by then."

We would depart as quickly as possible. Papa was willing to take any plane in any direction, as long as it got us out of Israel. He booked passage on two different flights to Europe. We would take the earlier flight if we could, but the second was our backup.

As I thought through the plan, I worried that someone might see me leave the apartment with the children *and* with baggage, and alert Chaim. I thought: I won't take anything with me—just my jewelry and a few clothes for the kids—whatever I can cram into two small nylon grocery bags. My mind spun. Mothers with three small children routinely carry grocery bags, but I was paranoid that somebody would take undue notice. I took the risk of confiding in my German-American friend, who agreed to take the bags and bring them to me at the clinic parking lot. That way, no one would see me leaving the building with the bags.

On Tuesday, I was in the bedroom, gathering some of the

children's things, silently repeating a litany: two days, two days, two days. Suddenly I heard the front door open and close. Chaim had come home unexpectedly! Quickly I dropped the bags to the floor and kicked them beneath the bed.

"What are you doing?" he asked. Was it suspicion in his voice or merely curiosity?

"Nothing—just putting some things away," I said. My heart pounded so fiercely I feared it would echo through the room. I went to the kitchen sink and began rinsing some glasses. "What are you doing home this time of day?" I asked.

"I forgot some papers I need," he said. "I'll only be a minute."

As he poked about the apartment, the minute stretched into thirty. I was sure that he suspected something. I was terrified that he would spot a corner of one of the bags, protruding from beneath the bed. I pretended to attend to the housework, hoping desperately that I could hide my nervousness. When he finally left, the sense of relief brought tears to my eyes.

That night, Chaim demanded sex. It was over quickly, and I thought: Phew! That's the last time!

Wednesday morning dawned and I immediately thought: One more day. But when I called my father at his hotel, he said, "Not tomorrow. I don't have the passport yet."

I wailed, "Papa, I cannot stand one more day. Cooking, cleaning, fighting, acting like I will be staying here when I know it will be over in two or three days, it's extremely hard. My head is somewhere else. I don't belong here anymore."

"Patsy, just try. Can you?"

One more day would be Friday, and then, what if it was one more, and one more? I could not take another weekend with Chaim. I was sure that, somehow, I would unwittingly alert him. "No, I cannot!" I cried. "It's too hard. I won't be able."

"I'm calling and calling everywhere," Papa complained. "No one will send the damn telex. But, okay, I'll keep calling and arguing until I get it done. We'll make it tomorrow." He said that he would rent a car and meet me at 9:00 A.M. in the central square of Karmi'el.

That evening I approached Chaim. "Moriah's therapy is tomorrow," I reminded him. "I will need the car to go to Haifa."

"Yes, yes, I remember," he said.

"And after that I will do some shopping for vegetables."

Chaim merely shrugged.

I woke on Thursday realizing that it was imperative—no matter how difficult it might be—that I stick to the daily routine. By now I was counting the minutes. I prepared breakfast for everyone, the usual fare of bread and jam, milk for the children, coffee for Chaim and me. I helped Marina get ready for school, even though I knew that she was not going. I cooked a lunch of chicken, small round noodles, and tomato sauce, so that it would appear to be ready and waiting. I threw a load of laundry into the washing machine, knowing that Chaim would return to find it damp.

Finally, it was time to go. We all climbed into the car and Chaim drove toward the shop. I felt as though the words *I am leaving* were emblazoned in bright neon letters across my forehead. I chattered on about inconsequential things, all the time worrying: Am I talking too much? Do I sound nervous? Does it show?

We reached the shop. Chaim got out of the car and I slipped into the driver's seat. I drove on ahead for several blocks. Only when I was sure that we were out of sight did I make a U-turn and head back to the apartment.

I left the children with my friend and ran upstairs to retrieve our nylon shopping bags from beneath the bed. Then I took a few moments to set a false scene for Chaim. I put my wallet into a spare bag and left my regular purse near the door. When Chaim came home, it would appear that the children and I had simply stepped out for a few minutes.

I paused in front of the door and shivered, suddenly struck with the reality of what I was doing. I thought: Patsy, you are taking responsibility for your own life, yes, but you are also making a big decision for the kids. Is it the right thing for them? I was uncomfortable with this act of sneaking out on Chaim and taking the children without his permission, but there was no other way to do it. If I tried to leave in a conventional manner, I knew that he would take the children from me.

A sudden thought intruded: Leah has been so good to me. How can I hurt her like this? But I lectured myself: Patsy, don't think about Leah. Think about yourself. I resolved: That's it. I'm leaving.

With emotional as well as physical effort, I pulled the door shut.

Without looking back, I hurried down to my friend's apartment and left the nylon grocery bags with her. We would meet in the clinic parking lot in exactly five minutes. I clutched Moriah in my arms. Marina and Simon stayed close, sensing that something unusual was happening. We returned to the car and drove to the clinic. My body moved, performing all the necessary tasks, but I felt detached, as if I were watching myself from someplace high above.

I told the children only as much as they needed to know and could understand. "We are going to meet your grandfather," I said, "and then we are driving off with him. We are going on a trip!"

I waited in the clinic parking lot with nervous impatience, constantly checking my watch. My friend was late! Had I misjudged her? Had she taken it upon herself to alert her husband or Chaim? Were we trapped?

She finally arrived, spilling out an apology, but I was too frantic to hear the reason for the delay. I grabbed the two grocery bags and tossed them into the car. "Good-bye," she said. "Good luck. I will follow you in my car until you meet your father." We sped off.

I drove as if in a trance. The route took me past Chaim's shop. I was thankful that the building had no windows, but I was concerned that, for some reason, Chaim might be out on the street.

It was a bit past 9:00 A.M. when we reached the central square. My father, too, was nervous over the delay. Seeing my car in his rearview mirror, he extended his left hand out the window and waved broadly, indicating for me to follow. From her own car, my friend waved farewell. We headed south out of Karmi'el in the direction of Tel Aviv. My hands shook as I gripped the steering wheel.

Once we were safely out of town, I motioned for my father to pull over. He did and I stopped my car behind him. "Papa, I'm afraid that I will have an accident because I am so nervous," I said. "Take the kids in your car."

He saw that I was shaking. "Don't be so nervous," he said. "Nothing is going wrong." Although the day was beastly hot, I saw that he too was shivering. His face was flushed, and small droplets of perspiration clung to his forehead.

The children barely knew their grandfather. I tried to explain calmly, "Okay, you will go in the car with him, and I will follow." With innocent trust, they obeyed. Leading the way, my father was careful not to speed or do anything that might attract unwanted attention. The children peered through the back window of the car to make sure that I was following.

My father took a coastal highway rather than the inland road, because it would bring us into Tel Aviv close to the Belgian Embassy on Hayarkon Street; he still did not have the passport.

We reached Tel Aviv in a bit more than an hour. My father stopped at a hotel and explained that I had to find someplace to park my car. "Leave the keys in the glove compartment," he suggested, "so that when Chaim finds it, he can drive it away." Papa said that he would rent two adjoining rooms in the hotel. He and the children would wait for me there.

I drove off quickly and found an open garage beneath a small apartment building. I pulled to the back, where the car was hidden from view. "You must leave. This is private property," a woman said angrily.

I snapped out a lie: "It's for two minutes."

The woman glared at me, and I decided not to risk trouble with her. Frustrated, I returned to the hotel parking lot, shoved the keys into the glove compartment, and rejoined my father and the children.

The children were hungry, so we ordered food from room service. As the kids ate, my father called the embassy. But the telex we were awaiting still had not arrived.

It was clear that we would miss both of the morning flights that my father had booked. He left for a travel agency to make new arrangements, and I settled all three children into one of the twin beds for a nap. They slept peacefully.

My father returned, having exchanged the tickets for two afternoon flights to Europe. Our first option was an Austrian Airlines flight to Vienna, leaving at 2:00 P.M. If we missed that, we were confirmed on a 4:00 P.M. Lufthansa flight to Frankfurt.

Papa handed me some money and said, "Patsy, we need some pictures of you. Could you please go get a passport photo taken?"

I scurried along the sidewalks of downtown Tel Aviv, searching for a coin-operated machine that could produce the necessary photos. In Brussels, these are common, but I could not find one here. I walked for many blocks, past one shop after another, not realizing how much precious time was passing. Finally, I spotted a photographer's studio. He snapped the photos quickly, but more minutes passed before the prints were ready. Then I lost additional time waiting for a bus back to the hotel.

"Where have you been? What happened?" my father asked anxiously when I returned.

But the delay did not matter, for a new complication had developed. The precious Foreign Office telex had finally come in to the embassy, but the employee who transcribed and decoded telexes was out to lunch. My father groaned, for he knew that in this country, lunch often included an extended nap or shopping trip. He ran off to the embassy, where he hovered until 2:30 when the decoder returned.

Embassy personnel reluctantly followed the Foreign Office instructions, preparing a passport for me that included the three children. But alongside their names, in brackets, it declared, "Not Belgian Citizens." "Maybe write it in Dutch, rather than French," my father suggested. That would make it less likely that an Israeli passport authority could understand it. But the pompous official refused and wrote the critical words in French.

Father returned to the hotel and relayed the advice of one of the few helpful people he had encountered at the embassy: "If they ask you questions, don't lie. Evade the truth, yes, but don't lie." My father advised, "Pretend that you don't understand Hebrew."

We checked out of the hotel. There was no way that we could make the 4:00 P.M. Lufthansa flight, so we went to the Air France ticket office nearby and booked passage on the early-evening flight to Paris, the last plane out to Europe.

Once more we packed the children into my father's rental car. We drove off toward Ben Gurion Airport but soon found ourselves in the midst of a huge traffic jam, the worst I had ever encountered in Tel Aviv. "It's okay, it's okay," my father said in a soothing tone. He checked his watch. It was past 5:00 P.M. "The flight doesn't leave until seven," he said. "We have plenty of time. Take it easy."

We arrived at the airport, calculating that we had more than an hour to spare. Once we had made it through passport control and were safely into the international zone, we planned to send Chaim a telegram, assuring him that the children were fine.

The five of us approached the security counter, where an unsmiling guard asked, in English, "How come you go to Belgium with three children and you don't have a suitcase?"

My father replied, "Ah, but she has everything she needs in Belgium."

"Where is the father? Why doesn't he travel with you?"

"He is working. He will join us later."

The guard paused to consider this, nodded, and waved us through.

Next, we arrived at the passport checkpoint. The children had picked up on the anxiety. Tired, scared, and confused, all three of them whimpered.

A uniformed woman at the passport-control booth glanced at our papers. Don't lie, I repeated to myself, Don't lie. She asked us a few questions in Hebrew. I tried to pretend that I could not understand and found that it was difficult. But I must have succeeded, for she switched to English.

"The father is Israeli?" she asked.

"Yes," I said slowly.

She held up my new Belgian passport with the children's names, and studied it carefully. "These children are Israeli," she pronounced.

The children were crying louder, creating a disturbance. Simon whined, "I'm thirsty."

"Let her go through to take care of the kids," my father suggested. Pointing toward a snack bar where I could get Simon something to drink, he nudged me forward to the metal detector, knowing that once we passed this station, we were technically out of Israel.

"Okay," the official agreed. But she held on to my passport. She studied it with care and then announced to my father, "These children may not go out of the country."

Trying to keep his voice calm, my father asked, "Why?"

She declared, "As Israeli citizens, when leaving the country, they have to pay tax!"

The relief on Papa's face was almost tangible, but he knew that he had to hurry. As long as the woman held my passport, it was possible for her to realize her mistake. Following instructions, he raced down the corridor to a bank office, paid the tax of fifty-five dollars per child, and returned to present the necessary receipt and reclaim my passport. Never before had he paid taxes with such a ready smile.

Father joined us in the cafeteria. After we satisfied Simon's thirst, we would send the telegram to Chaim. Suddenly a man approached. "Are you the Heymanses?" he asked. "Mrs. Heymans?"

I felt the blood rush to my face, and I saw my father react also. He found us already! Tentatively, I answered, "Yes."

"Your flight has been waiting for you for several minutes."

We had noted the wrong flight time. It was scheduled for 6:00 P.M., not 7:00 P.M. We ran to the gate, where an attendant rushed us on board. The door closed behind us quickly.

Within minutes, we were on our way to Paris.

Papa summoned a flight attendant, ordered a double whiskey, and drank it in a single gulp.

11

One month later, Chaim telephoned me at my parents' home on Avenue des Fleurs. They were reluctant for me to speak to him, for fear that I was too weak to stand up to the pressure. "It's okay," I told them. "I can handle it."

Chaim was contrite—full of apologies and professions of love. "Patsy," he said, using his softest, most persuasive voice, "you must come back to me. You know you love me. Tell me you love me."

I was unmoved. "No, I don't love you," I said.

The conversational tug of war continued. With the miles separating us, it was easier for me to stand my ground. Before we hung up, he told me that he was coming to Belgium and would convince me to return to him.

A few days later he arrived. His arms were full of pinkish-red roses.

"Don't talk to him, Patsy," my mother warned.

"Yes, I will," I replied.

"Don't do it. He will manipulate you. He will work on you until you change your mind," she insisted.

"No, I have made up my mind and that's it." I asked my parents to leave us alone—I wanted to handle this on my own—but I kept the living-room door open. Mother went upstairs with the children. Father hovered, out of sight but nearby. I knew that they were very concerned. I had spent five years under Chaim's dominance and it was difficult for them to believe that I had the strength to stand up to him now. They held their breath.

Chaim came into the living room. I did not sit, so neither did he. I looked at the roses. It was the first time in all the years I had known him that he had brought me flowers. "No, I don't want them," I said.

"Yes, take them, take them," Chaim insisted.

"No."

"Take them."

"No."

"I love you and you must take them."

With a shrug I accepted the bouquet, walked into the kitchen, and threw the flowers into the trash. Bloody roses, I thought. The physical act of throwing the flowers away infused me with confidence. I returned to the living room and told Chaim, "I took them, but I put them in the garbage."

He ignored this slight and continued his litany. "I love you," he said, "and I know that you love me. Tell me that you love me, Patsy."

I hesitated. I sensed the tug of his power.

"Tell me, tell me," he insisted.

"No, I don't love you," I snapped.

He refused to accept this. "Tell me, Patsy, tell me," he begged.

Why was it so difficult for me to defy this man? Finally I responded, "Okay, I love you—but it's a lie. Just shut up."

We began a heated debate. One by one I listed my grievances, and he attempted to refute them. My first complaint, of course, was the series of vicious beatings and the humiliations I had suffered. "It's your imagination," he argued. "Maybe it happened once or twice, but if it did, it was because you deserved it."

I let that subject go, and complained, "The kids were very unhappy."

"That is because you are a very bad mother." His contrite facade was slipping. I could sense his temper simmering beneath the surface.

There might be some truth to that, I thought; if the mother is not happy, the children suffer. But I forced my mind away from such thoughts. He was manipulating me again. "We never had enough money, but you always had money," I complained. "Eating chicken wings every day is not too healthy. I ate so many chicken wings that I felt like I had wings on my back. And there was never any money for even basic necessities for the children."

"Well, what can I do?" Chaim asked. "I've been trying to work, but nobody wants me."

At that moment I saw him clearly for what he was, a spineless bully who refused to—or could not—assume responsibility for his actions. I told him, forcefully, that our marriage was over. But I added, "I want you to know that you can come to visit the kids whenever you wish. You are their father. It's important."

The children did not concern him at the moment. After a month's absence, he did not even ask to see them, although he could hear them playing upstairs. He was more concerned with his own ego, which found it inconceivable that a woman would, or could, leave him. He had convinced himself that my father forced me to come back to Brussels. He could not believe that I had made up my own mind and acted upon my own wishes. To admit this, even to himself, was a crushing blow.

I was as direct as I could possibly be. "I have made up my mind," I said. "It's over. I've had enough."

But Chaim had the last word. He stared daggers through me and promised in a slow, menacing tone, "Whatever it takes, whatever it will cost, I will destroy your life. The kids, you, me, my life—I don't care. I will destroy your life."

I believed him.

With a desperate sense of urgency, I struggled to erase the past five years. I had forgotten the sweetness of freedom. I could come and go as I pleased, asking permission from no one, and I savored it. Chaim was out of my life—or so I hoped—and I wanted him out of my mind. At times this was difficult, for there were details to discuss.

My parents disclosed that they had learned from Samuel Katz in Tel Aviv that Chaim's discharge from the Israeli army was suspect. All Israeli soldiers are classified under a numbered profile. Chaim was classified as a Profile 21, a designation applied to individuals considered too unstable for military service; in some cases, such individuals were not even allowed to have a driver's license. There was some indication that Chaim had received this designation after he had a fight with an officer. This, not a skirmish with the enemy, was the source of his elbow injury. With the Profile 21 on his record, it was no wonder that Chaim had difficulty getting an Israeli driver's license and did not serve normal reserve duty. This also could explain some of his problems in finding a job. But I did not want to concern myself with this sort of speculation—and the discomforting emotions that accompanied any mention of Chaim. "It's done, it's over," I said to my parents. "I married him and it was a big mistake. I will turn the page now and start a new life."

My grandfather had died in December 1982, and I was shattered to learn why he had seemed to reject me. He had been sending me $350 each month for six months before his death, and I had never thanked him. He was so hurt that he had refused to speak to me and I had never known why. In fact, I had been unaware of the payments. Chaim had kept the money and fed us chicken wings. I felt very bad, because it was too late to apologize.

We skirted the issue of Chaim's physical abuse. My parents knew that Chaim had hit me. But they never asked me details of how often, and how severe, the beatings had been. And I never spoke about them.

The most painful subject of all was my telephone call relaying Chaim's desperate request for 360,000 Belgian francs in order to avoid a prison term. My father disclosed that he paid the money even though Chaim had neglected to sign a statement, drawn up by his attorney at my father's insistence, allowing me continued contact with my family. I could not believe that I had caused my parents so much anguish, and whenever the subject came up I wailed, "Don't speak about it. I'm too ashamed!"

My mind was so set against even thinking of Chaim that I neglected to follow the proper legal procedures. I wanted a divorce, but the inevitable side effect of a court case would be renewed contact with Chaim. I'll get around to it someday, I reasoned.

The children also seemed to want to forget. They never asked about their father. When we had been together, Chaim generally ignored them, so now they did not miss him. If someone asked them who their father was, they answered in childish innocence, "Jacques," "Eric," or "Géry"—choosing my father or one of my brothers as a surrogate.

By the end of the summer our pediatrician was very pleased with the children's progress. "We should have taken a videotape in the beginning," he said, "to see the evolution of these children. They open like flowers in the sun." Marina was much more relaxed. The bright, spontaneous smile returned to light up her small, round face. Simon, his trim, honey-colored body in constant motion, was still rambunctious but not nearly as aggressive. At ten months, Moriah could not sit; now, at fourteen months, she toddled about like any other child.

More than anything else, the four of us simply wanted normal lives.

In September I enrolled in secretarial school once again, taking a one-year, accelerated course of study that kept me extremely busy. My parents allowed me to use their Toyota for the commute, and my mother or Cousin Isabelle watched the children for me. The classwork was difficult, but I had three little reasons at home that motivated me to do well. I was grateful for my parents' support but determined to build a life of my own.

On September 26 we gathered in a small chapel at St. Paul's Roman Catholic Church, a few blocks away from Avenue des Fleurs. Père Albert, my father's cousin and the priest who had served our family for as long as I could remember, smiled down at the three small children, each flanked by a pair of godparents.

Marina, almost four years old, returned his smile with her special, broad, dimple-cheeked grin.

Two-and-a-half-year-old Simon was nervous, not knowing what to expect.

Moriah, at fifteen months, squirmed on my hip.

My parents stood behind us, pleased and proud, as Père Albert read from his missal. The service was brief and very nice. The priest took the children one by one and baptized them, "in the name of the Father, the Son, and the Holy Spirit."

Simon watched anxiously as Père Albert took a vial of oil, approached Marina, and made the sign of the cross on her forehead. When the priest turned to Simon, he gestured with his thumb and whispered, "My little sister first." He wanted to use her as a guinea pig, to make sure that the ritual was not painful.

The touch of the priest's slippery finger disturbed Moriah, causing her to whimper. This, in turn, brought tears of alarm to Simon's eyes. He flailed his arms to ward off the priest, but his godfather calmed him and held his tiny hands in check.

After the ceremony, we returned home, where Maman had prepared an elegant buffet to celebrate the event.

Now, if I wished, I could enroll the children in Catholic schools. Years from now, they could be married by a priest.

Chaim phoned occasionally from Israel—always collect—to ask for news of the children. Then, after a time, he began to call from various European cities. He had left Israel and appeared to be enjoying a comfortable life in Hiltons, Sheratons, and other expensive hotels. I had no idea why he was traveling or how he could afford the luxurious accommodations. I remembered his constant complaint in Israel: "We never have enough money."

I did not mind that he called to inquire about the children. He was their father. But a vague uneasiness settled over me after each conversation. The echo of his parting threat always hovered, but I pushed it aside, determined to get on with my life.

12

Marina and Simon scrambled eagerly into the backseat of the Toyota. I strapped eighteen-month-old Moriah into her car seat, and we set off on the hour-long drive to the Ardennes countryside.

It was shortly after Christmas 1983. I had successfully completed a difficult battery of tests at school. The second phase of the course called for a combination of classwork and on-the-job training. By happy coincidence, my father had acquired an interest in a small trucking company in the city of Mons, about forty miles south of Brussels, and he had agreed to hire me for the work-study program. My parents, planning to spend considerable time in Mons to oversee the new business, had rented a small house there. In fact, they were currently in Mons, fixing up the still-empty house.

The children and I had a holiday coming—a full five days alone at the country house in Nassogne. We were very excited.

An icy sleet peppered the windshield as I drove along the highway. There was very little traffic.

"Patsy, hold my hand," Marina requested.

I smiled inside. Here in Belgium everyone called me Patsy, so the children had adopted the habit also. I steered with my left hand and held my right hand back across my shoulder. As the Toyota cruised along the highway at a steady seventy-five miles per hour, only a few other cars sped past.

We sang "Frère Jacques" in French, then we sang a short Hebrew song about a van that delivers eggs in the morning.

After a time I became aware that a car was following close behind us. The distinctive pattern of its headlights illuminated the icy raindrops on my rear window. It appeared to be a powerful car, such as an Audi or BMW, and I wondered why the driver did not pass. I accelerated a bit, to put some distance between us, but the other car picked up speed also. I slowed, hoping that the other driver would pass, but he slowed too.

A shiver ran up my spine. Was this some crazy person who spotted a woman alone with only her kids? Could it be Chaim? Which would be worse?

The children wanted to sing some more. "Calm down," I instructed. "Marina, let's lock the doors."

"What's happening?" Simon asked.

"I don't know. Nothing. It's okay," I answered.

Marina asked, "Why do we have to lock the doors?"

"It's okay, it's nothing," I repeated. "We just have to be careful."

The children grew silent. In the rearview mirror I saw Marina's eyes grow wide with fear. I swallowed hard and fought back tears.

For many kilometers the other driver and I played a game of cat-and-mouse on the slush-covered road. I pushed hard on the accelerator pedal, taking the Toyota up to one hundred miles per hour, as fast as it would go. The car moved up to follow even more closely. Then I nudged my foot against the brake pedal, slowing to thirty-five miles per hour, barely crawling. Adrenaline rushed through me. I drove so slowly for so long that the other car was forced to go on ahead. As it passed, I glanced to the side and saw two men inside. From the profile of the driver, I thought that he might be Chaim, but I could not be sure.

I waited until the car had driven on ahead, out of sight. Then

I edged forward, cautiously. I knew that we were approaching a rest area with a *friterie*, where you could buy fried potatoes. It would be closed this late on a winter's day, but I decided to stop there, to give the other car more time to move ahead.

But as I approached the parking area, I saw that the other car was there. The driver was waiting for me to pass on the highway so that he could resume the chase.

If I had been thinking clearly, I would have turned back toward the safety of Brussels. But at the moment the only important thing seemed to be to keep the car in front of me, where I could see it. So I decided to pull into the rest area and wait for the other driver to go on ahead.

As I turned off of the highway, Marina asked nervously, "Why are you stopping?"

"I have to rest," I lied.

The other driver had stopped near the far end of the rest area. He had parked at an angle, so that his headlights illuminated the roadway. I stopped about three hundred feet in front of him. Scared to death and not knowing what else to do, I flicked my lights, signaling the other driver to move on. I thought: If anyone gets out, I will quickly drive past. The standoff seemed to last for hours, but, in fact, only a few seconds passed before the other car pulled out of the rest area, taking the ramp that led in the opposite direction, back toward Brussels.

I feared that the other driver might attempt to double back, so I drove quickly ahead and turned off at the next exit ramp, which led to Marche-en-Famenne, the town where we did our grocery shopping when we were in the country. The side road was very slick, but I had to hurry. I was very afraid that I would wreck the car and hurt the children. I hid the car in the anonymity of the Delhaize supermarket parking lot and hoped that my heart would stop pounding. It was about 7:00 P.M. The store was still open, but not many people were out on this dark, snowy evening. My eyes followed the traffic on the nearby road. After only about thirty seconds, I saw my pursuer speed past.

Okay, I lost them, I thought. Then I remembered: Chaim

knows perfectly well where the country house is. He has been there many times. If he is in that car, he knows I'm going to Nassogne. What do I do?

I drove carefully along slippery back roads, through the village of Ambly, in the direction of the country house. I stopped at the home of my friends Marie-Anne and Olivier to tell them what had happened. They lived with their three children in a tiny, cramped house, and I did not want to impose by asking if the children and I could spend the night. But Olivier agreed to escort me over to my parents' house, to make sure that we were safe.

Over the years I had come to love this country home because of its isolation. Stands of trees hid it from the view of the road; now, I wished that it was not so private. Usually I parked the car out on the road, but this night I pulled through the gateway and down into the drive. I waited there as Olivier checked the house and the grounds carefully. He assured me that there was no sign of trouble, and we hustled the children inside. Olivier promised, "I will come once in a while to check that everything is fine. Call if you need anything."

I pulled the heavy wooden outer door shut and bolted it. Quickly I grabbed the telephone and dialed a number in Mons. "I've been followed," I said to my parents. I gave a brief account of the incident.

"I'm sure it's nothing to be concerned about," my father said calmly. "Don't worry. Someone probably saw a woman alone on the road. They just wanted to frighten you."

Could it be true? I wondered. Had I panicked so completely that I had imagined Chaim's profile? Papa was so reassuring, so reasonable, that he managed to calm me.

But after I hung up the phone, there I was, alone with three small children in a secluded house. Racing about, I checked the wooden shutters on all the windows to make certain they were securely fastened. I fed and bathed the children, then tucked them into the front bedroom and assured them that I would sleep there too. I lit a candle next to my bed and turned off the lights.

Olivier called two or three times during the evening to report that he had checked the area and seen no one.

Before settling into bed, I went out to the foyer and pulled one of my father's shotguns from a gun rack. I was glad that he had taught me how to use it properly. I loaded it, but kept the barrel cracked open for safety, and placed it beneath my bed. If Chaim broke in and tried to take the children, I *knew* that I would shoot him.

The night hours crept past like a snail.

My imagination told me all the things that Chaim could do: He could cut the telephone lines. If he was determined, he could force his way through the shutters. Or he could simply lurk outside and wait for morning to—what? What was he doing? What did he want?

I got almost no sleep. Darkness accentuated the incidental noises of the night. Each time the house creaked or a branch cracked outside I was ready to scream, although I knew that no one would hear me.

The bright winter morning sunlight made me feel a bit foolish. The children were refreshed and ready for their holiday. Their light mood made the events of the previous evening seem like a bad dream. It was probably as my father said, just two men who wanted to find a woman alone on the highway, and I had run away from them. If Chaim really was in Nassogne, he could have come after me during the night. But nothing had happened.

We needed to stockpile groceries for our five-day stay, so we clambered into the Toyota and drove back to the Delhaize supermarket in Marche-en-Famenne. The road was straight and clear; last night's ice was gone. My mood grew brighter by the moment.

Then, quite far behind, I noticed a brown BMW. I was startled, but I calmed myself with the thought: Stupid! Here you go again. Patsy, you are not the only one driving to Marche today.

I was in a generous mood. Marina and Simon ran around the grocery shelves as I filled two full carts. After paying the cashier, I decided to take one cartload out to the car, along with the children. When I had them safely in the Toyota, I would come back for the second load of groceries.

Moriah sat in the child's seat of the cart and Simon and Marina walked alongside. The children chattered as we emerged from the store and rolled the cart to the middle of the half-empty parking lot.

Suddenly I glanced up.

Chaim!

He stood in front of my car, apparently alone. *Merde!* I thought. I was right yesterday. My heart pounded inside my chest. I called out to Marina and Simon, "You stay with me. Your father is there."

He walked forward, meeting us halfway.

"Hello," I said, attempting to maintain a civil tone.

"Hello," he responded politely. Then he ordered, "You come back to Israel with me."

"No way! After what you did, no way. I'm not going. You know it. Now leave us alone." I could see that he was surprised by the force of my answer. He still remembered the old, obedient Patsy.

In what seemed like one motion, he swept down upon us, plucked Moriah from the shopping cart, and ran toward the brown BMW that I had spotted earlier. I raced after him, grabbed at his shirt, and screamed, "He's kidnapping my child! Stop him!" Marina and Simon followed, shrieking in fear.

Chaim pulled away, reached his car, shoved Moriah in the backseat of the BMW, and quickly slipped in behind the wheel. I was no match for him physically, so I grasped my only chance. I continued to yell at the top of my lungs, "Help me, he's taking my baby!"

Around us, bystanders froze, staring. Marina and Simon, still screaming and crying and more alarmed by my own reaction than the presence of their father, ran into the arms of a kindly looking woman. I gestured toward the crowd and wailed, "He's running away with their little sister! Help me!"

Chaim tried to close the car door, but I lunged forward,

wedging myself halfway inside. My fingers grabbed wildly for Moriah, but she was so terrified that she squirmed away. Chaim could have pushed me out of the way, but he was suddenly shaking with his own fear. Still, no one would help.

Finally an older gentleman—probably in his sixties—broke from the crowd and came up behind me, reached into the driver's seat, and grabbed Chaim by the shoulder. Young, strong Chaim could have overpowered him easily, but he cowered in terror. Having noted the German plates on the BMW, the older man commanded in German, "Get out of the car."

Chaim, not understanding the words, stammered, "Uh, uh, uh . . ."

The gentleman eased Chaim out of the car. I scrambled into the backseat of the BMW and pulled Moriah into my arms.

The older gentleman stood protectively between Chaim and me. Others gathered about. Someone decreed, "You have to go to the police station."

In a shocked, tearful voice, I sobbed, "Yes, but people have to come with me. What if he runs away? What if he tries to take my baby again?"

The older gentleman reassured me; he would come with us.

The station house was nearby, just up an alley from the supermarket. We drove there in a caravan—the gentleman in his car, the children and I in the old Toyota, Chaim in the BMW. He was too intimidated to attempt an escape.

At the station house I gave the gentleman the telephone number of my parents' house in Mons and asked him to call. Mother was busy painting a room when the telephone rang. To her shock, she heard the voice of a stranger, who implored, "Madame, don't panic. Your daughter had a problem, but everything is all right." Mother, of course, panicked. She quickly drew the details from the caller. Then she called my father at his office and they set off immediately to come help.

The gentleman gave the police a brief statement and was allowed to leave. But before he disappeared he told me that the reason he got involved was because Chaim, with his black hair and bronzed skin, looked like an Arab. His voice exhibited the characteristic local Walloon accent as he said, "Those Arabic people, you never know . . ."

Chaim denied attempting to kidnap the children, claiming that he only wanted to speak with me. Skeptical of this explanation, the police confiscated his papers and locked him inside a basement cell as they tried to figure out what to do with him. Within minutes, he banged on the cell door and yelled, "I want coffee." A police officer sighed, poured a cup of coffee, and took it downstairs. Then we heard Chaim shout, "No, not that kind of coffee." He asked for a blanket, complaining that he was cold. When they brought it, he demanded a second one. He asked for food. "It tastes bad," he grumbled. From the looks that the officers exchanged, I knew that Chaim Yarden was not helping his case.

When my parents arrived, one of the officers smiled broadly. He recognized Jacques Heymans immediately, for he had hunted many times with one of my uncles. I was glad that this was an area of small towns, where everyone knew everyone else's business.

In the eyes of the police, this episode was a serious matter. They questioned me carefully and made several calls to trace Chaim's actions. His BMW had been rented in Germany, and the police were able to determine that he had not come to Belgium alone. Three other men were staying with him at his hotel. It appeared that they had devised a coordinated effort to take the children. My guess was that they planned to stop us the previous night on the side road leading from the highway to the country house. I had spoiled that plan by getting off the highway at Marche instead of Nassogne. Why had they not made an attempt to get into the country house during the night? I wondered. Perhaps they had seen Olivier with me and thought that he had spent the night. Or perhaps Chaim remembered that I knew how to use my father's shotguns. At any rate, the plan had changed. This morning, when Chaim attempted to act on his own, he had botched the job. He knew me as a weak, submissive woman and probably reasoned that I would quickly agree to bring the children and return to Israel with him.

One officer asked me who had legal custody. "No one," I admitted.

Hearing this, the officer was confused and concerned. It appeared that Chaim had not broken any laws.

The officer called a youth court judge in Brussels, who agreed to handle the case. Then he explained to me that they could take no official action against Chaim. We were still married and, in the absence of a formal custody agreement, Chaim had as much right to the children as I did. The officer lowered his voice and advised, "Okay. You leave and go hide somewhere. We can only keep him locked up until evening."

I must have been in shock, for all I could think about were the two carts full of groceries that I had left in the supermarket parking lot. "Go get the groceries. Go get the groceries," I begged my mother.

But the larger question was: Where would we take the groceries?

13

"Your father wanted to take you because he wanted us to go back to Israel," I explained. Simon, always ready to act out his emotions, went on a destructive rampage, venting his rage at Chaim by smashing his toys against the wall, yelling, "Bad father! Leave us alone." Moriah was too young to understand what had happened. But Marina, like me, kept her anxiety buried inside. She had never before sucked her thumb, but now she took up the habit. She started wetting her pants several times during the day. Overnight, she soaked her bed. Her once-careful drawings reverted to childlike scrawls. Her pediatrician prescribed a mild tranquilizer for her, but I was reluctant to use the medication on a child so young. Instead, I let her stay with my mother for a few days, and in the familiar and safe surroundings she calmed considerably.

The young court judge acted quickly. Since I was the one who had originally fled with the children, the judge was reluctant to grant me custody without investigating the case. Nevertheless, Chaim's attempt to snatch the children back, and their obvious terror of him, convinced the judge that the children were in jeopardy. On January 17, 1984, the Brussels court issued a provisional order, granting temporary custody to my older brother, Eric, until the final disposition. But the judge knew perfectly well that the children were living with me.

We moved into my parents' rental house in Mons. It was a pleasant, small, brick row house at the intersection of two streets. A small convenience store was next door. Due to the heavy traffic, we always used the rear entrance, which was enclosed by a chain-link fence. I kept the gate locked at all times. I told the children that the name of the town was Gand, and they were too young to know the difference. If their father, or someone on his behalf, spoke to them, I hoped the information would mislead any pursuers, since Gand is about forty miles north of Brussels, whereas Mons is southwest of the capital.

I found a tiny, two-room school less than a quarter of a mile from the house, which made it convenient and provided me with a sense of security. One of the classrooms was a kindergarten for ages two through six; the other taught children aged seven to twelve. When I enrolled Marina and Simon, I presented both of the teachers with copies of the custody order and told them that under no circumstances were they to release the children to Chaim.

For the next few months I lived with constant tension. I grew extremely anxious whenever any one of the children was out of my sight, even briefly. I instructed them to play only in the backyard, where I could keep an eye on them. I cautioned them against speaking to strangers and reminded them that only my parents, brothers, or I would ever pick them up from school. I was concerned about turning them into frightened rabbits—and I did not want to paint their father as a monster—but what else could I do? I constantly walked a tightrope with my fears on one side and the children's emotional health on the other.

Friends and family treated my phone number as a state secret. Papa, or another family member, stayed with us throughout the nights; I could not bear to be alone. If friends came to visit, I issued strict instructions to make sure that they were not followed. On the road between Mons and Brussels I used various exit ramps and often parked on the shoulder for a few minutes to see if there was any evidence of someone following me. I realized that, like a sixth sense, I had learned to memorize the license plates of suspicious cars. My father kept a licensed pistol in the house, on top of the bedroom cupboard, and he made me practice loading and unloading. He wanted me to handle the pistol enough so that I would feel comfortable with it.

On April 3, 1984, the Brussels court amended its original order and granted custody of the children to me. The court also granted Chaim visitation rights, but only under unusually strict conditions. The visits were to take place on Monday and Wednesday afternoons at my parents' home in Brussels. I was to be present at all times. Noting Chaim's previous attempt to take the children, the judge ordered that Marina, Simon, and Moriah's names should be scratched from his passport; the names were not to be removed but visibly crossed out, so that any border official would immediately question Chaim if he attempted to travel with small children.

One day a registered letter arrived for me, addressed to my parents' house. By chance, I was there in case Chaim wished to exercise his visitation rights, so I signed for it. I glanced at the oversized envelope and saw that it was penned in Chaim's hand and had been mailed right here in Brussels. I opened it to find a pamphlet describing an organization to aid lonely women. This is ridiculous, I thought. Why did he send such a thing to me by registered mail? I threw it out, classifying it as one of Chaim's sick jokes.

A few weeks later I was again at my parents' house at the appointed time for Chaim's visitation. He never arrived, but another registered letter did, once again addressed in his handwriting, once again mailed in Brussels. Inside, wrapped in cardboard, was a sample vial of Clair de Lune perfume. This is too much, I thought. It makes no sense. But my instincts warned me to keep both the perfume and the envelope, although I did not know why.

* * *

I glanced nervously at the bright-blue Toyota in my rearview mirror. It had been behind me for several minutes, following at a distance. Only mildly concerned, I pulled off the highway. The Toyota followed. Quickly I turned into the parking area of a small market. The Toyota sped past. Patsy, you are too nervous, I told myself.

But I saw it again a short time later. I was sure that it was the same car. Again, I parked quickly. Once more, the Toyota sped past.

Then, just as I pulled into the side street where we lived, I saw the same car drive by.

It cannot be Chaim, I reasoned. The Toyota was a brilliant blue. If someone was following me, he would not use a car that was so easy to spot. Someone who lived near me in Mons must have bought such a car.

Moriah began kindergarten in the autumn of 1984 and we developed a smooth daily routine. Each morning I took all three children to school and then drove to work. We spent the evenings playing with flash cards or jigsaw puzzles. After the children were asleep, I tended to the housework and concentrated on my studies. We were happy in our little home, and our lives were brightened by two new family members: Max was a standard dachshund; the other, a midget dachshund who reminded me of Princesse, was so ugly that we named her after the movie alien E.T.

On the morning of October 17, I was on an errand, buying office supplies, when my father received a phone call from one of the children's teachers. She sounded frantic. "You've got to get to the school right away," she said. "The father is here, and he wants to take the kids!"

Papa raced to the school; Eric called all over Mons, trying to find me.

My father arrived at the school to find Chaim arguing with the teachers and waving a document in the air. Papa called the police.

Meanwhile, when I finally returned to the office, Eric said, "Get over to the school right away." I drove over quickly and found a chaotic scene.

It took some time to realize what was happening. Chaim had somehow obtained a letter from a Belgian attorney stating that *he* had custody of the children. So he had simply walked into the school, announced that he was the father of Marina, Simon, and Moriah, flashed the attorney's letter, and demanded the children. Clasping Moriah's hand, he said, "Let's go. We go to France."

But Chaim had not counted on resistance from the teachers, who had seen the court order granting custody to me. Moriah's teacher pulled her away from Chaim and gathered the three children around her as she called out for help from the second teacher. The man who taught the upper grades came running. As he argued with Chaim on the legalities of the respective documents, his colleague had called us.

The police compared the legal papers and easily concluded that a court decree took precedence over an attorney's letter, and they released the children to me.

As we left the school, we noticed a car outside. A man sat in the driver's seat, obviously waiting. We approached, and my father asked what he was doing.

The man was embarrassed and upset but talkative. He introduced himself as a private detective and explained his role in this affair. Sometime earlier, Chaim had come to him and identified himself as the uncle of three Israeli-Belgian children. He said that the three were living with an extremely abusive mother. As a favor to the children's Israeli father—Chaim claimed to be his brother—Chaim had promised to locate the children and check on their well-being.

The detective had agreed to help. It had sounded like a noble cause.

They had watched my parents' house until I showed up. Then they had placed me under surveillance (the bright blue Toyota! I remembered) until they established that I was living in

Mons. The detective had systematically telephoned all the schools in Mons and finally located the Yarden children.

The detective had gone into the school with Chaim, intending to see how the children were. Only then did he learn that Chaim was the father, not the uncle, and that he planned to take the children away with him. He had angrily stormed out of the school and simply waited outside to see what would happen.

"That man is no good!" the detective raged. "He lied to me." He realized, now, that Chaim had planned carefully. "We have another car parked nearby," he said. It was obvious that Chaim had planned to switch cars and drive the children to the nearby French border.

The detective wanted no further part in this mess, at least on Chaim's side. He gave us his telephone number and told us that he would help in any way he could.

Once I realized that Chaim knew we were living in Mons, I faced a difficult decision. Should I move once more to another secret address?

After much careful thought, I decided: No, I will not keep running every time Chaim tries to make trouble. I will not disrupt the children's lives because of him. But I would be very, very careful.

Each time Chaim reappeared in my life I was forced to revisit the terror that pervaded our marriage. Sometimes I was conscious of its effect on me; sometimes the fear burst out with surprising force from a reservoir that I kept hidden even from myself. One weekend my parents hosted a huge hunting party. The country house at Nassogne was so filled with guests that my brothers Eric and Michel had to sleep at the old cabin in Grune.

In the evening, after a day in the outdoors, my father was exhausted. He compounded his mood by drinking a bit too much. After the guests were gone, we fell into a bitter argument over something trivial. We screamed at one another and he slammed a door in frustration. That's it, I thought, I'm getting out of here. I drove to the cabin in Grune to visit my brothers.

To my surprise, Papa followed me. We continued our argument, and my father grew so agitated that he pushed at me. It was only a slight shove, but the mere act of a man raising his hand to me set off a chain reaction of dormant fears. Suddenly I was once more under Chaim's control. It was Chaim who had shoved me and I knew that more blows—many more—would follow.

I bolted from the cabin and ran into the woods. Everyone in Grune must have heard my screams.

Eric and Michel gave chase. When they finally caught me, I was babbling out stories about Chaim, reliving some of the worst events from our marriage. They pushed me into Eric's car, and Michel had to sit on me to prevent me from jumping out the door. Eric drove quickly to a doctor's office. Throughout the ride, I gasped out stories of Chaim's bestial behavior toward me and the children. My brothers had not heard these details before. They had thought that Chaim had, perhaps, slapped me a few times, but nothing more. They were horrified.

The doctor had to come out to the car to administer two shots of Valium, right through my clothing, before I began to calm down.

Later, some friends said to me, "Patsy, why don't two, three, or four of us take him into woods, you know . . ."

Eric felt the same way. He said, "He just needs for someone to break his face once or twice and he will understand to leave us alone."

Even my father agreed. "What we should do is break both his elbows," he suggested. "That will give him time to think about all the trouble he is making for us." Remembering Chaim's exaggerated sense of modesty, Papa fantasized, "Someone would even have to help him go to the bathroom."

14

The month following Chaim's second kidnapping attempt, his Belgian lawyer contacted us and disclosed that a court in Haifa, Israel—months earlier, on June 10—had granted custody of the children to Chaim. Now, the lawyer said, Chaim had retained him to make the judgment valid in Belgium also.

This was preposterous, I responded. How could an Israeli court make such a decision without notifying me or hearing my side of the story?

Our attorney obtained copies of the Israeli court papers, and it was true. Chaim had accused me of abusing the children, and the Israeli courts had believed him, without giving me an opportunity to defend myself. This explained why he was so emboldened as to attempt to take the children from school. If he could get them to Israel, they were his!

My father and I put together the pieces of this puzzle. In most countries, a legal agent must serve a subpoena on any party in a lawsuit, but in Israel, the plaintiff simply must show evidence that he notified the defendant of the suit. When we asked Chaim's Belgian lawyer for proof that I had been notified, he displayed copies of the receipts I signed for the strange registered letters he had sent me.

We lodged a complaint with the Police Judiciaire, the investigative arm of the Brussels prosecutor's office, charging that Chaim had used false papers to obtain the Israeli custody decree. I sifted through my belongings until I found the perfume sample that Chaim had sent, along with the envelope, and I presented these items as evidence. That stalled Chaim's legal battle.

Now I decided to take the offensive. I did not care about Chaim's money, but I filed papers for a legal separation and asked for child-support payments. On February 28, 1985, the Brussels court reaffirmed its earlier decision awarding me permanent custody of the children. Because Chaim would not grant me a divorce, and I had no proof of his abuse, I would have to wait until we had been separated for five years before I could file for divorce. The judge ordered Chaim to pay support of seventy-five hundred Belgian francs (about two hundred dollars) per month, per child.

Chaim never sent a single franc and I did not expect him to do so. But now I could threaten to have him jailed for nonpayment.

This seemed to work. For a time, he left us alone.

We spent an April weekend at the country house. It was the second anniversary of my independence from Chaim, and I said to myself: Patsy, you cannot keep on like this. You should be grown up enough to go home alone. Even the court has put you in charge now. And so, for the first time in four months, I did not ask my brothers or Papa to come home with me.

It was twilight when the children and I arrived back in Mons. The moment I entered the house I was overwhelmed by a very strong sense that someone had been there. The feeling was so strong that I could almost *touch* it. Nothing was out of place, no doors were tampered with, no windows were broken, but the atmosphere simply did not feel right. I said to the children, "You stay in the kitchen. If I scream, run to the neighbor's."

I walked through the kitchen and the living room to the steep, narrow staircase. There were no windows here, and the darkness closed in on me. I was terrified. I clutched at my stomach, worried that I would vomit. I checked each of the bedrooms and peered into the closets. My jewelry was there. The pistol was undisturbed atop the bedroom cupboard. Patsy, I said to myself, you are nervous because this is your first night alone. Nobody was here. It's your imagination. Get hold of yourself before you frighten the children.

The kids were tired from their weekend in the country. We all prepared for bed and I tucked them in early. But by 11:00 P.M. I was still nervously awake.

The quiet of the night was broken by an insistent pounding on the front door.

My open bedroom window was directly above the door. I peered through the thick curtains to see two uniformed policemen on my front steps, illuminated by yellow streetlights. One of them held an open passport in his hands. Instantly, I recognized Chaim's picture. Oh, my God, I thought. I was right. Something is happening.

When I opened the door, the officers told me that Chaim was outside, sitting in the backseat of the police cruiser. "I don't want him in here," I said.

One of the officers got right to the point: "Your husband tells us that you use and sell drugs and that you beat and torture your children. He says that you cut their fingers and their ears." He asked politely, "Look, we don't have a warrant, but do you mind if we go and see the kids?"

"I don't mind," I agreed. "I have nothing to hide. Just go ahead." I took them up to the girls' room, switched on the light, and whispered, "Look. You can count their fingers, their ears, everything."

One glance at my peaceful, sleeping daughters satisfied the policemen. They did not even bother to check Simon.

One officer continued to chat with me as the other puffed on a cigarette and moved about quietly. He did not open drawers or check closets, but his eyes were very busy.

The search found nothing, and the talkative officer commented apologetically, "You don't look like you use drugs."

"If you want, I can go to the station and you can give me a blood test," I offered.

"We are not authorized to do that. You'll have to go to an independent clinic for that."

As they were leaving, they instructed me to bring the children to the police station after school the next day.

My old fears returned with full force. Chaim was back, and I did not want to be alone in the house, so my mother drove down from Brussels in the morning to offer support. That afternoon, she waited at the house as I took the children to the station.

The police specialists were very professional. Calmly, gently, they escorted the children to a room where they had games and toys available. As the children played, the police asked seemingly casual questions.

Meanwhile, in a separate room, an investigator asked me politely, "What did you do on Sunday?"

"I was in Nassogne. Friends were there. They saw me. You can ask them." A typist recorded my answer.

The questioner countered, "Your husband says he saw you on Sunday afternoon in the center of Mons, selling drugs." They told me that Chaim had come to the police station on three separate occasions, repeating his allegations. Each time, his information was more specific.

I was not even nervous. The accusations were so unbelievable that I knew this episode would amount to nothing. I offered honest, credible answers to every question.

One of the investigators asked, "Did he ever speak to you about using drugs?"

I said, "I remember once in Tel Aviv, he showed me a place where he said you could buy drugs."

"Do you think he would be able to cause you trouble by putting drugs in your house?"

"No," I said. "I doubt that he would go that far."

Once the authorities were assured that the children were safe and in good health, we were allowed to leave. On the drive home, I started thinking: It is not like Chaim to be so persistent. In the past, when one of his tricks failed, he gave up quickly and disappeared. Why would he go back to the police three times? Why was he so sure of himself this time? When we arrived home, I suggested to my mother, "You take care of the kids. I'm going to look through the house."

I conducted a haphazard search through closets and cupboards downstairs, but I found nothing suspicious. Still, I felt uneasy. It occurred to me that if Chaim had tried to plant evidence in this house, he would seek out my bedroom. I turned, made my way upstairs to my bedroom, and began searching systematically. The small nightstand next to my bed held two drawers. One was for my private things; the other was what we called the "secret drawer," where the children often left special messages for me. When I opened the secret drawer, I spotted a small, yellow-paper package, folded at the edges. My first reaction was: Oh, the kids left me a surprise. I opened up the folds of the paper and found a quantity of a grainy, grayish-yellow, sandlike substance. This cannot be from the kids, I realized. The paper was folded too carefully.

I immediately called the police station to report what I had found. "We are closed," someone reported. "You will have to bring it over in the morning." I wrapped the mysterious packet in foil and placed it on top of a cupboard, where the children could not get to it.

The next morning I took the packet to the station house. The duty officer told me that he would send the powder to a lab and would have the results within a few days. A few days, I thought. What if there is more of this poison in my home?

I had been home for only a half hour when four police cars surrounded my house. The attitude of the officers had changed dramatically. At least one investigator did not need to wait for a laboratory test to recognize heroin.

The officers regarded me with fresh suspicion. They asked to see my arms. I rolled up my sleeves. The inner sides of my elbows revealed small scars from needle punctures. "I give blood," I explained.

Skepticism showed on their faces, but they were satisfied when I displayed my donor card. One of them said, "Well, if you give blood, you've been tested. They wouldn't accept you if you used drugs." They sat at my dining-room table and prepared an official report, asking further questions, noting my answers carefully.

I reassured them further by telling them that, in case someone had hidden other dangerous drugs in my home, I wanted them found before my children came across them. "Listen, you do me a favor," I said. "Tear apart my whole house. Bring dogs—I don't care. If you find something, good for you, because I'm afraid for the kids. Take whatever you want."

Soon after this, I voluntarily submitted to private blood and urine tests. The results indicated that I had eaten fish for dinner the night before the tests, and that I drank a lot of coffee. There were no traces of illegal drugs.

The police said nothing to Chaim about this. Instead, they listened carefully as he came to them two or three additional times, repeating his allegations. They were not as gullible as Chaim had supposed. Their response was to search Chaim's car, taking it apart bit by bit. They found no drugs, but they did find a map of Europe, with every major drug-distribution center highlighted. Unfortunately, this was not sufficient evidence to arrest him.

But I was beginning to wonder if Chaim had found a way to finance his threat: "I will destroy your life."

Every Monday and Wednesday I made the forty-five-minute drive to my parents' home to honor the terms of Chaim's visitation rights. Sometimes Chaim showed up, but he did not come to the door. Once, a neighbor alerted me, complaining that Chaim was standing in her garden, watching our house. On several other occasions I saw him on the sidewalk across the street, pacing back and forth, but he did not attempt to visit. He was playing a diabolical game, and I did not know the rules.

Finally, one afternoon about three weeks after the incident with the drugs, Chaim's car appeared on our street in Mons. He drove back and forth several times, slowly, making no attempt at secrecy. Moriah was playing in the garden. I made her come inside. Chaim parked across the street, came to the gate, and banged on the iron bars to get my attention.

Cautiously I approached the locked gate and asked him what he wanted.

"I came to see the kids," he said.

"Wait here," I ordered. I went inside and discussed the matter with my father. Chaim's legal visitation rights were very specific. He could see the children on Monday and Wednesday afternoons, but only at the Brussels house on Avenue des Fleurs. "It's not the right day," I said. "It's not the right place."

We decided to call our lawyer. The attorney did not know what to do either. He advised, "Well, it's not the legal way. If you want to be nasty, you can say no. If you want to be nice, you can say yes."

I had almost decided to allow Chaim inside when Papa advised, "Hey, but first check his passport."

"Yes." I was shivering with apprehension when I returned to the gate and demanded, "Let me see your passport."

Chaim presented the document and held it up so that I could view it through the wide spaces of the bars.

"I need to see inside," I said coolly.

With a sneer on his face, he opened the cover. He spoke to me as if I were a baby: "Well, on the first page you have a number. On the second page you have the picture. On . . ."

I reached through the bars, snatched the document from his hand, and raced back inside the house. Chaim yelled angrily at my back.

Inside, I examined the passport carefully and announced to my father, "Look, it's fine. The kids' names are not in here."

"Let me see," Papa requested. He studied the booklet, turning the pages slowly. "Patsy," he said, pointing, "there is a page missing. He has torn out a page."

Once again we called the lawyer. He reminded us: "The court order clearly states that the children's names have to be *scratched* from the passport."

I returned to the gate and told Chaim, "No, you may not come in. You took a page from the passport. The kids are not in it."

"That's it!" he raged. "You will not let me see the kids. Give me my passport."

"No."

"Okay, I'm going to the police station."

"Just go. But I'm keeping your passport."

He ran off. I hurried into the house and called several different police officers, to warn them, "Chaim Yarden is coming in."

I happened to be speaking to one of the officers who had investigated the drug incident, when the man said, "He just came in. I will call you back."

Several minutes later, the officer reported that Chaim had displayed a proper passport which did, indeed, contain the scratched-out names of the children. The policeman said, "He said he has two passports because he knew you would do something wrong. He says you tore the page out."

"It's a lie," I said.

The officer was sympathetic, but he asked me to bring in the suspicious passport.

By the time I arrived at the station house, the police had decided to see if they could force us to settle our differences. "Okay," an officer said, "we will put you together in a room so that you can talk."

I did not wish to be alone with Chaim, but I apparently had no choice. We sat across from one another at a square table in a cold, bare conference room.

I was determined to be polite. I was certain that the police were listening to us, and I wanted to show Chaim a Very Strong Patsy.

Chaim took the offensive and repeated old complaints. According to him, it was my father who forced me to leave Israel. He never beat me, and if he did, it was only because I made him do it.

As the minutes passed, it became very difficult for me to hold my temper. At one point Chaim finally goaded me into an angry outburst.

"Ah, Patsy," he said smoothly, "don't be so impolite. You are an extremely bad woman. How can you raise the children correctly if you are so impolite?"

After forty-five minutes of useless discussion, a police officer entered the room and asked Chaim for his identification papers. Chaim handed over a document and the officer turned to leave. I asked, "Do I need to stay here with him? I'm getting very nervous and it is not accomplishing anything."

The officer shrugged and I followed him out the door.

Chaim remained inside the meeting room as the officers attempted to inspect his ID. It was written in Hebrew and they could not understand a word. I studied it and told them, "It's not an ID card. It is his reserve card for the army."

It was about this time that the police computer reported that Chaim Yarden had already been evicted from Belgium once. He had attempted to kidnap children, and he was a suspected drug dealer.

That was enough. Two policemen put Chaim in a car, drove him to the French border, and kicked him out of the country.

But, of course, in Europe, borders mean nothing. Chaim could walk or drive back into Belgium anytime he wished.

In June, the trucking company in Mons declared bankruptcy and we moved back to my parents' home in Brussels. I set a goal: By September, when it was time for the children to return to school, I would have a job and a house of my own.

After answering several newspaper ads, I was hired for a clerical job in the administration office of Olivetti, the Italian-owned typewriter company. The pay was minimal and I hated the work, but I was proud to have found something on my own, outside my father's sphere of business contacts. The office was in a modern—ugly, I thought—white building on Boulevard du Souverain, across from the headquarters of Royale Belge Insurance Company.

My job was to file invoices. I sat for eight hours a day in the midst of a crowded, noisy floor. For some time I was not assigned to a permanent desk, so each day I had to move my particular pile of paperwork to a new spot.

I soon discovered that in the professional world of Brussels I suffered from a language deficit. Much business was conducted in Dutch, rather than French, and the Dutch-speaking office bureaucrats tended to snub those who only spoke French. For example, I had a few clashes with Walter Boghaert, a project leader in the marketing division. On several occasions I picked up the phone and heard him rattle off a request in Dutch. "Speak French!" I snapped, hanging up the phone. Moments later the phone on the desk in front of me would ring, and Mr. Boghaert would request the same information, in Dutch, from a more accommodating employee. If Mr. Boghaert and I happened to meet in the hallway, we avoided one another.

Nevertheless, I advanced on the job. My temporary position was extended, and I was given new duties, working with computerized inventory control.

Keeping to my timetable, I leased a small town house at Nine Rue Verte, in the Kraainem district of Brussels, a middle-class neighborhood fairly close to my parents' home. The town house was dark and narrow, but it had three floors and five bedrooms, and it also featured a small courtyard in back. It was an important step for me to sign the lease, for it was the first time that I had assumed total responsibility for my children and myself. Patsy is finally on her own, I thought. Now I can raise my children like a real mother.

After my clashes at work with the laconic, Dutch-speaking Walter Boghaert, I decided that my children would become bilingual. If they were to thrive in Brussels, a mastery of Dutch was essential. I enrolled Simon in the Dutch-language section of Sint Jozef's College, a Roman Catholic school situated on Boulevard de la Woluwe, not far from Olivetti. I found another Catholic school for the girls, called Mater Dei. I presented both principals with copies of the custody order and instructed them that the children were not to be released to anyone without my permission. I stressed that if there was ever any change in plans, if one of the children was ill or we had to be away, I would always write a note or call.

I bought a used Citroen Visa. Its green exterior was faded by the sun, but it got me where I needed to go. Each morning about 8:00 A.M. I dropped all three children inside the gate of Sint Jozef's and continued on down the boulevard to my job. A woman friend, who also had children in both schools, picked up Marina and Moriah and drove them on to Mater Dei. I worked hard all day, taking only a half-hour break for lunch—if I had any shopping to do, I crammed it into this brief time—so that I would be able to pick up the children by 5:00 P.M., one hour after school ended. I picked up Simon first and then drove the hilly back streets to get the girls.

By 5:30 or 5:45, depending upon the traffic, we were home, and I had to handle every aspect of parenthood throughout the evening. I supervised the homework for Marina and Simon, helping them, and myself, with the unfamiliar Dutch. Moriah's kindergarten did not assign homework, so I prepared pretend lessons for her. She was very proud to color a page just as instructed. Then I made sure that all four of us had a bit of time to play together; we particularly enjoyed doing jigsaw puzzles. Some of my best memories are of these evening activities. Then we had baths and supper. The children were in bed by 7:30; only then did I turn my attention to such things as ironing and cleaning.

The new routine was difficult for Simon at first. A perfectionist, he often grew frustrated as he struggled with his Dutch-language homework, crying and tearing up a paper when his letters were not perfect. He was assigned to clip letters from a newspaper, and he was very upset when he did not cut them out with precision. I sometimes found him sitting sideways on our small couch, sucking his thumb, with E.T. on his lap and Max at his side. After a time I realized that he was just too full of energy and stress from the long days of concentration. Every day when we returned home I encouraged him to spend about fifteen minutes in the courtyard, kicking a soccer ball. He was much better after that.

As the only male in the household, Simon seemed to envision himself as a tiny chieftain. On his own, he decreed that the girls could not enter his bedroom. "Okay," I agreed, "they may not. But you may not go into their bedroom, then." Unwilling to accept the deal, he finally agreed that the girls could enter his room.

Thanks to Belgium's thirty-eight-hour work week, I was able to take off every other Wednesday afternoon, when the children were out of school. Sometimes we rented a boat and paddled about the lake surrounding Val Duchesse, the palatial meeting hall of government ministers.

Gradually we found a comfortable rhythm to our new life, a sense of routine that the children found reassuring.

One incident showed me how close they had become to one another. I discovered that someone had tried out a new pair of scissors by cutting holes in some of our clothing. I suspected Simon, but I could not be sure. I gathered the three of them together and said, "Who did this?" The three of them answered in unison, "It's me."

I had to laugh at the way they protected one another. I said, "If the person who did this admits it, I won't get mad, because he told the truth."

Slowly, sheepishly, Simon raised his index finger.

I was very proud of them, and of myself. I thought: Patsy, you can do this.

We did not hear directly from Chaim for more than a year. The children grew and thrived. As she neared her seventh birthday, Marina was a delightful girl with a bright, dimpled smile. Five-and-a-half-year-old Simon was getting better and better at dealing with a Dutch-speaking world. At four, Moriah was learning all the tricks of being the baby of the family.

We began to relax.

15

The Belgian countryside is peppered with small villages like Nassogne. They are tightly knit and people watch out for one another. There are few secrets. One Saturday in the summer of 1986 we received a telephone call at the country house from the owner of a service station, warning me that he had seen Chaim. "He's looking very different," the man said, somewhat puzzled. "He has a full, busy beard and wears a flat-brimmed black hat." The description held no significance for me, but I filed the information in my mind.

That same day the police in Nassogne saw Chaim driving. They pulled his car over and questioned him closely. They could find no reason to arrest him, but they wanted him out of the area. One of the officers made sure that Chaim got a good look at his Uzi machine gun. Then they ordered him to leave.

On a September morning, my mother experienced a premonition. She could not say why, but she sensed that something was amiss. The air about her held the eerie sensation of the calm before the storm.

As she drove the narrow, winding roads from the country house toward Marche, she passed a car traveling in the opposite direction. Immediately she recognized Chaim at the wheel. It was true that he had changed his appearance dramatically. He had grown the beard and did indeed wear a hat, but the eyes that caught her own were Chaim's. Is it some sort of disguise? Maman wondered.

Once, long ago, Chaim had worn a mustache for a brief period of time, but I could not envision him with a beard. And why a hat?

These reports disturbed me greatly. I did not want Chaim back in my life or anywhere near it. But my uneasiness was caused by more than his proximity. The beard and hat represented some sort of mysterious change in Chaim's life that I did not understand. I assumed that he was trying to disguise himself so we would not recognize him.

For a time I was apprehensive. I took extra care with the children. But weeks passed, then months, and Chaim seemed to have disappeared once more.

Early in December, I was alarmed by the suspicion that a car had followed me. I discussed this with friends and with my parents. I realized that the most vulnerable part of the day was the short time span in the morning when I left the children together at Sint Jozef's.

"From now on," I said to my parents, "I'm going to take all the children to their schools myself. I will take Simon to his school and then I will take the girls to their school. Just me."

My father tried to ease my mind, reminding me I had no proof that Chaim, or anyone else, was following me. "You cannot do it all," he said, "you cannot surround them every minute of every day."

He's right, I said to myself, it's only a feeling. I cannot live my life ruled by daily fears.

December 11, 1986. I awoke at 7:00 A.M., showered quickly, and dressed for work. Knowing that Simon was the most difficult of the three to get going in the morning, I tried to rouse him first. "Simon, Simon, get up!" I called, gently shaking his shoulder.

Marina was up and already getting into the blue skirt, white blouse, and navy-blue sweater that comprised her school uniform. As I made my way to Moriah to dress her, I passed Simon, still huddled under the covers. "Up, Simon, up!" I called.

Moriah was sleeping next to her favorite doll that she called *ma poupée,* a floppy-armed infant with a soft, cloth body, plastic head, and big blue eyes that opened and shut. The doll showed the marks and stains of being constantly cuddled and well-loved by a four year old. Moriah awoke cheerfully and I helped her get dressed.

As always, I had set the breakfast table the night before. Simon, wearing jeans and a blue sweater with pale-yellow stripes that I had knitted for him, finally came into the dining room. The four of us ate a quick meal of bread and jam, with coffee for me and milk for the kids.

I cleared the kitchen table while the children checked their book bags and packed their snacks. Typically, Marina fussed over some small detail with her hair. I reminded her to hurry. Then we all slipped into our coats. By 7:45 we were ready to go.

We stepped outside into the cold, damp winter air. The children piled into the backseat of the car, with Marina and Simon flanking Moriah. My small, two-horsepower Citroen did not have childproof locks, and it was their job to keep Moriah's little fingers from courting disaster. Within five minutes, we arrived at Sint Jozef's. I parked directly in front of the gate, got out of the driver's seat, walked around the car, and opened the door for the children.

" 'Bye, Simon," I said, kissing him on the cheek, "have a nice day."

" 'Bye, Moriah," I said, with a quick hug and kiss.

"Marina," I said, kissing her good-bye, "*bonne chance* with the tests!"

As I pulled the Citroen back into traffic, I felt extremely good. Things were falling into place so nicely. When we lived with my parents, my role was confusing for the children. With so many adults around, they had been able to get many of my decisions sidestepped or overruled. Now, in our own house, in our own small world, we had developed structure in our lives. My children were flourishing, and I knew we were going to be just fine.

16

Marina's Story

Patsy kissed us good-bye and watched until we were inside the gate. Then she drove away. My little brother started to walk to his classroom as I waited with Moriah for the lady who always drove us to our school.

But Patsy was barely out of sight before two men got out of the car that was behind hers and walked toward us. They were kind of strange-looking. They wore long black coats. On top of their heads they wore flat black hats. They had long dark beards and funny-looking hair, like pigtails, hanging down over their ears. I didn't recognize either one of them.

One of the men spoke to me. "I want you to call Simon," he said.

"Why?" I asked.

The man spoke quickly. "Because the school is going to see a movie today and there isn't any room on the bus for you. We are supposed to drive you there."

I thought it was funny that he seemed to know us, but I didn't think we should go anywhere with him. "My mother told me we are not allowed to get into cars with strange people," I said.

"No, it's all right," the man explained. "If you don't come, you will be alone here all day."

I didn't want to be alone in the big school all day. Maybe we should go, I thought. I called down the hall for Simon, and he turned and came back. At first he didn't want to come with us, but I told him it was okay.

We all like movies very much.

The man who knew us sat in the front seat and the other man drove the car. We rode in the back. Two of their friends followed us in another car.

The man gave us presents. Simon got some small plastic soldiers. Moriah and I played with a little bunny rabbit that had a drum. You could make it sing by turning a small switch.

We drove for a while and then the man said that he had to make a phone call to see if the other children had arrived at the cinema. I hoped we wouldn't be late for the movie. The driver stayed with us in the car, but he didn't like to talk.

When the man came back he said that the movie had been canceled because one of the buses had broken down. We were very disappointed. "Are we going back to school?" I asked.

"We'll see," the man said, "but first there is a place we want to check to see if the bus is there."

We never found the bus. Instead of going to the movie, we went to a big house and met a very old man with a long gray beard. He looked at us and asked some questions. He didn't seem to like us very much. The old man made a telephone call and then spoke to the man who was supposed to take us to the movie. We had to get back in the car and drive some more. Finally we went to an apartment and met a man named Mr. Armoni. He had long dark hair and smiled a lot.

Whenever we asked about the movie, the man who took us said, "Tomorrow . . . tomorrow . . . tomorrow . . ."

17

At 5:00 P.M. I left Olivetti and followed my usual route back along Boulevard de la Woluwe. As always, I parked across from Sint Jozef's and hurried along the crosswalk past six lanes of rush-hour traffic. Then I walked to the first-floor classroom where children remained after the school day, under the supervision of a teacher.

Several children were still in the after-school study hall, but there was no sign of my son. "Where is Simon?" I asked the teacher.

"I haven't seen Simon," he replied.

"Did you see him after school?"

"I didn't see him."

"Maybe he's in the back, playing soccer," I said.

The teacher shrugged. Both of us knew that, when the weather was good enough for soccer, many of the boys would be on the playground.

I hurried out to the play area, but it was deserted.

I was alarmed but searched my mind for a logical explanation. Ah, I thought, my parents came back from London today. Perhaps they came for the children. I will check at the girls' school.

I drove hurriedly along several small, winding streets up to Rue au Bois. Swinging the wheel wildly, I jogged the car left and right and left again, past the sports center where all the girls from

Mater Dei took swimming lessons. From Avenue de l'Aviation, I pulled into the parking lot of Mater Dei and raced to the back door. The girls were not there.

I searched in panic until I found a teacher. "Have you seen Marina and Moriah?" I asked.

The nun reported, "We haven't seen them all day."

"Marina had her tests," I said. "You didn't see her for the whole day and you didn't call?"

The confused nun had no answer.

I ran from classroom to classroom, searching, asking. No one had seen the girls.

Finally I found the principal. She checked the attendance roster and reported, "No, they were not here."

"But I didn't write a note!" I protested. I could hear panic rising in my voice. "I didn't call. I didn't say anything." This was highly unusual, especially during Christmas tests. Someone should have called me at work to see why the children were absent. "Maybe it's my parents," I repeated, knowing it was not. By now I was shaking. My body had already told me what had happened, but my mind refused to accept it. I used the school telephone to call my mother and father.

Mother heard the desperation in my voice as I demanded to know, "Did you pick up the kids?"

She was thrown on the defensive. "No, no, it's not my turn," she said.

I blurted out: "Well they are not here! Chaim took them! They were not in school all day."

"Patsy, Patsy, where are you?" my mother asked. But I had already slammed down the phone.

Mother stood frozen for a moment, staring at the telephone receiver, trying to comprehend the information she had just received. No, no, it can't be, she thought. There must be some explanation. She called my father and told him what had happened.

"I'll call the police," he said. "You go to Patsy's house."

*   *   *

Where would he take them? I asked myself. *Where?* Clearly, he would want to get the children out of the country as quickly as possible.

I jumped into my car and raced for the airport, only a short distance away.

At the airport, I parked the car quickly and ran inside, shoving my way past luggage-toting travelers. My thoughts were scrambled. Where were the kids? How could I find them? I ran to the police office near the passport-control station on the lower level. This was where refugees and other passengers with questionable papers were taken. A gendarme tried to understand my dilemma, but words tumbled out of my mouth in an incoherent pattern. The most I could get out was, "My husband took my children." I pointed over a low partition on the other side of the passport-control station and said, "I want to check all the gates."

"You may not," the officer answered.

"But my kids are gone!"

The officer raised his hands, palms upward, and said, "What can I do for you?" His tone conveyed the answer: nothing.

My body shook furiously. I flailed at the policeman with impotent fists. Then I turned and ran from him. I scrambled onto a chair and tried to climb over the partition. "Let her go," someone said.

I ran down the long concourse leading to the flights. Racing from gate to gate, wailing, I asked everyone, "Have you seen a man with three small children?"

I encountered a group of passengers emerging from a flight. One of them, a man who appeared to be Arab, asked, "What's wrong?"

"My husband took the children!" I screamed.

"You are divorced?"

"We almost are."

"It's good. It's normal," the man declared. "The children should be with the father."

The world blurred.

*   *   *

My mother paced back and forth in front of the window of my house for nearly two hours. Her heart was torn with pain. And she was afraid for her grandchildren. Finally she saw my car turn the corner onto Rue Verte, traveling the wrong direction on the one-way street. The car came safely to a stop. She saw me get out, alone, and went to the door to meet me, but I did not come inside.

Confused, she came outside and viewed a scene that nearly destroyed her with grief. I was walking, as if in a trance, up and down the narrow street, crying. In my arms, I clutched two items that my children had left in the car that morning: Simon's jacket and Moriah's doll, *ma poupée*.

18

Maman called my younger brother, Michel, who was an intern at nearby Saint Luc Hospital, and he came quickly. Together they drove me to the emergency room. I sat in a wheelchair, crying for what seemed like hours. When I tried to speak the words were incoherent. As I squirmed, my skirt inched upward and I became obsessed with pulling up my knee-high stockings. Between sobs I babbled: "Moriah will miss her doctor's appointment. Everything was so good. They were getting along. Moriah's ears— they mustn't get wet!"

The next thing I knew, I lay on a small bed, still crying. My old friend Didier arrived and offered words of comfort. I could not respond.

"Help her," my mother said to a psychiatrist. "Can't you give her something to let her sleep?"

"No," he said, "for now it's better if she lets it all out." Mother pleaded with him, but again he refused.

Papa vowed the hunt of a lifetime: If he did nothing else as long as he lived, he would find Marina, Simon, and Moriah and return them to me. He would never give up.

In the morning, my mother drove me to her home, but I was largely unaware of what was happening around me.

The next afternoon we returned to the hospital to speak with the psychiatrist. My mother was allowed to remain with me during the session, and that made me very uncomfortable. The meeting left me more nervous, miserable, and wracked with guilt than before. "I don't need this," I announced. "I will do this by myself." The psychiatrist gave me a prescription for tranquilizers and some medication to help me sleep. Then he prepared a report declaring that I would be unable to work for six weeks; Olivetti would have to allow me this time off.

Eric and his wife, Caroline, took me to the country house in Nassogne. I carried a photograph of Marina, Simon, and Moriah with me everywhere. It was taken at Nassogne, shortly after my father had mown a patch of very long grass. Marina and Simon had covered Moriah with the clippings, like they would bury someone in sand at the seashore; they were all grinning broadly. Every time I looked at the photo, I cried inconsolably.

An entire week passed in a dismal, weeping fog.

As I languished, aware of nothing, my father swung into action. The very day of the kidnapping he filed a formal complaint with the police. They agreed to notify, through Interpol, all the passport-control stations throughout Europe. But these were generally located in airports. There was no way to prevent Chaim from driving the children across an open border.

That same day my father visited with Josef Hadad, the Israeli ambassador in Brussels. Vice-consul Miriam Resheff was present also. When my father explained what had happened, Resheff reported that Chaim had visited the embassy on December 2—nine days before the kidnapping—and asked for an extension on the expiration date of his passport. Resheff had met Chaim before, and she said that she was surprised by the change in his appearance. He was in the garb of the devout Hasidic Jew, with a full beard, the extended, black sidecurls called *peiyot*, a severe black suit, and the flat-brimmed black hat known as *shreimel*.

Embassy officials already viewed Chaim as a troublemaker, so Resheff was reluctant to fulfill his request. But she recognized that, as an Israeli citizen, he had a legal right to the extension. She explained to my father that she had extended the passport for one month—the minimum she could do. "We will do our best to find the children," she promised. For his part, Ambassador Hadad said that he would contact all other Israeli embassies and consulates in Europe and North America, and ask that they immediately advise him of any request by Chaim to extend his passport further. Chaim would have to do so by January 2, unless he returned to Israel.

My father visited Sint Jozef's and interrogated the principal. He learned that two men in Hasidic garb had been to the school a few days prior to the kidnapping. They had spoken to several children, asking seemingly innocent questions, perhaps to gain their confidence, perhaps to study the scene of the planned crime. When confronted by maintenance man Mark Plovie, one of them had asked, "Is this a Jewish school?"

Plovie had responded, "No, it is a Dutch/Catholic school." The two men had left the school yard immediately.

Father solved another mystery. Every morning when I dropped off the children at Sint Jozef's, the mother of one of Marina's classmates picked up the girls and drove them to Mater Dei. She knew about my security concerns. If Marina and Moriah were not waiting for her that morning, why did she not call me immediately? Father discovered that, by a ghastly coincidence, the woman could not run the errand that day and had sent another friend to take her place. This second woman did not know my children personally and was not aware of what their absence could mean.

Four days after the kidnapping, on December 15, my father received a call from Miriam Resheff, the vice-consul of the Israeli Embassy, who reported that Chaim had telephoned her. "Chaim and the children are fine, and they are in Israel," she said.

It made sense that Chaim would take the children directly to Israel, where, as far as the Israeli courts were concerned, he had legal custody. In addition, he would not have to get another passport extension.

My father also wanted to make sure that I would have no legal problems in Israel, since I had initially taken the children without the father's permission. He booked a flight to Tel Aviv for December 17 and reserved a suite for us at the Sheraton Hotel.

I would follow him as soon as I was physically able.

19

The line at the El Al ticket counter was long and slow-moving. I wished that I had worn more comfortable shoes.

Nothing seemed real. I was strangely relaxed, not comprehending the effects of the tranquilizers. I comforted myself with positive thoughts: I have Belgian law behind me. I have legal custody. We will find them in Israel and bring them home. Papa already has an Israeli lawyer and private detectives on the job. We are prepared to act quickly. In one month I will have them back.

A well-meaning friend had coaxed me into going shopping with her. As a result, I was dressed more formally than usual, in a calf-length knit dress. It was stylish and fairly expensive, but it was gray and drab, like my life. Over it, I wore a thin, gray knit sweater.

Two flights were scheduled to depart for Israel, about one hour apart. I was booked on the first of them, but there were so many people in front of me that, when I finally arrived at the head of the line, the agent informed me there were no seats left. The airline had overbooked, so I was bumped from the flight. As consolation, I was given a seat in the business-class section of the second flight.

As I waited, I noticed Walter Boghaert—the project leader at Olivetti who had always insisted upon speaking Dutch—standing a few feet away. He was tall and solidly built, dressed in jeans and a shirt. His sweater appeared expensive, but it clashed with the rest of his outfit. A shock of wavy dark-brown hair fell across his forehead. We avoided one another at work, but here, in this change of venue, his familiar face was a welcome sight. I went over to speak with him.

He greeted me with a noncommittal shrug, surprised by the coincidence of our meeting. As I suspected all along, he spoke French well enough to maintain a conversation. He explained that he was going on holiday to Israel, and he asked why I was going. Calmly, as if I had misplaced my car keys, I said, "I'm going to pick up my children. They've been gone several days."

As we spoke, I glanced at my airline ticket and noted that the date was Friday, December 19. It took several moments for me to realize what I was reading. Eight days ago! It was an eerie feeling to realize that a week of my life was lost in a fog. What had happened? What had I done with those days?

Once airborne, I buried my nose in a book, as I often did to escape reality. We had been flying for about twenty minutes when Mr. Boghaert's voice broke into my thoughts. "Do you mind if I join you?" he asked.

I looked up to see him standing in the aisle beside me. "Of course not," I replied politely. But I kept the book open on my lap, ready to return to my reading as soon as the interruption was over.

He took the seat next to me, to my left. He insisted that I call him by his first name, Walter. I felt a bit self-conscious to be found in the business-class section, and I explained, "There was a problem with my reservation, so they put me up here." Walter said that, in his previous job, he had traveled frequently and normally enjoyed the perks of business class or first class, but on holiday he was spending his own money, so he chose to book economy. He told me about his plans; he would spend a few days in a youth hostel in Tel Aviv, then he wanted to see the southern resort town of Eilat. During the course of the conversation, I again mentioned that I was going to Israel to pick up my children but shared nothing of the details.

Soon it was dinnertime. A flight attendant approached and told Walter that he would have to return to his seat. By now, I was enjoying the company.

"Why?" I asked. "That seat is vacant. What's the harm?"

"If we allow one passenger to move up, others may want to also," she replied.

Walter rose to leave. "It's all right," he said. "If you'd like to join me in the back after dinner, the seat next to me is empty."

I nodded, and Walter disappeared into the back of the passenger cabin.

For a few minutes I picked at the food on the plate in front of me, but I had no appetite. Once again I tried to read, but I grew restless and decided to accept Walter's invitation. I found him in the very rear of the airplane, sitting quietly, staring out the window. He smiled when he noticed me. He did not seem nearly as serious and officious as he did on the job at Olivetti. I sat down, and we resumed our easy dialogue.

Walter had traveled extensively. "Normally, I take my vacations in Africa," he said. He spoke of how much he enjoyed observing different cultures. "I'm not one to lie on the beach and bake in the sun. I'd rather see things, do things."

"So this is your first visit to Israel?" I asked.

"Yes."

I assured him that he would find the country beautiful and interesting. He brightened when I told him that I could speak Hebrew. Although he was fluent in four languages, Hebrew was not one of them.

I learned quickly that twenty-seven-year-old Walter Boghaert was a man of few words. He was content to allow me to chatter, as he nodded his head. Something about his manner was very stabilizing and relaxing. The tranquilizers I was taking, and the shock that still enveloped me, caused me to speak easily. I wondered whether he could sense that something was amiss. If he did, he did not push for an explanation.

*   *   *

That evening, when we arrived in Tel Aviv, my father waited for me at the arrival gate. He had a rental car ready. I introduced him to Walter and suggested that we drop him off near the youth hostel where he was staying, since it was on our way to the hotel.

Once we were alone, my father filled me in on his activities thus far. He had met with a lawyer in an attempt to have the old 1984 Haifa court decision—granting custody of the children to Chaim—revoked. He was certain that we would be able to retrieve the children quickly if we could just straighten out the paperwork.

Throughout his career, my father had developed a vast network of business contacts that stretched across the continents. He told me that one of those contacts had recommended a respected private-detective agency. Those operatives were ready to work with us.

That evening, Papa, as was his custom, went to bed very early. By 8:00 P.M. I was staring at the walls. Even with tranquilizers, I could not sleep. I decided to take a walk and soon found myself heading in the direction of the youth hostel.

Walter was jolted out of a deep slumber. "There is somebody here who wants to talk to you and it's urgent," the young receptionist said. His eyes blinking at the light, Walter stumbled out to the lobby. He thought that something terrible must have happened. Was there an accident? Was someone ill?

"I need to talk" was all I could say.

"Okay," Walter replied. He asked the receptionist if I could come inside. When the young man explained that women were not allowed in this area, Walter excused himself to find a jacket. I waited for him outside.

A few moments later he returned, suggesting, "Let's walk." He gestured across the street to a park with a long, narrow pathway adjacent to the Yarkon River.

We walked for a short time then stopped to sit and rest. The moon reflected off the tranquil water. Eucalyptus trees bent in the breeze. The serenity of the scene was in sharp contrast to the angry, bitter words that now burst from my mouth. In my illogical state, I threw fragments of my story at Walter. Tragic scenes of my marriage and its aftermath tumbled about like so many pieces in a giant, macabre jigsaw puzzle. Why, I wondered, was I able to share these things with someone I barely knew, when I could rarely even speak of them to my family? This was not like me. Walter asked gentle questions, helping me to place the pieces into a coherent pattern so that he began to understand what had happened.

Reliving so many stories—the beatings, the humiliation, and the final assault of taking my children—caused my body to shake. I felt as if I would explode.

Walter glanced at my clenched fists and offered quietly, "If it would make you feel better, you could hit me."

The suggestion was so kind, so unexpected, that it broke through my barriers. My eyes filled. My fingers relaxed. I leaned against Walter's shoulder and let the tears spill quietly down my cheeks.

Later, as we walked back to the hostel, Walter reminded me that he would be leaving for Eilat soon. "If you'd like to join me, you are welcome," he suggested. "It might be good for you to relax and think of other things."

I thanked him for the invitation, but I told him that my father and I planned to visit my mother-in-law on Sunday, to see if she might disclose any information about my children.

"If you need to talk, call me," Walter said. He gave me the address and phone number of the youth hostel in Eilat where he would be staying.

Although we came from very different backgrounds, Chaim's mother, Leah, in her own restricted way, had always been pleasant and supportive. But I wondered how she would react to me now. From her perspective, I had run away from her son, taking her three grandchildren with me. On the face of it, this was true. But at the time there was no court order restraining me from taking the children. Beyond that, I had made no secret of the fact that the children were living in Belgium and I would allow Chaim to see them whenever he wished, as long as he complied with the legal restrictions. There was a huge difference between what I had done and what Chaim had done, and I hoped that Leah recognized it.

Fortunately, she seemed to understand my pain. She invited us in—a private detective, my father, and me—and agreed to talk. I was relieved that Shlomo was at work.

Leah confirmed what Miriam Resheff, the Israeli vice-consul in Brussels, had told my father—that Chaim had returned to Israel sometime in 1985 and "become religious." At least he had changed his appearance and now wore the somber garb of the conservative Hasidic Jew. Leah admitted that she was unsure whether the change was genuine. For example, even after he adopted the mode of dress, Chaim continued to sidestep some of the restrictions of Shabbat and did not go to the synagogue regularly.

I nodded, remembering when the police in Nassogne had stopped his car. That incident had occurred on a Saturday, when those who keep Shabbat may not drive.

When pressed for details, Leah said that Chaim had befriended members of an ultraconservative sect of Hasidic Jews known as Satmars, who judged every issue of life by a simple formula: Anything Jewish was good; anything non-Jewish was bad. "Those people are extremely fanatical," Leah warned. "They would help him if he joined them."

Like Leah, I doubted Chaim's sincerity. Had the man who sneaked cigarettes on Shabbat and eagerly devoured "the meat I like" actually adopted the philosophies of the Hasidic community, or was he using these people as he had used so many others?

During my years in Israel I had, of course, seen many Hasidic Jews. Although I had paid little attention to them, I had always respected their beliefs. Now, I could only hope that they would display the same generosity toward me.

As Christmas approached, my father declared, "Patsy, I have to go back to Belgium, but you can stay if you wish." It would be difficult to accomplish much here during the holidays. Papa had to attend to his business matters, and I had to be on hand to speak with private detectives and attorneys. I felt frustrated. My father knew that I was still in shock, still dependent upon tranquilizers, and he worried about me staying all alone at the hotel over Christmas. On the other hand, he also knew that being at home for Christmas, without the children, would be torture. He suggested, "Why don't you go to Eilat? Join your friend Walter, so that you won't be alone."

I decided that this might be a good diversion until the private detectives could devise a plan of action, so I searched through my purse for the scrap of paper containing the number of the youth hostel in Eilat, and placed the call.

"I've decided to come," I told Walter. "I'll take the bus first thing in the morning."

"Fine," Walter replied. "I will wait for you."

Walter greeted me with the statement, "It's a different Patsy."

"What do you mean, different?" I asked.

"From BC/BG to this!" He smiled, gesturing at my jeans and T-shirt. BC/BG was a familiar expression in Belgium, meaning *bon chic/bon genre*, a reference to a stylish, upper-crust appearance, like that represented by the knit suit I had worn on the airplane. "I like this better," he said.

Unfortunately, Eilat turned out to be a garish mosaic of disco clubs and noisy night spots. It was a tourist trap and I hated it on sight. I also discovered that Walter did not lack for companionship. He had already made two girlfriends in Eilat—one Swiss and one German—and he was enjoying himself. I was pleased for him, since I was interested only in friendship, not romance.

After spending Christmas Eve and Christmas Day with Walter and his friends, I could stand Eilat no longer. "You do what you want," I said to Walter, "but I'm leaving by noon tomorrow." I had come to Israel to look for my children, and I was impatient to resume the search. One of the private detectives had suggested that I visit some of the Hasidic communities scattered about Israel. He figured that if I watched the little Jewish children going to school, I might see one of my own. The chance of success was small, but it was something that I could do as I waited for leads to develop.

Walter decided that he wanted to explore some of the more open parts of the country, but he did not know Israel well and he spoke no Hebrew. "Why don't we make a trip together?" he suggested. "We could combine your search with my sightseeing."

I agreed and went off to buy food—bread, olives, cream cheese, tuna—that we could take with us.

The next day we took a bus north, along Highway 90. The route continued along the Jordanian border toward the Dead Sea, until we saw our destination, the massive, rocky bulk of Masada, rising in the distance. This was the historic hilltop where, two thousand years ago, Herod the Great, King of Judea, built an impregnable fortress.

The bus left us off at a kibbutz, from where we climbed the steep, narrow trail called the snake path, until we reached the gate of Masada.

At the tip of the rock is Herod's Northern Palace, a monumental three-level structure. The upper level, reserved for Herod's residential apartments, ends in a semicircle, where you can look down upon the two lower terraces. We were so high that birds soared below us.

In A.D. 70, two thousand Jewish zealots took refuge here after the fall of Jerusalem and held out against the Romans for three years. When defeat became inevitable, the besieged Jews achieved a victory of sorts by committing mass suicide rather than allowing the enemy to capture them.

In the distance, we could see the ruins of the old Roman camps, where the enemy lived as it besieged the doomed people inside. It was a solemn feeling to imagine the Jews looking out at impending death. Walter and I stood quietly here for several minutes. There were no words to describe the sense of reverence and history.

A modern flight of steps on the west side took us to what

was left of Herod's glorious life here. We roamed the site for hours. Other visitors came and went, but our plan was to stay right here all night long, to witness the fabled glory of the sunrise at Masada.

"It's time for closing, it's time for closing," said the young Yemenite Jew who served as the guard at this ancient site.

"We want to stay here," I said in Hebrew. "We want to sleep here."

"You may not."

I stared into his eyes. I reached out and touched him lightly on the arm and said softly, "Oh, you know, it is so nice here. We just want to stay. You can do us a favor."

His mood softened, but he explained, "For security reasons, you know—we are very close to Jordan—and you never know when terrorists will come across."

"Ah, we are not afraid of terrorists."

"But you know you have a lot of snakes here."

I shrugged and muttered, "Ah." At my side, Walter was unable to follow the conversation, so I explained, "He says there are snakes here." Walter shrugged also.

The guard eyed me with new suspicion. He asked, "How come you speak Hebrew so well?"

"Because of my husband."

The Yemenite's gaze moved toward Walter, a burly European. "He is not Israeli," the guard said.

Once more I touched the guard lightly on the arm and confided softly, "He is not my husband."

Suddenly a grin of understanding crossed the man's face. "Okay," he said. "You may stay. But you may not make a fire. The army will see a fire where no one is supposed to be, and they will come and I will be in trouble."

"Okay," I agreed, "no fire."

Walter smiled and nodded at the guard when I announced, "We can stay."

The guard instructed, "Stay in the tower until it is dark, so nobody sees you. I will 'forget' to check the tower."

That evening, as we walked around the ancient, silent rooms, Walter and I could almost see, hear, and feel the tragic Jews of so long ago.

The solemn, peaceful atmosphere relaxed me and loosened my tongue further. We played the simple card game called "War" and talked. I was able to tell Walter my story in a much more calm and reasonable way than before. He had quickly become a good friend, and perhaps that was what I needed most.

By 1:00 A.M. we decided to get a few hours of sleep. Walter was not accustomed to the chilly nights, so I gave him one of my blankets. The cool air felt wonderful to me.

We awoke well before the sunrise and heard voices below. A few other visitors had arrived to witness the moment, but Walter and I had the special view from the tower.

Darkness gave way slowly. We stared to the east, toward Jordan, where the black of night became pink and then bright orange. A small bird flew in front of us.

But the awakening day, as spectacular as it was, filled me with deep sadness. Images of Marina, Simon, and Moriah filtered in, mixing with the colors of the sky.

From Masada, we hiked to the kibbutz at Ein Gedi, where we spent the night at a youth hostel. The next morning we caught a bus north to Jerusalem, where our efforts to search the Hasidic community were hampered by a torrential rainstorm. Then it was on to Tel Aviv to check in with the private detectives; they had no news.

We continued our journey north, sometimes walking, sometimes hitchhiking, sometimes traveling by bus. We inspected several small Hasidic communities. Throughout the trip, we enjoyed an easy, comfortable camaraderie.

Gradually, with Walter's gentle encouragement, I reduced my intake of the tranquilizers that had left me so vacant. Withdrawal brought on sleeplessness, but I felt myself returning to reality. We were in Haifa on New Year's Eve, and the youth hostel was filled with rambunctious, celebrating teenagers. I was certain that sleep would be impossible. But in spite of the noise they created, I fell into a deep slumber; my first natural night's sleep in a week. I awoke refreshed and ran around bubbling to everybody, "I slept so well! Did you sleep well, did you sleep well?" Everyone looked at me through bloodshot, sleep-deprived eyes. The raucous teenagers had kept them awake all night long. They looked as if they wanted to strangle me, but I felt so rested that I vowed to myself, "Never again will I take these medications."

We visited additional Hasidic communities in northern and central Israel. The more I saw of the Hasidic children, the sadder I became. Little girls were completely covered with long coats, thick socks, and heavy shoes. Many of the pale, serious faces— particularly the boys—stared out at the world through tiny, square eyeglasses. To me, they appeared not like children but like little old people. There was not a hint of spontaneity in their actions. Will my children be raised this way? I wondered. I pictured Marina's smiling face as she drew colorful pictures at our dining-room table. And Simon, expending his excess energy on a soccer ball. Moriah was hardly old enough to know the meaning of play.

My head echoed with the memory of Chaim's threat: "Whatever it takes, I will destroy your life."

A week after New Year's Eve, Walter's vacation ended and he had to return to Brussels and his job. I was very grateful for his companionship during this painful time. We had become good friends, but I viewed the relationship as peculiar to the time and circumstances. Often, during our journey, I had cautioned him about my complicated life and told him that I did not expect anything from him in the future. In Belgium, we had our own separate lives.

Before he left, I said once again, "If you want to stay in contact, fine. If not, that's fine too. Don't feel you have to call me."

My father returned to Israel, ready to resume the hunt. Upset because the private detectives had uncovered no leads, he fired them and engaged the services of a company called International

Consultants for Targeted Security. Known as ICTS, they had operatives in New York, London, Paris, Brussels, and many other places throughout the world. ICTS was owned and operated by Danny Issacharof, a short, heavyset man who did not look the part of an ex-agent of the Israeli government security agency Shein Beth, but he was. The company's specialty was airport security contracts, but Issacharof agreed to work on our case, since he was my father's longtime business associate and friend. He promised that he would never give up until we found the children.

I reacted strongly and differently to Issacharof's colleagues. Eitan Rilov was a skinny, nervous man, who treated me as if I were invisible and directed all of his comments to my father. His long, sinewy body seemed to be in constant motion. He spoke quickly and with great pomposity. His manner suggested that he was the one with all the answers, the smartest, the most cunning of the lot. I tried to treat him politely, but I was keenly aware of his general disdain for women.

Eitan Rozen, on the other hand, was open and warm. He was a short man but obviously in better physical condition than the other two. He was based in London and would work the case from a European perspective.

I was despondent to realize that one month had passed since the kidnapping. In the beginning, I had convinced myself that I would have the children back by now. My one-month deadline had spurred me to action. Now, I told myself: In six months, they will be back.

One of the ICTS detectives advised me, "There is nothing more that you can do now. We will be working."

My father and I agreed that it was time to return home.

20

Marina's Story

After a few days in Mr. Armoni's apartment, the man who took us from the school told us that he was our father! He looked so different from what I remembered.

"But where is Patsy?" we wanted to know.

Papa said, "I wanted all of you to come, but she didn't want to."

I missed Patsy, and it felt uncomfortable to be around all these strangers. I remembered my grandmother's telephone number in Belgium, so I decided to call her. One day I picked up the phone and dialed the numbers, but all I heard were funny noises and a voice saying the same thing over and over. Papa found out that I tried to use the phone without permission and he was very angry. He said that I cannot use the phone again.

We all missed Christmas. Instead, Mr. Armoni and his wife made a dinner to celebrate another holiday. There were lots of candles and they read some prayers in a language we didn't understand.

We sat together on a sofa, with Moriah on Papa's lap. Mr. Armoni sat with us and had Simon and me crawl onto his knees. His wife took a picture of us.

We didn't like to stay inside all the time. The only time we got to go out was once, when Papa and Mr. Armoni took us to the zoo.

*   *   *

One day Papa said we were going on a trip. Mr. Armoni drove us to the airport. It was exciting and a little scary on the big airplane. We landed at a busy airport in a big city. Papa said it was London.

We stayed in Stanford Hill in a place called the Jewish Community Center. It was a neighborhood full of small homes, attached to each other in long rows. Everyone who lived here was Jewish. Papa said we were Jewish too. I never knew that before. There was a big park at one end of the neighborhood with two lakes.

All of a sudden, there were lots of new rules to follow. On Friday night, something called "Shabbat" started, and we were not allowed to ride bikes or even turn on a light until the sun was setting on Saturday. Papa said there was a lot we had to learn.

A holy man called a rebbe taught us prayers to say before we ate or drank anything. We began to learn the rules for eating kosher, but there were so many rules that it was confusing. We also learned about a great tragedy for the Jews, when six million of us were murdered by an evil man called Adolf Hitler. He killed us simply because we were Jews. But it taught a great lesson to those of us who survived. It taught us that Jews must look out for one another, and never, ever, place our trust in non-Jews.

Papa told Simon it was time to begin to grow *peiyot*. That's what he called the long curls on the sides of his face.

One day there was a big meeting. We said many prayers. Then a rebbe told us that we had new Jewish names. Instead of Marina, Simon, and Moriah, we were now called Sarah, Josef, and Rachel.

At first it was hard to get used to the names. But Papa got very mad at us if we made a mistake.

A lot of things changed. Rachel and I had to wear long dresses and heavy socks that itched. Josef got a small cap to wear.

21

When I arrived home from Israel I found a note in my mail-box. "Call me," it read. There was a telephone number and Walter's signature. But I decided to ignore the request. I had too much else on my mind.

With a deep ache in my heart, I opened the door of the little town house that I shared with my children. My mother had been there to make sure that the kitchen was clean, the laundry done. She had dusted and vacuumed, but she could not remove the most depressing sights. Marina's drawings sat on the dining-room table, alongside some play jewelry that she had been fashioning out of colored paper. Simon's soccer ball rested in a corner, motionless. Moriah's lunch box was on the kitchen counter. The refrigerator door was covered with their drawings. This house was once filled with activity, laughter, and chatter; now, the silence was suffocating. It was not the big things but the small details that hurt the most.

In one corner, neatly arranged, was a stack of Christmas presents awaiting the children.

Solemnly I placed the children's belongings where they would expect to find them when they returned.

I cried for hours.

*   *   *

When I tried to return to work, my boss at Olivetti informed me that I was no longer employed. "Your doctor ordered six weeks' sick leave, but we learned that you went to Israel," she said. "So you took some vacation; you are not sick." She chose her words carefully, but the unspoken message was clear: A woman who had just lost her three children could not be expected to be a productive employee.

"Listen, my life is destroyed, " I said. "I've lost my children. Don't think for a moment that losing a job means anything to me."

I stormed out of the office, muttering to myself, "ugly woman." I walked toward the elevator and was startled to see Walter standing there. We did not greet one another in the presence of the other employees, but he followed me to the underground parking garage. He told me that word of Olivetti's decision had already spread throughout the office. Many of the other workers were upset with the management. "People say that this is no way for them to act," he reported.

I realized how much Walter's support meant to me, and I decided that, yes, we would continue our friendship.

The Israeli Embassy in Brussels confirmed that Chaim had not renewed his passport, and the ministry of the interior in Tel Aviv reported no record of his reentry into the country. This meant that as of January 2, wherever Chaim was hiding, he had become an illegal alien.

Since the largest Hasidic community in the world is located in New York State, my father went to the U.S. Embassy in Brussels and asked whether Chaim had applied for a visa. To our dismay, we learned that the records were not computerized, and officials said that it would take some time to check the microfiche files. They promised to give us an answer by the end of February.

In Israel, ICTS detectives were busy checking every possible data bank that might contain a reference to Chaim or the children. They studied Social Security and health-services rolls. They examined school rosters. They searched bank records. The work was tedious and, ultimately, fruitless. Chaim and the children had simply vanished.

There was little that I could do on a day-to-day basis. The children could be anywhere: Israel, America, England, France, Holland, Austria, Germany, Canada, Mexico, Brazil, Argentina— or a dozen other countries that had Hasidic communities. Without any direct evidence, we could search the world with little hope.

Paralyzed by my grief, and unable to face life alone in my empty house, I took refuge in my parents' home. Some mornings I woke knowing that I had dreamt about the children, but I could remember none of the details. I felt cold and ill. In the immediate aftermath of the kidnapping, I had lost weight. Now I began to gain rapidly, until I was much heavier than normal.

I said nothing to my family of my friendship with Walter, and I did not want to see him in my parents' home. But we began to spend time together, meeting at the end of Walter's workday in the parking lot of the Musée d'Afrique. If Walter was late, I walked in the park surrounding the museum. After he arrived, he drove me through the rush-hour traffic to his apartment in Leuven, a small university town close to Brussels; he shared the apartment with four students. We often spoke late into the night.

It took Walter some time to realize that, although I could speak of events, it was almost impossible for me to express my feelings. Long ago, Chaim had beaten emotion out of me. I could be warm and loving to children, but I remained aloof with adults. When something in particular was bothering me, I grew very quiet, and he had to work gently to pull information from me. For example, he finally got me to admit that my mother was confused and frustrated because I refused to cry on her shoulder. Tears were her outlet for either happiness or sadness, and she ached to provide the same solace for me. "I cannot," I said to Walter. "I just cannot."

Walter's response was, "Is that it? Is that all? The problem is really small."

I let out a deep sigh and agreed. Not being able to cry on my mother's shoulder was not the end of the world. It was something I could handle.

Walter had a wondrous ability to impart his strength to me. Whenever he sensed that my resolve was drained, he said firmly, "Look at you. What are you doing? You must fight back. Be strong."

22

Sarah's Story

We only stayed in London for about three weeks. Then Papa sent Rachel and me on another long plane trip. A Jewish man came with us to keep us safe. We flew all the way to America, to a place called New York City. Papa said that he and Josef would join us soon. Rachel and I stayed with a family that we didn't know, until Papa and Josef arrived, about a week later.

Some things were very confusing. Papa kept changing his name. Most of the time he said he was David Mizrarhi, but different people called him by other names too. He didn't like it when we asked too many questions.

All of a sudden Papa said we were going to move again. This time we went to a place called Mexico.

For a while we stayed with another family; then Papa got us a house of our own. The Jewish community was pretty small.

Mexico was cold and Josef's hands got all red and cracked.

People were speaking Spanish, and it was hard to learn our lessons at school. The children in the school fought a lot and once someone stole my new scissors and eraser.

Papa was always in a bad mood. Sometimes he got very mad at us. When we were bad, he slapped our fingers with a pencil, over and over again. It hurt. Once, when Josef was playing with a ball and Papa told him to stop, he didn't and Papa grabbed it from him and slashed it with a knife.

We got really tired of eating only Rice Krispies and cornflakes all the time. Papa made us pick up all the specks of dirt on the floor with our hands. "Girls have to do the cleaning," he said. He got angry with us if we said anything about Belgium, so we didn't. We didn't like it when he was mad.

Back at Mr. Armoni's house, Papa had been really nice to us. But now I didn't like living with him. He hit us very often. If we made a small noise while he was sleeping, he would smack us, but if one of us wanted to take a nap and it was noisy, he just laughed. I didn't think it was fair. And before, back in Belgium, I could take a bath by myself. Now he was washing me together with my brother and sister, and I didn't like it. I didn't feel comfortable.

23

"I cannot stand this situation anymore," I declared. Our family doctor, Jean-Luc Vossen, listened carefully to my complaints. He asked direct, simple questions and allowed me to speak for a long time.

"I have failed at everything in life: my studies, my marriage, and my responsibilities as a mother. I am just a big zero," I said flatly. In the space of one month, my weight had ballooned from one hundred and twelve pounds to one hundred and forty-three pounds. I had no energy, no desire to face the morning. Each night I went to bed thinking about Marina, Simon, and Moriah; each morning I awoke thinking about them.

Day after day passed with the clock ticking like a time bomb. The detectives were searching. The police were watching. But nothing happened. No one told me anything. There was nothing I could do. I felt myself slipping. I wanted the world to say, Poor Patsy, have pity on her.

Dr. Vossen gave me a sample packet of medicine, an emergency supply of a strong tranquilizer that I resolved to take only if I reached a moment of extreme crisis. But he prescribed more basic medicine for my daily life: a strict diet and a suggestion that I engage in some form of strenuous exercise at least twice a week. "Get busy," he advised. "Do something during the day, so that every day you can see that you accomplished something."

I hate swimming, but every Monday, Wednesday, and Friday I forced myself to go to the nearby community pool and swim laps. At first, I could manage only a few, but I gradually increased my stamina until I could complete more than fifty laps of the Olympic-sized pool in a single session. The workout took about an hour and left me exhausted, but with a great feeling of accomplishment. For a time I became obsessive about losing weight, eating a maximum of only fifteen hundred calories per day and pushing the exercise to excessive levels. Still, as the extra pounds burned away and an extremely thin, even gaunt, Patsy emerged, I looked into the mirror and saw the same overweight young woman.

My brother Michel suggested another outlet for my days. At Saint Luc Hospital, where he was an intern, there was a constant need for volunteers. Perhaps I could assist in the playroom of the children's ward.

I started immediately, and I found my heart captured. Most of the volunteers came to the hospital only once a week, but I was there every day, reading storybooks, helping with crafts, playing games. The little patients were wide-eyed and happy, despite their ailments. As a university hospital, Saint Luc's treated children with very serious illnesses, and I grew concerned about those in isolation. I said to the woman in charge of the playroom, "My being here is nice. But what about the kids who can't come here? They need to play too."

"Sure," she said. "Go play with them."

So I packed a boxful of books, puzzles, and craft supplies and began to visit the most seriously ill patients. When I walked through other wards I heard adult patients grumbling and complaining. But here was a six-year-old boy, suspected of having tuberculosis, constantly coughing up blood, who always had a ready smile for me. Here was a boy with a severe case of kidney stones, suffering through painful surgeries without a complaint.

I said to myself: Patsy, stop complaining. Your kids are not with you, but they are probably healthy and safe. Look around you. Some situations are worse than yours.

I took a particular liking to a little Moroccan girl battling leukemia. She had lost her hair as a result of chemotherapy, but she remained cheerful. She had been to the hospital many times before and knew what to expect. Together, we decided to transform her dismal room into an aquarium. She colored pictures of fish and cut them out. I tied strings to them and hung them from the ceiling. Soon, so many fish were "swimming" about that a cleaning lady complained. We ignored her and spent several days creating paper seaweed.

One morning I put on a smile and entered her room, but the bed was empty. The fish and seaweed still decorated the area, but the girl was not there. I found a nurse and asked, "Where is she?"

"They have moved her to intensive care," the nurse replied.

I found the room. Following instructions, I dressed carefully in sterile clothing and entered through a double set of doors. The girl lay quietly in the bed. Tubes and wires were attached to her body. Her eyes were open. I tried to speak with her, but she seemed not to hear.

The next morning, her bed in the intensive-care ward was empty. I hoped that she had recovered sufficiently to return to the "aquarium."

"Where is she?" I asked a nurse.

"She's gone."

"Home? Another room? Tell me the number and I'll go see her."

The nurse repeated, "She's gone, she's gone, she's gone."

After careful thought, Walter asked if I would like to move into his apartment until I could sort out my future. I accepted the offer, but it was more like running *away* from something than *to* something. We continued to keep our relationship quiet. No one at Olivetti knew that Mr. Boghaert was keeping company with me.

My brutal honesty was one of the initial personality traits

that attracted Walter to me; but at times this caused difficulties. I explained to him that our relationship was not a big passion. "I love you," I said, "but you're like my best friend and I feel comfortable with you. If I want to get mad, I know I can get mad. I feel safe and secure with you. Chaim was my big passion and, after a time, that goes away. I had one in my life, and nobody is going to get me a second time. Never again."

I found a thousand ways to avoid painful discussions concerning the children. If Walter asked me a leading question, I jumped up and said, "I have to go to the store because I forgot to buy butter . . ." or "Oh, I have to clean the bathroom . . ."

One day Walter lectured, "Patsy, it's really time for you to start working. You don't do that much to look for your children."

"I can't," I wailed. "What more can I do?"

"Work," he advised. "Keep the money to try to look for your children. Help your parents with that. But start working. Get back to a normal life."

His advice shook me. I knew I could never stop looking at the past, but I realized that I also had to begin looking toward the future. As usual, Walter had chosen his words carefully. Earning money to help search for the children was the motivation I needed. It was a goal.

I searched the newspapers for jobs. I found a low-level position, similar to the post that I had held at Olivetti, and began to write the necessary letter of application. When I showed it to Walter, he said, "No, no, no. You've got to aim higher. Start over." We read the newspaper ads together, and Walter buoyed my confidence by encouraging me to apply for more challenging jobs that offered better pay. His faith in my intellect and abilities was contagious, and my self-esteem grew.

Job applications had to be handwritten, and sometimes Walter forced me to rewrite simply for neatness. He showed me how to make subtle changes in my resumé to make it more impressive, and coached me on job-interview techniques, advising, "When they ask how much you want to earn, don't tell them. Ask, 'Well, what's normal for that kind of job?' "

*   *   *

On May 26, Belgian TV, at the request of the police, broad-cast a public appeal to anyone who could provide information on the whereabouts of my children or the circumstances of their dis-appearance. The next morning, a U.S. Embassy official, a certain Mr. Leider, called to say that, for an entire month, he had been in possession of information but had simply forgotten to tell us. The television spots had jogged his memory. What he had learned was that Chaim had applied for a visa for himself and the three chil-dren—offering some excuse as to why the mother was not travel-ing with them. The embassy had accepted the application and issued the visas on December 2, 1986, the same day that the Israeli Embassy had renewed Chaim's passport. Chaim had listed his address as Mercator Straat 56 in Antwerp.

As it happened, the same day ICTS agent Eitan Rozen brought us more news. He had been concentrating his search in Antwerp, about forty miles distant from Brussels. We felt that if Chaim had received help from the Hasidic community in Belgium, it had to come from Antwerp, where the Hasidim oper-ate a large diamond exchange, and a more informal "rumor ex-change."

Now, Rozen came to my parents' home and declared tri-umphantly: "New York!"

Then he explained further. In Antwerp, an informant had told him that a man named Moishe Aaron Reich had helped Chaim prior to the kidnapping. In fact, Reich's home was the Mercator Straat address that Chaim had listed on his U.S. visa ap-plication. This was confirmed by Rozen's discovery that a car rented to Chaim Yarden had, indeed, received a ticket for illegal parking in front of Reich's home, around the time of the kidnap-ping. The informant said that Chaim had represented himself to the Hasidic community as a poor, abused Jew who had the mis-fortune to marry into a wealthy, politically powerful Belgian fam-ily, and he needed help to rescue his children from their evil influence and from a physically abusive mother.

In such a milieu, Chaim's considerable powers of persuasion

served him well. He displayed the Haifa court decision granting him custody. He reported that I had placed the children in Roman Catholic orphanages. He claimed that I was crazy and that he needed help to rescue his children from such a mother. The three young innocents must not be allowed to be lost in the abyss of Christianity. Chaim's Satmar friends asked for no proof; they simply accepted his word.

Hasidic agents canvassed from house to house pleading Chaim's cause. The collectors took out cuts for themselves, but they presented Chaim with ten thousand dollars to make good his escape. And, finally, the informant declared that the children were now in New York with people who would make "good little Jews out of them."

Rozen managed to speak with Reich, who confirmed that Chaim had become a member of the Satmar sect. He said he believed that Chaim and the children were being sheltered in one of the Satmar communities in New York—either in the Williamsburg section of Brooklyn or one of two small towns in upstate New York, Monroe or Monsey.

The realization that my children were being raised as Jews did not concern me, but the qualifying words, "good little," did. It was the fanaticism that saddened me—whether Jewish, Christian, Muslim, or anything else—not the faith. I saw in my head the faces of the Hasidic boys and girls in Israel, as serious and dour as old people. Poor kids, I thought.

Nevertheless, we finally had leads. "We know that the kids are in the States," my father said. "Let's celebrate." He uncorked a bottle of champagne. I generally do not drink, but this was a special occasion—our first solid information on the whereabouts of the children—so I made an exception. The emotions of the moment, combined with the small amount of alcohol, sent me reeling. I stumbled off to a bedroom.

Walter told me that he found me at an open window, screaming.

24

Sarah's Story

Finally Papa said we would go back to the States because the people in Mexico were bad people.

Papa lied to the people at the airport. He said we had been in Mexico for a three-week vacation, but I knew we had been here longer than that. When the passport man asked his name, my brother said "Josef," and that made Papa very angry because "Simon" was written on the small document. He slapped him hard. We wished Papa would make up his mind, because it was very hard to be two people all the time.

We moved to a town called Monsey and stayed at Eight Maple Terrace, with Mr. and Mrs. Borochov. It was a split-level house and we had a room in the basement.

I had a shock one day when I overheard Papa talking with a rebbe. He was talking about me. From the words I could understand, I thought he said: "Her father was another man but Mr. Jacques Heymans forced me to marry her mother anyway."

I decided that I did not want to hear these things. It was like I took a big, dark blanket and covered my memories.

25

I vacillated between being silent and sullen or aggressive and impolite to everyone; this, I figured, would prevent them from asking too many questions.

Walter knew I was troubled and tried to get me to talk about what was on my mind. But I refused to say anything. Finally, during an hour-long drive to the country house, when he knew that I could not run away from the conversation, he coaxed me until I opened up. Moriah's fifth birthday was coming up on June 7. I wanted to buy a small gift, some kind of remembrance that would be there for her when she returned, but I could not bring myself to do it. It was too painful. I could not buy a cake to take to her school. I could not invite her friends over to celebrate. I could not even send her a card.

"Just cry, Patsy," Walter urged. "Let it out. It will make you feel better."

I felt tears forming, but I held them back by chanting to myself: *un, deux, trois . . .*

I had cried an ocean of tears since the children had been taken from me. It was enough. I had to be tougher, I told myself.

A few friends called on June 7 to offer their sympathy. I was grateful that they remembered, but their well-intentioned comments twisted at my insides like a sharp knife.

Four days later another milestone occurred. June 11 was the six-month anniversary of the kidnapping. Another emotional deadline had come and gone. I'm not setting any more deadlines, I thought. It will take time. It will take time.

Armed with the knowledge that Chaim had been granted a U.S. visa, ICTS detectives checked with the U.S. Immigration Office in New York to see if he had used it. We were told that Chaim and Simon had taken a Pan Am flight from London to New York's JFK International Airport on February 7.

This news raised some questions. First, why was he not stopped? We knew that his Israeli passport had expired and that the Belgian police had promised to broadcast an alert to all European airports. We asked a local policewoman who specialized in family disputes to investigate. She reported, "I've been checking through your file, and I didn't see anything about it." Evidently the alert had not been issued as promised. The policewoman issued it now, but it was far too late. If it had been in effect on February 7, diligent British passport agents would certainly have detained Chaim, and the children would be home by now.

The other disturbing issue was that there was no record of Marina and Moriah making the trip. The fact that Chaim had obtained visas for all the children seemed to indicate that he would keep them together. I hoped so, desperately. Perhaps the immigration office had simply not recorded the girls, or perhaps they had traveled under false names.

While I waited, I continued my search for employment. I interviewed for a job in the administration department of IES, a small information-systems company. General manager René Vanderheynde asked, "How much did you earn in your job at Olivetti?"

Following Walter's advice, I countered, "I expect what is normal for this job."

Vanderheynde named a figure twice as high as my Olivetti salary. I accepted, then I told him what Olivetti had paid me. His mouth dropped open in surprise; he was impressed with my clever performance.

My job was to follow each customer order, from the moment it came in until it was shipped and paid for. Shortly after I arrived in the office, I told Vanderheynde that I would need a computer to accomplish this task. With a wry comment that I was manipulating him—no one else in the office had a computer—he agreed. In the evenings, Walter helped me create programs to track the orders.

Meanwhile, my father continued to orchestrate the hunt. Our intention was to remain active on all fronts. ICTS geared up for an all-out search of New York's Hasidic neighborhoods. Papa tended to legal details, so that when we did find the children, we would have the authority to bring them home immediately. Unless there was absolutely no other alternative, I was against the idea of a counter-kidnapping. I wanted to keep everything legal, and I did not want my children to be put through the trauma of being taken by force—again. I felt this could lead to a never-ending series of snatchings and counter-snatchings. I would not consign my children to such a fate.

Father asked me to sign an affidavit at town hall, formally granting my permission to have the children's names added to his passport. Then he obtained U.S. visas for them. Now, if he found them, they could legally travel with him.

With those tasks accomplished, my parents engaged the services of a New York attorney, a religious Jew named Franklyn H. Snitow, to begin the process of obtaining legal custody of the children for me under U.S. law. I already had custody in Belgium, but a U.S. order would strengthen our position. We also hoped that Snitow's work would pressure the Jewish community. Certainly the Hasidim would not wish to be seen as accessories to kidnapping.

I was at my desk at IES when one of my co-workers approached and showed me an article that had appeared in the Brussels newspaper *La Dernière Heure*. The piece was vague and inaccurate. It stated that three children had been kidnapped by their father and that their mother, a woman identified only with the initials P.H., was also missing—and the authorities had been searching for her for more than a year. It implied that I was not looking for the children, as if I did not care.

"This is crazy," I said, "I haven't disappeared. I'm right here and I'm looking for my children. Who wrote this?"

I asked my boss if I could take off work the next morning. He agreed and, the first thing the next day, I charged into the newspaper office and demanded to see the reporter responsible for the article. I introduced myself and said in a hard tone, "When you do your job, do it correctly or don't do it at all!" I felt my face grow red.

"What are you talking about?" the young man asked.

I shoved the newspaper article at him and told him how much damage false information like this could cause me in my search for the children. "Now you have to rectify what you said. You've caused me a lot of trouble by saying that I'm missing too. I'm right here."

"But I couldn't find you," he protested.

"That's your job! To search for information and to find people is what you do! It's not for me to come to you!" I was very angry. He asked me to sit down and tell him the entire story.

The following day the newspaper ran a full feature article on the front page, accurately detailing the kidnapping and my search for the children. Other reporters picked up on the story and called me for interviews. It can only help us, I thought. People will know about the case. Perhaps someone will read about it and come forward to help.

I was still paying rent on my unoccupied house at Nine Rue Verte. I could not bring myself to give it up, because I wanted the children to be able to return to the life they knew and not have to adjust to major change. I was terrified by the illogical thought that if, somehow, they managed to escape from Chaim and return to Brussels, they would not be able to find me. "If they come back, they have to have their place, they have to have their things," I explained to Walter. "This house belongs to the children. I cannot touch it."

But we knew that it was unwise to pay rent on two different places. When Walter's apartment lease expired on August 15, we moved to my house. We packed up the stack of unopened Christmas presents and stored them in the basement, where I would not see them every day.

My father traveled to the U.S. in August and met with New York–based ICTS detective Arik Arad to establish a search program. Arad introduced my father to police investigators in various areas where the Satmar congregated, such as the Williamsburg and Borough Park areas of Brooklyn and the towns of Monsey and Monroe in upstate New York. The police expressed appropriate sympathy, but my father doubted that they would provide us with any active help. Like police agencies all over the world, they tended to dismiss a case such as this as a simple domestic dispute.

Accompanied by Arad, Papa walked the streets of Williamsburg, searching for anyone who might help. In a kosher restaurant they showed photos of the children to patrons, asking for information. One Hasidic man's face showed a flash of recognition. He said that he knew Chaim!

Arad asked quick questions: How did he know Chaim? Where was he? Did he have the children with him?

The man realized that he had already said too much. He refused to answer the questions and scurried from the restaurant.

"Stay here," Arad commanded my father. He followed the Hasid at a careful distance. When he returned to the restaurant a few minutes later, he flashed a small notebook, displaying the license plate number of the man's car.

The license plate traced to an address in Monsey.

Father hired yet another detective, an ex–New York police officer named Ben Jacobson, whose company, Peregrine, Incorporated, specialized in investigating business fraud. Jacobson's job was to concentrate on Monsey.

*   *   *

One day at work, René Vanderheynde said to me, "Patsy, sometimes you come into my office and I ask myself, 'What is she going to get me to do now?' I make up my mind to say no and suddenly I'm saying yes." He pointed out that this was a talent. I had the ability to motivate people, to get them to do what I wanted them to do. I thanked him for the compliment. The words were a welcome encouragement, for my self-esteem remained very low. I realized that I was maturing into a very different Patsy than the young girl whom Chaim had so successfully manipulated.

Vanderheynde assigned me a new task: to create a system of inventory control. Until now, the company had no way of knowing what happened to each item in stock—and Vanderheynde suspected that some items had disappeared. He wanted answers. I enjoyed this new challenge and set to work, devising a standard stock-inventory form that everyone in the company was obliged to use. In my first month at the task, I located records of merchandise that had been delivered but never invoiced, and thereby recovered more than one million Belgian francs for the company. Vanderheynde called everyone together to celebrate. He uncorked a bottle of champagne and forced me to climb onto a desktop to accept a congratulatory toast. I was embarrassed but very pleased.

Every month I allotted the smallest possible amount of money for living expenses and another small sum for recreation and relaxation. With fierce discipline, I stashed the remainder in my bank account. Often, when my mother suggested that I go somewhere or buy something, I replied, "I'm sorry, I can't do it. I don't have the money." She looked at me with confusion, for she knew that I earned a good salary.

I wanted to be very careful. I did not know how long my parents could handle the costs of the investigation. The private detectives were very expensive. Israeli and American lawyers charged even more.

And we had no idea how long this nightmare would continue.

26

Sarah's Story

Papa introduced us to his new friend, Iris. She had a big nose.

We thought she was the cleaning lady, but Papa said that she wasn't. He said that he was going to marry her. Josef cried because he said that he didn't want her as a mother.

One day Iris came with us as we drove to a place called Washington, D.C., for a holiday. Iris took a picture of us in front of an iron fence surrounding a big white house. Josef hated to have his picture taken and tried to run from the camera. We laughed at him.

27

"The Duchess" was tiny, dressed in conservative Hasidic style. She moved with surprising agility for an older woman as she darted through the lobby of the Hilton Hotel in Amsterdam. She would not meet with us directly. Rather, ICTS detective Eitan Rilov would act as intermediary.

As the woman waited in another part of the hotel, Rilov explained why he had called us here. The Duchess claimed to be the widow of an extremely important Hasidic rebbe. Rilov had promised not to reveal her true identity to us, so he had devised the code name. She was a French woman, born and raised a Christian, who had converted to Judaism. After a previous marriage that produced a son, she had married one of the leaders of the most religious of the Hasidic sects. She had gradually become ultrareligious and was both revered and reviled among her people. Rilov knew that she had contacts deep within the Hasidic community, and he felt certain that she could help us.

The obvious question was: What did she want in return?

Rilov disclosed that, after the death of her husband, the unnamed but obviously influential rebbe, some of his most important and personal documents had been stolen. The thief was now attempting to blackmail the Duchess.

What sort of damaging information could be in the papers of a deceased rebbe? I wondered. Did they document illegal activities or immoral behavior? We could not know, but the Duchess was desperate to get them back. Here was an indication that, at least in some segments of the Hasidic culture, not everything was "kosher."

Rilov explained that the Duchess wanted to hire ICTS to retrieve the papers, but she could not afford the five-thousand-dollar fee. Here was the deal: If we would pay the ICTS fee for her case, she would search the Satmar community for the children.

My father tried to hide his reaction, but I could almost feel him wince inside. He had already paid ICTS a great deal of money, and now they wanted him to come up with another five thousand dollars.

"This is an opportunity," Rilov declared. "She's a Hasidic lady, very strict. She doesn't have any money and she needs us." He held up his fists and shook them for emphasis. "I am going to manipulate her. Don't worry. I know how to do it."

During the course of our conversation, Rilov made a slip of the tongue, calling the Duchess by her real name. My father and I ignored the blunder and said nothing but mentally filed the information.

Papa asked: could the Duchess provide us with any preliminary information, to convince us of her sincerity?

Through Rilov, the Duchess responded. She said she knew that Chaim had brought the children right here to Amsterdam immediately after the kidnapping. They had stayed in the apartment of a carpenter, a man surnamed Armoni; she did not know his first name.

We would see if this information was useful. Then we would decide whether to cut a deal with the Duchess.

In the subsequent days, Rilov and another ICTS operative narrowed the search to three families in Amsterdam named Armoni. The most likely suspect was Zvi Armoni, an Orthodox but not fanatic Jew married to a formerly Christian woman. The detectives fashioned a plan, loosely based on Chaim's well-known bank-fraud case in Israel. Posing as employees of an Israeli bank, they approached Armoni and told him that they were looking for Chaim Yarden. They said that he had embezzled money from the bank, and they were here to recover it.

Armoni was coy. He admitted that Chaim and the children had stayed with his family for about a month. He hinted that he could tell the agents much more, but he would do so only if they offered him a cash reward.

Once the detectives revealed their true identity to Armoni, we faced a series of decisions. The man had admitted to the criminal act of harboring three kidnap victims, and we could bring charges against him. But, rather than revenge, we wanted his cooperation. For his part, Armoni realized that he was enmeshed in a delicate situation. To protect himself against prosecution, he agreed to a thorough debriefing by ICTS operatives.

Finally, through Armoni's interrogation, we were able to retrace the events that occurred following the kidnapping. In a two-car caravan, the children were driven to the small Belgian city of Mechelen and then on to Amsterdam, to the home of a certain Rebbe Averat. Apparently the children did not measure up to the rebbe's strict standards. "They were almost Christian in their manners and behavior," Armoni said, explaining why the rebbe did not want them in his own house. Rebbe Averat persuaded Armoni and his wife to take them in, calling the act a mitzvah, a good deed for God. Apparently, Armoni's apartment was to serve as a sort of Hasidic halfway house, where the children would begin their education in Judaism, first with the celebration of Hanukkah.

Armoni said that Chaim had arrived with ten thousand dollars to finance his travels. The case was not unique; other children, too, had been "rescued" by the Satmars.

While in Amsterdam, Chaim forged an extended date on his Israeli passport and, in addition, purchased a false French passport.

Traveling on the false French passport, Chaim took the children to London on January 11, 1987—exactly one month after the kidnapping—where they remained for several weeks, supported by the British Satmar community. They stayed in a Jewish community center in Stanford Hill, where they were formally converted and given new names. Marina was now called Sarah. Simon was Josef. And Moriah was Rachel.

For the final leg of the trip to New York, Chaim used his genuine Israeli passport—with its illegally extended date—because that is the one which held the visa allowing entry into the U.S.

By this time, nearly a year after the kidnapping, Chaim must have felt very secure. He had the backing of an insulated community committed to the righteousness of its cause, with safe neighborhoods situated at various points all over the globe. Some of his new friends had the ability to produce all manner of false documents and identification papers. An outsider, looking for Chaim, would encounter great difficulty in this impenetrable environment.

Armoni had five or six photographs of the children. Several were taken inside his house and showed the children praying during the Hanukkah festival. Another photo was taken at the Amsterdam zoo. After bartering with my father, Armoni sold the photos to us for five thousand dollars.

A jumble of emotions washed over me as I held one of the five-by-seven Hanukkah photographs in my hands and stared into the faces of my children. Against the backdrop of a stark white wall, on a worn brown sofa, Moriah was sitting on her father's lap like a little rag doll. Her arms and legs were outstretched in a posture of weariness and her gaze was downward, but I thought I detected a faint smile on her face. Chaim's hands, fingers clenched, were visible under her arms, as if supporting her. He was a study in darkness with deep brown eyes beneath the brim of a black felt hat. His ebony beard seemed to disappear into the shoulders of a suit of the same color.

Armoni sat to Chaim's left. He had a generous mop of black hair. Large dark glasses shrouded his eyes. But he had a warm smile as his head tilted down, looking at Simon and Marina, who sat on his knees.

Marina wore a black sweater and a long brown skirt. She clutched something in her hands, perhaps a flower, but I could not be certain. Her usually luminous, big brown eyes looked confused and sad. She had dark half-circles under her eyes; we call them "suitcases," because you can carry everything in them.

Simon was centered in the photograph, wearing a blue sweater with red-and-white trim, which offered what appeared to be the only color relief in the room. He was the only one whose eyes bore straight into the camera, unsmiling and trancelike. A dark yarmulke rested atop his coal-black hair.

Our American private detective, Ben Jacobson, learned that the children had, indeed, been in Monsey, in one of about a dozen houses on a certain private road. He was able to give us the address of a school where, he believed, Marina and Moriah had been enrolled. But word of our search had spread through the community, and Jacobson could find no evidence that either Chaim or the children were still in the area.

The local police promised to search the neighborhood and to remain on the alert.

28

Sarah's Story

It was time to move again. From Monsey we were taken to a place called Lakewood, New Jersey. Papa said that this time he would not be able to live with us, but he promised to visit often.

At first we all stayed with Mr. and Mrs. Brown, but then Josef went to live with a local school principal and his wife and three children. We liked it better when we were all together, but the families were friends, so we got to see Josef often.

Rachel and I didn't like it at the Browns' house because we weren't allowed to do many of the things that their children did. Each time they went away for the weekend, or to a wedding, we weren't allowed to come along. We had to stay with friends instead. So it felt like Mr. and Mrs. Brown liked their own children better than us.

At first Papa came to visit us twice a week. Then he came only once a week, and pretty soon he wasn't coming at all. Josef asked the principal, "Why doesn't he come?" Josef was told that Papa was working somewhere very far away and could not come to visit.

Josef got his first pair of eyeglasses. They cost a hundred dollars. The glasses made it easier for him to read the prayer books.

29

Suddenly, so many things seemed to be happening. My father and I flew to Tel Aviv for a meeting at ICTS headquarters, and we discussed a variety of ways to proceed. We had three separate agents available to infiltrate the New York communities.

First was the Duchess. Her tip concerning Amsterdam had proved useful, so we had reason to trust her further.

Our second hope was Zvi Armoni, the Orthodox Jew from Amsterdam who had originally harbored Chaim and the children. In need of money, he agreed to travel to the U.S. and to circulate among the various Hasidic communities. He would approach people whom we knew had met Chaim, and he would claim that Chaim had offered him a job. As proof of his association, he could flash photos showing himself with Chaim and the children.

The third possibility was a man whom the ICTS agents referred to only by the name Nechemiah. They made vague references that he was retired, either from the Israeli police or the Mossad, or both. In any event, Nechemiah's unique background made him the perfect undercover agent. He had been raised in a Hasidic household but had broken away from a religious life. As a law-enforcement agent, he had specialized in infiltrating clandestine and Hasidic groups and monitoring their activities. Now, he was willing to do the same for us.

My father and I discussed these proposals in private. Papa had difficulty admitting that he was running short of cash. He knew that Mizou might have to sell some of her jewelry to cover these new expenses. Every time someone mentioned a fee, it was usually five or ten thousand dollars—and always American money. My father asked ruefully, "Isn't there an amount of money in the world less than five thousand dollars?"

We decided that we would work with the first two infiltrators and hold Nechemiah in reserve. My father agreed to pay the five-thousand-dollar fee so that ICTS could handle the Duchess's case—with the stipulation that we would not actually pay the money until the missing papers were secured. And he agreed to pay Zvi Armoni a substantial fee, which included travel and living expenses for him, his wife, and baby.

The holiday season approached and there were painful reminders of the children everywhere. December 6 was Saint Nicolas's Day, when the happy, bearded, red-suited man visits schools and homes to distribute presents to children. December 11 was the first anniversary of the kidnapping. Then came the memory of last Christmas in Israel, desperately seeking any news of my children. The start of the new year meant another year without the children, and January 2 would be Simon's seventh birthday.

But there was good news. ICTS located the stolen documents and returned them to the Duchess. My father paid the promised five-thousand-dollar fee, and it was time for the Duchess to live up to her end of the bargain. She was extremely well known in Hasidic circles, and we knew that she would have no difficulty making discreet inquiries. We were very excited and hopeful. I thought: She is a woman, she is a mother, and she is religious. She would not, could not, lie to us.

Through Eitan Rilov she relayed a message to us: "I'm going to the States. I will do something for you."

Waiting was difficult. A week passed with no news from the Duchess. Then a second week passed. Soon it was a month. We heard nothing from her. There was nothing we could do except wait some more, and the entire family felt the stress.

No matter what I did I felt torn. If I did not spend every waking moment thinking about the search, I felt guilty. If I took some time off to spend with Walter or on other matters, I was ashamed.

Friends and relatives called my parents frequently, asking if there was any news. I appreciated their interest and support, but we had nothing new to report.

On occasion, someone would ask my parents, "Why doesn't she just give it up and stop looking? Wherever the kids are, they are used to their new situation now. Why doesn't she just move on and start a new life?"

To some extent I understood their concerns, but I also felt that it would have been more honest if they had made these comments to my face.

Friday, February 12, 1988. Danny Issacharof spoke quickly as he ate his lunch. Walter and I listened carefully. ICTS had certain papers that had to be delivered to Zvi Armoni in Amsterdam. The delivery had to be made in secret, in order to protect Armoni. The detective agency was going to charge my father a substantial fee for the delivery, but Walter had insisted that he could do it as easily as anyone else. So here we were at a hotel restaurant in Paris.

Issacharof handed Walter a yellowish-brown envelope, small enough to fit into a jacket pocket. "Do not open it," he instructed. In two days, precisely at noon, Walter was to approach the concierge at the Amsterdam Hilton and announce that he had a meeting with Mr. Armoni. He would identify himself by a code name, Peter Feltham. The concierge would point out Mr. Armoni. Issacharof instructed, "Verify his identity. Give him the papers. Don't answer any questions."

When we arrived home from Paris, Walter immediately

steamed open the envelope and found airline tickets and Israeli passports in the names of Armoni and his wife, complete with U.S. visas. For some unexplained reasons, Armoni had been unable to get a U.S. visa, but ICTS had supplied it. Walter wanted to make copies, but, concerned that we had disobeyed Issacharof's instructions, I said, "No, don't touch. Leave that alone."

On Sunday morning we made the three-hour drive to the Amsterdam Hilton. All I could do was stay in the car and wait.

Walter walked off, dressed in jeans, a T-shirt, and a light jacket. The envelope, resealed, was hidden in his jacket pocket. He climbed the stone stairs and entered the large, sprawling hotel lobby.

"My name is Feltham," he said to the concierge. "I have a meeting with Mr. Armoni."

"There is no Mr. Armoni here," the concierge replied.

"I will wait," Walter said. He looked about, spotted a quiet corner, pointed, and said, "I will be over there."

He settled into a chair and picked up a newspaper. As he pretended to read, his eyes studied every movement in the lobby. As time passed, he grew concerned that he had said or done something incorrectly and frightened Armoni off. Then he found anger building inside. He knew that Armoni had conspired with Chaim to harbor the children. He suspected that Armoni knew much more than he had told ICTS. He thought: Rather than give him the papers, I would prefer to wring his neck.

More than an hour passed before three strange individuals—a man, a woman, and a baby—entered the lobby. At first, Walter thought they were hippies. The man was dressed in sloppy jeans and a shirt. The woman wore a brown poncho with a diamond-shaped Aztec motif. She had shoulder-length, straight blond hair that Walter suspected was a wig. Then he noticed that the man wore a skull cap.

Rising, Walter approached and asked, "Are you Mr. Armoni?" He identified himself as Peter Feltham.

"You're from the police!" the woman charged.

"No, ma'am, I'm not from the police. I'm just a messenger."

"You're from the police!"

"No, I'm sorry. I was just told to give you this." Walter produced the envelope. "I don't even know what I'm giving you," he lied.

Armoni opened the envelope and inspected the contents. He seemed satisfied, and the woman's attitude softened. She asked, "What's the weather like in New York?"

Walter said that he thought it would be colder in New York and suggested that she take warm clothes.

Armoni thanked Walter for the delivery. Then he said, "You stay here for five minutes after we leave."

The little Jewish family hurried out the door.

Walter forced himself to wait for about thirty seconds, then followed. He emerged onto the street in time to see the Armonis scurry around a corner. But by the time Walter reached the corner, they had disappeared.

Armoni spent a full month in the U.S. trying to track Chaim under the ruse that he had been promised a job. If he learned anything about Chaim and the children, he did not report it to us.

On March 11, 1988, an Israeli court finally canceled the order granting custody of the children to Chaim. Now I was the only one, anywhere, who had a legal right to them.

The Duchess surfaced briefly, mumbling excuses. *Now* she was going to New York, she said. *Now* she would work for us.

She did go to New York. But instead of asking quiet questions, the Duchess simply stormed about the Hasidic neighborhoods, flashing photos of the children, crying out, "Have you seen them? Have you seen them? We are looking for them."

Too late, we realized what she was doing. In effect she was saying: "Look! They are searching for these children! They are close! Hide them deeper!"

Rilov had promised to manipulate her, but it was clear that

she had turned the tables. Still, the ICTS detectives wanted us to pay for her to travel to additional locations.

"No!" I argued. "Wasting more money on the Duchess is useless."

Several people seemed quite surprised by my vehemence, particularly Rilov, who always spoke directly to my father, never to me. Reluctantly, my father backed my decision. It was the first time everyone had listened to me, the first time I had the last word.

30

Armoni had discovered nothing. The Duchess had mocked us. Now, we resorted to the Israeli undercover agent known as Nechemiah.

His arrival in Monsey caused no alarm, for he appeared to be a typical Hasidic man. His long black coat and flat-brimmed *shreimel* were authentic. No one knew that his *peiyot* were fake. No one knew that the cash he deposited on an apartment had been supplied by my father.

Nechemiah's initial inquiries found no one whom he could identify as Chaim. There was no sign of Marina, Simon, or Moriah. He played a waiting game, keeping his senses alert, but not pushing too hard for information.

He quietly sought out the man who had led us to Monsey, the patron whom Arik Arad and my father had encountered in a kosher restaurant in Williamsburg. He had recognized Chaim's picture because he operated a transportation service company and had employed Chaim occasionally. Now, he said that he had not seen Chaim for a while and had no idea where he was. During the conversation, Nechemiah learned that the man most likely to know something about Chaim was Rebbe Ezekiel Tauber, who was in charge of a shul (a synagogue) and a yeshiva (a school).

After a time, Nechemiah reported very disturbing news. Apparently, one or more local police officers had alerted certain Satmar leaders—possibly Rebbe Tauber himself—that we were looking for the children in Monsey. It was very difficult for us to believe that the police would do such a thing, but apparently it was true. That very day, Chaim had once more fled with the children. Nechemiah did not know where they were, but he learned that the Satmar congregation in Monsey had supplied Chaim with nine thousand dollars in traveling money.

The news that we had been so close to them, yet missed connections, was agonizing.

"I am representing myself in this case." I explained.

The judge frowned. In Belgium, as elsewhere, the courts much prefer to deal with a trained attorney. But I was desperate to conserve money and determined to handle this task myself. The judge allowed me to continue.

I explained the background of the case. I emphasized that when we finally found the children, I wanted the full force of the law on my side. I asked that, upon his apprehension and return to Belgium, Chaim receive the maximum sentence of one year for parental kidnapping.

On June 27, the judge levied the one-year sentence *in absentia*. An international warrant of arrest was issued for Chaim Yarden. Interpol circulated this among the world's police forces.

Now, all we had to do was find him.

By law, the court was obligated to inform Chaim of his conviction and sentence. Since his whereabouts were unknown, they sent the papers to his next of kin, Shlomo and Leah Edwar. Leah returned the papers to Brussels with a notation declaring that her son was living somewhere in the U.S.

Business fell off, and IES was forced to lay off a number of employees, including me. My boss staged a small, sad farewell party and bought me perfume as a parting gift. He also gave me an excellent recommendation, and I was fortunate to find another job very quickly.

Display Point manufactured quality mannequins, patterned after top fashion models. I was responsible for administrative duties and for controlling the stock. It was a small family firm, run by a husband-and-wife team, but it had offices in both Brussels and Paris. As I had with my previous boss, I explained my situation in the very beginning, so that no one would be surprised by the complications in my life.

Walter was fascinated by the dynamics of our family. My father had instilled in us a tradition handed down through generations of Heymans. That tradition was that, in times of crisis, each family member would rally around the others—no matter what. Walter was impressed at how we had drawn together in a common effort to retrieve my children. My brothers never raised any objections concerning the money that my parents spent to help me in the quest. Instead, they were there to help me at every opportunity. We were so close that it was difficult for Walter, or anyone who was not a blood relative, to find a place. Walter coined an affectionate nickname for us: "Heymans's Mafia."

Somewhat excluded from the inner circle, Walter found an auxiliary but invaluable role. If we needed a document or a letter copied, he ran off quickly to handle the task. If my parents or I needed extra money to pay for some aspect of the search, Walter loaned it without hesitation. If we had to travel, Walter's responsibility was to remain at home and manage our everyday lives. My job was to search for the past, but Walter's task was to plan for the future, to create a stable and comfortable life that would be ready, at a moment's notice, to include Marina, Simon, and Moriah.

It was still extremely difficult for me to be alone in the house that was once filled with the laughter and sweet chaos of three small children. Every afternoon, Walter and I spoke to one another from our respective offices, coordinating our movements. If Walter had to work late, I went shopping or to dinner with a friend, not arriving home until I was sure that Walter would be waiting for me.

I could not have managed without the support of my family, but Walter was truly my rock.

Nechemiah made a bold move. He went directly to Rebbe Tauber in Monsey and lied, "Chaim Yarden's father is very ill. Can you tell me where he is? The family wants to locate him." Nechemiah was armed with enough information to make his story convincing.

Tauber could have checked this statement very easily by calling Chaim's brother Asher in Israel, but he did not take the precaution. He seemed to accept Nechemiah's words at face value. He said that he had spoken with Chaim only two days earlier. The Rebbe told our informant that Chaim was, at this very moment, staying with Tauber's brother-in-law, and that his last name was Stroh.

In London.

Immediately we focused our energies. My father initiated legal action in a British court, just as we had in the U.S., to make sure that we would have the cooperation of the local authorities. London's resident ICTS agent, Eitan Rozen, directed the investigation.

Nechemiah traveled from Monsey to London in order to work undercover. He visited Stroh, wearing a hidden recording device. During their conversation, Stroh acknowledged that Chaim had been at his home here in London, and Rebbe Tauber had called him from New York to report that his father was ill.

During a subsequent high-court session, Stroh denied under oath that he had seen Chaim in London. We all knew that he was lying, and we had a tape recording to prove it, but it was not admissible evidence. Stroh's testimony did add one tantalizing bit of information: He admitted that his own children had played with mine during a vacation trip to Monsey.

My job was twofold. First, I would try to get British press coverage of our story, to put pressure on whomever might be helping Chaim. Second, I was determined to search personally through every inch of London's Hasidic community.

We hired a public relations firm that was successful in getting several newspapers to run articles about the missing children; they also arranged a radio interview with my father.

I made frequent weekend trips to London, staying as a guest in Eitan Rozen's home. He and his family were very sympathetic and supportive. From the Rozen house, I rode the subway for one hour and fifteen minutes, then walked about another half mile to the Stanford Hill area, a self-contained neighborhood of Hasidic families. I approached through a large park, where children often played. If there were children about, I walked toward them, coming as near as I could without alarming them; they were raised to view any non-Jew as a possible enemy who would threaten their way of life.

After surveying the park, I strolled the maze of streets, where Hasidic families lived in block after block of English town houses. Rather than attempt a systematic search, I watched for groups of people and moved toward them. I knew that the chances of finding my children this way were slim, but I felt compelled to do something.

Often, after such an exhausting day, my sleep was tortured by a recurrent nightmare: I walked and walked through the streets, regarded by everyone as a hostile invader. I passed a group of children. One of them was mine. In the nightmare, it was sometimes Marina, sometimes Simon, sometimes Moriah. But I did not recognize my very own child! In the unreal world of the dream, I somehow knew my child's thoughts: *It is my mother, but she pretends not to see me because she doesn't want me.* I always woke from the nightmare at this point, nervous and fearful. I would grab the photo that I kept next to my bed and study the faces of Marina, Simon, and Moriah as they played with my mother's black mongrel, Goupi.

I told Rozen that this nightmare was my biggest fear. The children were young and growing fast. The more time that passed, the more their appearances would change. Whenever I went out to search, I made sure that I took the photograph with me.

A British television station decided to produce a short feature on the case and sent a film crew to Belgium. This was an extremely difficult experience for me. For the past twenty months, ever since the children had disappeared, I had avoided driving past Sint Jozef's, because it was the last place I had seen them. It was too painful. Now, the crew asked me to re-create the drive I had taken on the morning of December 11, 1986.

Two members of the film crew jockeyed for position in my small car as I drove from Nine Rue Verte to Boulevard de la Woluwe. Then I had to get out of the car and point to the very spot where I had last seen Marina, Simon, and Moriah. The crew then spent some time interviewing teachers, filming Simon's classroom and the small field where he played soccer. They did not need me for these sequences, and I slipped off to one side, where I could cry privately.

Afterward, I took a quarter tablet of the tranquilizers that Dr. Vossen had given me for just such an emotional emergency. It was soft like a marshmallow. I placed it between my teeth and gums. Within seconds I felt much more relaxed.

After filming in Belgium for several days, the crew returned to London and asked me to accompany them. We journeyed to Stanford Hill, to film basic scenes of Hasidic life. Groups of angry Hasids gathered around, and their comments rang in our ears:

"We don't like you here . . ."
"We don't like to be on television . . ."
"You just go away from here . . ."

Alone, I approached the park. It was yet another Saturday in London, another Shabbat here in Stanford Hill. In the late summer heat, the park was nearly deserted, but a group of six or seven girls stood together at the edge of a lake. I walked the path around the perimeter of the park and approached.

The girls were dressed in sensible frocks, with sleeves that covered their arms to the wrists and mid-length skirts over long, thick socks. They girl-talked in Yiddish, smiling and giggling. As I walked past, my eyes met those of the youngest girl, who stood in the midst of the group.

I was already past the girls when my body began to react. I shivered. My heart pounded so violently that I feared it would burst through my chest. My head reeled as if I had been punched. Only after a few moments did my mind register what my body was telling me.

Moriah?

Had I just stared into her eyes?

Moriah!

31

I moved ahead, warning myself not to alarm the girls. Then I turned—casually, I hoped—and walked back. When I came past the second time I was able to approach within six feet of the child in the center of the group. I tried to study her face without staring too obviously.

Moriah was only four years old when I last saw her. Now she was six. How would she have changed? With just a glimpse, it was difficult to be sure. Would she even remember me? I had to fight the impulse to scoop the girl into my arms, lest I frighten her and her companions and send them fleeing.

I made yet another circular track about the park. When I returned for the third time, some of the older girls, noticing my stares, drew in close, surrounding the youngster in the center, encasing her in a protective cocoon. I looked for a key detail. Moriah's nose was slightly off-center so that, when she was a baby, she appeared to be somewhat cross-eyed. Oh, my God, yes, I realized, *it's the same nose!*

I could not speak; Moriah's name lodged in my throat. I wondered if these girls could hear the pounding of my heart. I did not know what to do. I did not want to frighten them away, but I was close enough to touch my daughter and my hand longed to reach out. The group inched away from me warily. I wanted to laugh, to cry, to run.

She doesn't know me, I realized. Two years ago I was overweight; now, anxiety and stress had melted twenty pounds off my body. When she last saw me, I wore my hair long and straight or in a ponytail; now, it was much shorter and curly. Then, I still had the blemished complexion of an adolescent; now, the blemishes had been replaced by fine worry lines around always-searching eyes and a mouth that seldom smiled.

My entire body began to shake.

As the children edged farther away, I faced a dilemma. I knew that I had to get help, but I did not want to let my little girl out of my sight. Time began to play tricks with me. Seconds felt like minutes, and minutes felt like hours. I did not want to draw further attention to myself by running, so I walked quickly to a telephone booth in the park, about six hundred feet away. Still, my body felt weighted. I panicked when I realized that I could not see the girls from here. Somehow, despite fingers that could not stop shaking, I managed to insert coins and dial the home number of Eitan Rozen. When he was on the line, I became hysterical: "I saw Moriah! Moriah, she's here!"

He tried to calm me, but the timbre of my voice told him that I was in shock. "Are you sure?" he asked.

"Yes, yes, I'm positive." Tears gushed from my eyes. My body trembled. "Help me!" I wailed.

"Where are you?" Rozen asked. When I told him, he said he would call the police immediately and assured me that he would arrive as soon as possible. He told me to walk back to the main intersection at the edge of Stanford Hill and wait for him there.

I hung up and followed instructions. I waited at the intersection, pacing, for what seemed like a lifetime. It took hours for the second hand on my watch to make a full circle. A single thought echoed through my mind: I saw Moriah . . . I saw Moriah . . . I saw Moriah.

When Rozen finally arrived, we ran back to the spot where the girls had been standing. But they were gone.

Several police officers arrived within minutes. I told them what I had seen, and Rozen quickly briefed them on the background of the case. I emphasized the fact that the older girls seemed to be protecting Moriah. "Don't frighten her," I warned.

One of the policemen asked, "Are you sure it was her? If you have a doubt, tell us. It's normal. It's okay."

"No," I answered. "I'm positive."

In an unmarked car, the police officers drove us systematically through the rectangular grid of the neighborhood streets. My eyes searched carefully. Finally, as we turned a corner onto a street close to the park, I saw a few of the girls. Moriah was still with them, and we watched as she entered a town house with a small front yard.

I wanted to run in after her, but the police would not allow it. "We have no warrant," one of them warned. They took note of the address. Then we drove a short distance to the station house to consider our next course of action. I immediately called my parents in Belgium. Almost before I hung up, my father was out the door and on his way to the airport to catch the next flight to London.

The police inspectors asked question after question. Rozen provided them with copies of the necessary legal documents.

Over and over the police asked, "Are you sure?"

I explained about Moriah's nose. I showed them the photograph that I carried, and I vowed, "I've never been so certain of anything in my life."

Finally, the police arranged to take my father and me to visit the house the next day, so that we could see the child for ourselves, to make certain that she was Moriah. They told me that I would have to make a positive verbal identification. Again they reminded me: If you're not sure or if you've made a mistake, it's okay. Just say it.

I was terrified that if they knew Moriah had been spotted, whoever was keeping her would spirit her away once again. But we had no choice; we had to do as the police directed.

My father arrived from Brussels. Thinking quickly and

clearly, he had brought additional photographs of the children as well as a folder of legal documents. I spent the evening staring at the pictures, burning every small feature of Moriah's face into my memory.

As Papa and I walked toward the small town house, flanked by Rozen and two policemen, all I could think was: We are so close. So close.

The police spoke to the man and woman of the house and told them that I had identified the little girl as my daughter. Icily, the man contended, "No, she is our daughter."

These were light-skinned Jews, the kind known as Ashkenazi; they probably traced their ancestry to Russia, or somewhere else in eastern Europe. They agreed to let us inside, but they asked me not to upset their daughter by speaking directly to her.

As the adults conversed, the girl huddled under a table, obviously frightened. The man of the house said quickly, "She always does that when somebody comes."

A police officer asked, "Why doesn't she go to school, when all the other kids go?"

"She has been sick, so she couldn't go."

The atmosphere in the house was chilly and tense. I spoke very little, allowing the police to take the lead.

It was difficult for me to get a good look at the frightened child who cowered under the table, but I persisted. Yes, she was the right age, the right size, the right coloring. Her skin was dark-hued, like Chaim's, not like these Ashkenazi "parents." The police agreed that she had Moriah's nose.

"Are you sure?" the police asked.

"Yes," I replied and looked at my father.

He nodded his agreement. "Yes," he said. "It's Moriah."

"No," the man of the house protested. "She is our daughter."

An officer guided me gently toward the door. "Okay, okay," he said, "it's time for you to go to the car. We will take care of this."

Outside, I found myself surrounded by a sort of vigilante

band of hostile Hasidim, as well as some Orthodox Jews; news travels fast in a neighborhood such as this. They did not menace me openly, but they were clearly agitated. A venom-filled voice shouted, "How can you take somebody else's child?"

I wanted to shout back, to rage at anyone who dared to support my children's kidnappers in the name of religion. But I did not. I sat in the backseat of the car, with my eyes staring straight ahead.

When my father emerged from the house, he spoke with some of the assembled onlookers and attempted to explain our position. A few feigned sympathetic interest, but their eyes were hollow.

We drove off quickly. The morning had ended in a stalemate. There was nothing to do now but ask the courts to decide the issue.

As we rode, Rozen tested me again. He said, "Patsy, it's still not too late to say that you made a mistake. We will understand."

They must have said that a million times, I thought. "No!" I snapped.

Our British barrister immediately arranged a court appearance before a judge who must have felt like Solomon, hearing two mothers claim the same child.

The judge asked to see a birth certificate. The "parents" said that they did not have one, but I did. The judge asked, "Do you have pictures of her when she was younger?" The "parents" did not, but I did.

I testified that Moriah had a small birthmark on her chest and produced an old photograph showing the circular brown patch. The judge then ordered the child taken into another room to be examined. I remained outside, pacing, for the court would not allow me to approach the girl, but they permitted my father to go in. There was no birthmark, but in its place was a small scar.

"It proves nothing," the "parents" insisted. "She had some heart trouble. It's from a surgery."

The judge was truly confused. There were many coincidences, yet not enough to prove, beyond a shadow of a doubt, that this little girl was my Moriah. He ruled that the couple, the girl, and I would undergo DNA testing at a London laboratory, and he would make his final judgment when the results were available in six to eight weeks. The judge placed me under a restraining order, prohibiting me from contacting the family until the test results were in. But he also assured me that the Hasidic family would not be allowed to flee.

Six to eight weeks loomed ahead of me like a dark, endless tunnel.

The next day I visited a laboratory, where a technician drew a small blood sample from my arm. Afterward, I encountered Moriah's professed "father" in the hallway, as he arrived for his test. We passed one another without speaking.

"They will run away with her," I wailed to Rozen and my father. "We will not be able to get her."

Both men tried to reassure me. The court had too much data. If the family tried to run, they would be in a great deal of trouble. I reminded them that a Belgian court had said much the same thing to Chaim. The problem was that at least some of the Hasidim believed they answered only to a higher authority.

Back home in Brussels, I lived for weeks, as we say in French, "under a glass cover," as if I were isolated from the world about me. I forced myself to imagine the worst possible outcome, so that bad news could not destroy me. I refused to prepare Moriah's room in anticipation of her return. I refused to speak to anyone—including Walter and my parents—about Moriah.

Time passed at an excruciatingly slow pace.

Finally my father called with the news. He had received a letter from our London lawyer; the DNA testing had proved beyond any doubt that the little girl was *not* Moriah.

My first thought was a paranoid suspicion that someone had tampered with the test samples. Patsy, I told myself sadly, stop doing this to yourself. It was not your eyes that saw Moriah; it was your heart.

32

The thin, pocket-sized book appeared to be cheaply printed. The brown cover was unimaginative. The quality of the paper was poor. There were no pictures. I stared at it carefully and wondered what I could learn from it. This was the memoir of the Duchess; an ICTS detective had managed to locate an old copy. I opened it and read carefully.

During the Duchess's childhood in France, she realized that she wanted nothing to do with Christianity. She wrote of her discovery of Judaism and the lengthy process of conversion, which involved years of study, exhaustive tests, and grueling, interrogation-style examinations by various rebbes. She wrote of her move to Jerusalem, of her betrothal to a powerful rebbe, and of how difficult it was for her to gain acceptance within the Hasidic community; even though she had converted, she was a Christian by birth and therefore forever suspect.

Over the years, her faith had deepened and her fervor grown. She was impressed with the Hasidic system of education, which required boys of kindergarten age to spend their days repeating Biblical texts by rote. Young girls were trained to manage a proper kosher household. This, she said, was the very best education possible, but to me it sounded like brainwashing. Images of my three children trapped in such a system were extremely painful.

According to the Duchess, division of the sexes is rigidly enforced; for example, a young Hasidic boy may not touch his mother and is forbidden to enter her bedroom, lest he catch a glimpse of her body through the thin, chin-high, full-length undergarment that is worn beneath the dress.

I took special note when the Duchess wrote of what she saw as the "rescue" of young Josef Shumakher. According to this account, Josef's Hasidic grandparents fretted that their son and daughter-in-law were not raising their small grandson in accordance with strict ritual laws, and had arranged to have the boy taken from his parents. Following the kidnapping, the Duchess played an active, central role. She took Josef from place to place within the community, constantly changing his name and sometimes dressing him as a girl to conceal his identity.

Of course, what the Duchess believed to be a rescue, or even a mitzvah, was a kidnapping to most of the rest of the world. Apparently, such cases are not so rare within this cloistered world. Usually, however, the squabbles are kept quiet, for they pit Jew against Jew and are handled with discretion. It was only because my children and I were Christians that our story had leaked from behind the veil of secrecy.*

In her narrative, the Duchess noted that the Hasidim had considered plastic surgery to alter Josef's appearance, and this raised grave moral questions in her mind. Jewish law forbids such a practice; man is not to change what God has made. Josef was not subjected to the surgery, but the Duchess declared that it is permissible for a good Hasidim to break the laws in order to "save" someone. If she were confronted with the same situation now, she wrote, she would favor plastic surgery to assure that a child was safe from recovery and, thus, "properly" trained. This

---

* Later, I was told that the Mossad hunted for Josef Shumakher for more than three years before they managed to locate him by means of a blackmail scheme. They followed an important Hasidic rebbe to a rendezvous with a prostitute and took incriminating photographs. Threatened with exposure, the rebbe led them to Josef.

passage in the book chilled me; it gave me nightmares that my children's captors might change their appearance so drastically that I could never recognize them.

With pride the Duchess wrote about the many people she had helped convert to the religious life. These included thieves, murderers, and people with obvious mental deficiencies. All of them seemed to be social misfits, people who could not find their places in a normal world. The Duchess was unconcerned about the converts' past behavior because, she claimed, once they joined the society of ultrareligious Jews, they were transformed into "good people." The Hasidim did not ask penetrating questions. As long as a convert outwardly followed the rules, his motivation did not matter. As a new member of an exclusive fraternity, he was protected from outside society.

The more I read, the more agitated I became. My anger intensified. What is this kind of world? I wondered. What kind of person is drawn into a life such as this?

With a shudder, I threw the book onto the floor. I could not bring myself to discuss what I had learned by reading the memoir, even with Walter. To speak of it made it all too real.

33

Monday, January 16, 1989. Danny Issacharof, the head of ICTS, telephoned my father from Tel Aviv to tell him about "a guy from the West Coast named Abraham." Abraham claimed to have a contact within one of the New York Hasidic communities who could locate the children. Danny said that Abraham was willing to assemble several former colleagues and mount an operation to reclaim the children and smuggle them out of the States.

His asking price was three hundred thousand dollars.

Reacting to the exorbitant sum, my father responded, "Danny, are you joking?"

But Danny was not laughing. "No," he said, "I think you should listen to him. I know the guy. He's an ex-ranger and he works with a detective agency. He's done a lot of work with Jewish people. I think he has some good contacts."

There was no way that my father would—or could—pay three hundred thousand dollars. But Papa knew the ways of business and was aware that anything is negotiable. After considerable discussion, he agreed to meet Abraham in New York, and he further agreed to pay the man's travel expenses from the West Coast.

My father arrived in New York one day before the scheduled meeting. The local agent, Arik Arad, had arranged for a briefing with U.S. marshals who, because of the existence of the international arrest warrant, could take Chaim into immediate custody, if and when we located him. The federal agent in charge bore the unlikely name of Tony Crook. He was a stocky, rough-looking character with a medium build and shaggy brown hair; my father thought that, indeed, he looked more like a "crook" than a marshal. But he and his partner, Mike Hollander, were very likable. Crook and Hollander would be present at the meeting with Abraham, but they would pose as ICTS detectives. Crook suggested that my father bring a supply of cash with him in case Abraham demanded a down payment.

My father called me at work and summarized the situation. He was greatly encouraged by the presence of the marshals. Their enthusiasm was infectious. We knew that they would not commit their resources to this episode unless they believed there was a good chance of success.

The call left me extremely anxious, but I tried to concentrate on my work as if nothing was happening. The pain of my experience in London was still fresh. Once more, I could not allow my hopes to rise.

Abraham was about thirty-five years old, fairly tall, with dark, closely cropped hair. Casual clothes covered a trim, athletic build. Sitting across from my father at the bargaining table, he outlined the details of his proposed three-hundred-thousand-dollar commando operation.

"We are totally against taking the kids by force," my father interrupted. The children had been through enough trauma in their young lives. "The law is on our side, and we are perfectly entitled to take them out of the country legally," he pointed out. "There is no need to smuggle them out of the country. All you have to do is tell us where they are—and that should not cost three hundred thousand dollars."

Abraham's face registered deep disappointment, and he quickly lowered his asking price.

The two men fell to bickering. The give-and-take continued

for hours, sometimes in calm tones, sometimes with raised voices. My father was sickened. Marina, Simon, and Moriah were priceless, and here he was, bartering for them as if they were items in a bazaar. The chilling reality was that he had only dwindling resources. Finally he said that the most he could pay was thirty thousand dollars, and he would pay only upon the return of the children. Abraham said that he would agree to that amount for himself, but his informant also wanted five thousand dollars. My father, emotionally drained, snapped at the ICTS detectives, "Aw, you work it out." He rose to leave.

Realizing that the entire deal was about to be blown, Abraham blurted out an address: Eight Maple Terrace, Monsey, New York. Every morning at 8:30, he said, a car picked up the children there and drove them to school.

That evening, filled with optimism, my father bought presents for the children: a game for Marina, a truck for Simon, and a teddy bear with a music box for Moriah.

Very early the next morning, a four-car caravan of unmarked vehicles left New York City en route to Monsey. They carried ten U.S. marshals, Arik Arad, and my father, who was disguised with a false mustache, wig, and sunglasses, so that Chaim would not recognize him. His job would be to make a positive visual identification of the children before the marshals moved in.

By 7:30 A.M., the cars were in place. Agents were able to observe Eight Maple Terrace from four different viewpoints. The marshals kept their distance, watching quietly.

One hour passed. A few cars came and went. But at Eight Maple Terrace, there was no sign of Marina, Simon, or Moriah.

Another hour passed. It was 9:30, and all the schools were open. Where were the children?

The marshals drove off slowly to a coffee shop at the edge of town. As prearranged, Abraham waited there in eager anticipation of his thirty-thousand-dollar reward. My father was livid. He threatened to sue Abraham for attempted extortion. "You know where the children are and you won't tell us!" he accused.

Agitated and frightened, Abraham caught the first available flight back to the West Coast.

My bitterly disappointed father made plans to return to Belgium the following day.

But that same afternoon, the New York ICTS office received a telephone call from a man identifying himself as Abraham's contact. "Listen, sir," he said, "I thought the children were there. Obviously it's not true. Obviously it's a mistake, but I assure you that I can find the father. I can put my hands on him."

Tuesday, January 24. My father and Arad, along with Marshals Crook and Hollander, met with the man we now referred to as "Judas," because he claimed to be Chaim's friend yet was willing to betray him. Judas was a Hasidic Jew in his mid-thirties, average in every way, with a tinge of red in his hair.

Once again my father was in the distasteful and awkward position of bartering for his grandchildren. "We know from Abraham that you were working for five thousand dollars," he said. "We will give you the five thousand even if it's just for Yarden and not the children."

Judas said that he wanted more money.

"Go to hell!" my father responded. "You'll get nothing and we'll inform the police of your involvement."

One of the marshals jumped into the conversation, reminding Judas that he was the one who had started this whole thing. Through Abraham, he had claimed to know where Chaim and the children were. Now, if he did not produce at least Chaim, he could be charged as an accessory to kidnapping. He was already committed, so he had better carry through to the conclusion.

Judas realized the seriousness of his position, but he had a sudden, very strong attack of conscience. "How can I give you this information for a price?" he asked my father. "Chaim Yarden is my friend."

"You can, because what the man has done is very wrong," my father responded.

"But he is my friend. And he is a Jew. You are not. A Jew may not give another Jew to a non-Jew."

They argued for hours until my father's patience wore thin. At the end of this exhaustive day of negotiations, their only point of agreement was to meet again in the morning. Judas asked my father for money to return to Monsey for the evening. Apparently he did not even have enough cash to fill his car with gasoline for the trip. "Nothing before you lead us to Chaim," my father said firmly. "Not even one dollar."

That evening, my father and the detectives devised a plan. In the morning, Papa went to a bank and withdrew five thousand dollars in hundred-dollar bills. When Judas returned to the ICTS office, my father placed the money on the table where the informant could see it. Judas was allowed to touch the cash. His eyes grew huge and hungry. Suddenly my father scooped up the money and placed it in his suit pocket.

Judas began to talk. He said that he could contact Chaim through a certain Mr. Borochov in Monsey. He disclosed that Chaim found sporadic work as a painter, taking his payments in cash so that he would not have to report income which could be traced.

Based upon this information, the marshals formulated a plan. Judas was to contact Chaim—through Borochov—and convince him that he had a friend who wanted to renovate a restaurant in the Williamsburg section of Brooklyn. He would ask Chaim to accompany him there to give an estimate. Judas was to deliver Chaim to the corner of Ross and Lee streets at precisely 10:30 A.M. on January 27—two days from now. The arrest was purposely planned for a Friday; the impending arrival of Shabbat would tend to disrupt any organized response. The marshals' instructions were very specific, designed to keep the pressure on Judas; nothing would be left to chance. They told Judas what side of the street to walk on, what shops to pass, and the precise place to stop, so that my father could make the identification.

Papa called me at work. In a voice full of confidence, he told me of the plan.

This time I could not bury my optimism.

There were many details to handle. If Chaim was arrested, we were certain to locate the children within a matter of days. I checked airline schedules. It would be late Friday afternoon before I received any news. And if that news was good, I would have to wait until noon Saturday to fly to America.

I had no idea how long I would have to stay. How long would the legal process take? How difficult would it be for the children—and me—to adjust? When could I bring them home? Would they accept me as their mother or reject me as a stranger? With trepidation I remembered: They have been educated never to trust a non-Jew.

January 27. My father sat nervously inside an unmarked Cadillac. He was surprised that the marshals would use this sort of luxury car, but Crook and Hollander explained that it had been confiscated from a drug dealer. Three other cars full of marshals waited at various positions around the intersection of Ross and Lee streets. The agents all wore jackets emblazoned on the back: US Marshal. Arik Arad was there too, clutching a bag filled with my father's five thousand dollars.

Papa peered through the dark-tinted windows of the Cadillac, eyeing the diverse mix of people who walked past. Many were Hasidic; some were not.

At precisely 10:30 A.M., Judas and another man came into view. A marshal asked, "Is it him?"

"Let him walk by," my father said.

The two men moved past the Cadillac and stopped at the exact spot where the marshals had directed.

"Is it him?"

My father stared. The difference in appearance was dramatic between this man and the Chaim my father remembered. The garb of the Hasid, the dark suit and hat, the long beard, and the curly *peiyot* dangling down both sides of his face, all served to obscure the features. My father realized that he could not be certain—but he would not take the risk of letting Chaim slip through his fingers.

"Yes, it's him," he said forcefully.

An official voice echoed on the police radio, "We have positive ID. Let's go to it!"

Seven men jumped from the waiting vehicles and rushed toward Chaim. One pointed a gun directly at his nose. Others commanded him to lie flat on the sidewalk. Judas was pushed to one side.

A crowd of inquisitive Hasidic bystanders gathered quickly. To avert trouble, a marshal screamed, "This is a murderer. He has murdered people in Israel!"

The marshals quickly searched Chaim and handcuffed him. As they hustled him into the backseat of a car, Arad, in full view of the crowd, shoved the envelope full of money at Judas.

In the car, the marshals were disgusted to realize that their prisoner—the cunning and arrogant man who had promised to destroy my life—had soiled his pants.

Arad used his cellular phone to report to the ICTS office on Fifty-seventh Street.

The office notified Danny Issacharof in Tel Aviv.

Issacharof immediately called Brussels.

Within minutes of Chaim's apprehension, the phone on my desk rang and my mother's voice announced, "They've got him!"

"And the children?" I asked quickly.

"Nothing yet, but it won't be long now."

The room began to spin. We did it! I thought. My heart pounded.

I took a few deep breaths, determined not to allow myself to become hysterical. But my joy and excitement burst through as I explained to my boss, "Chaim has been arrested and I need to call Walter!"

"Sure," he said, sharing my happiness.

"And I need time off to go to the States."

"Sure."

"I don't know how long it will be."

My boss told me to attend to my children. They came first.

During the ride to the U.S. Marshals' office in Brooklyn, agents tried to get Chaim to talk. They jostled him a bit and stared at him menacingly. One of them asked, "Where are the kids?"

Chaim replied, "The children are in Israel. With my wife."

Chaim was taken to the Manhattan Correctional Center. Belgian authorities immediately began the process of requesting his extradition.

Meanwhile, detectives learned that he had been living in an apartment on Forty-third Street in Brooklyn, leased by a Yemenite Jew named Iris Buttel. She had disappeared suddenly.

Investigators immediately petitioned a judge to issue a search warrant. Clearly, there was probable cause; Chaim was a convicted kidnapper who refused to disclose the exact whereabouts of the children. But to everyone's surprise the judge refused to issue the warrant.

To my father, this was evidence of the political power of the Hasidic community. He had already seen how the authorities in Monsey cooperated with the Hasidim. Now, he was convinced that they had influence within the Brooklyn court system as well. If there was any evidence in Iris Buttel's apartment, we could not get to it.

The Saturday flight was unusually crowded. The gentleman sitting next to me, a Swiss diplomat, wore a strong, penetrating cologne that aggravated my asthma. I spent the nine-hour flight wheezing and coughing. By the time we landed, I had a debilitating headache.

New York City was overwhelming, but I was too concerned about my children to worry about the well-known dangers of this great metropolis. I managed to find a bus that took me from JFK

International Airport to a stop on Forty-second Street. The driver stayed with me until a shuttle bus arrived to take me to the hotel near Times Square where my father was staying.

My father, nervous and impatient, was waiting for me. He gave me a complete rundown of everything that had happened. I was disappointed to learn that the children had not yet been located, but we felt that they were close by, despite Chaim's claim that they were in Israel. We were sure that Chaim would break down soon and tell the police where they were.

That evening, we were in a relaxed, celebratory mood. We laughed over the name of the chief marshal, Tony Crook. My father showed me the gifts he had bought in anticipation of the long-awaited reunion.

We were still awake after 11:00 P.M. when the phone rang. A man's voice informed my father that he was in the lobby and asked him to come down. He said he could easily be identified because he was a Hasidic Jew. Papa dressed quickly and went to the lobby. A Hasidic man approached, handed him a thick envelope, turned, and left immediately.

Back in his hotel room, we found, to our astonishment, that the envelope contained many of Chaim's personal documents.

Several papers revealed that Chaim had been using a mixture of identities. He had managed to obtain a Mexican driver's license and U.S. credit cards under the false name of David Mizrarhi.

Photographs showed Chaim and the children on the sidewalk in front of the black wrought-iron fence that surrounds the White House in Washington, D.C. Chaim stood in profile, a white shirt breaking the monochromatic black of his clothing. His hands were thrust into the pockets of his overcoat. Marina and Moriah, wearing identical green-and-black-plaid winter coats, stood on either side of him. Both girls were smiling and appeared to be looking at something in the distance. Judging from their heavy clothing and the brown and orange foliage in the background, the picture appeared to have been taken in autumn, and a date on the photo confirmed that conclusion. On the back of

the print, someone had written "Oct. '88" and, in Hebrew, identified the children by their Hasidic names. The writer noted, "As
usual Josef is running away." I grinned. That was Simon all right;
he always hated to have his picture taken.

Another photo, apparently taken at the same time, showed
the children eating sandwiches. In the background was a van with
darkly tinted windows.

Chaim's personal phone directory contained the addresses
and telephone numbers of Rebbe Ezekiel Tauber, who had told
our infiltrator, Nechemiah, that the children were in London, and
a certain Y. Borochov—the man who had put Judas in contact
with Chaim. Borochov lived at Eight Maple Terrace, the Monsey
address that Abraham had originally supplied. There was also a
letter to the Hasidic community from Rebbe Tauber, which declared that I was the one who had illegally kidnapped the children. The document read:

> This letter is to prove that the holder of it is Chaim
> Yarden. It is in fact unthinkable to admit that his three
> children had been kidnapped (his two girls and his son)
> against their will and taken to another country and placed in
> a Catholic orphanage.
>
> After months and years of strong efforts, Mr. Yarden,
> with the help of God, has succeeded in taking them back
> from the clutches of those who retained his children in
> unpure places, in order to entrust them to religious Jewish
> institutions so that they will be educated following the Jewish
> rules.
>
> On top of this, Mr. Yarden had been obliged (no other
> choice) to take his children to a religious Israeli family where
> the children can get the teaching of the Torah as told by our
> ancestors.
>
> With the help of God, we can see how the children are
> blooming and how their beauty and how the grace of the
> Israeli people reflects on their faces.
>
> Unfortunately, all this takes a lot of money because Mr.

Yarden has to provide all the needs of the children, because
he wants their education to be done in the best conditions
possible.

This is why we ask our Israeli (religious) brothers to
help Mr. Yarden so that he can continue to educate his
children as to the rituals of Israel; for this mitzvah, God will
protect us as well as all the Israeli people.

The letter bore the official rabbinical court stamp and the
signature of Rebbe Tauber.

Another document indicated that Borochov had housed the
children in his Monsey home.

There was a wedding invitation sent to Chaim and the children, indicating yet another address in Monsey where they must
have lived for a time.

Still other papers indicated that Chaim, although he had
never divorced me, had married Iris Buttel, the registered tenant
of the Forty-third Street apartment where he had been living.

We did not know what to make of all this. But we realized
that we now had a number of important leads and wondered who
our mysterious benefactor might be. This was a very strong signal
that some of the Hasidim were on *our* side.

34

Sarah's Story

It seemed like the phone had been ringing all evening, ever since Shabbat ended. Something was going on, but I didn't know what. Finally, Mrs. Brown told Rachel and me to pack our suitcases. "Someone is coming for you at nine o'clock," she said.

"Is it our father?" I asked.

"No, someone else."

"What about Josef?"

"Josef is going too."

At nine o'clock a man came to pick us up. Rachel carried her favorite doll with her to play with in the car. First we went to pick up Josef. Then we drove for a long, long time. The man did not want to talk to us. Every time we tried to speak, he gave us a piece of moon-shaped candy to eat. We offered him one of the candies, but he just said, "Uh-uh," and kept on driving.

Finally we arrived at what seemed like a very safe place, because there was a guard at the gatehouse entrance.

Inside the gate, we stopped at a large house. The driver was in a hurry. He made us get out of the car so fast that Rachel forgot her doll on the ledge of the backseat. She was very unhappy.

The big house belonged to Mr. and Mrs. Jacobovich. All the

furniture was covered in plastic. As soon as we got there, they told us it was time to go to bed, so we did. We were very tired.

In the morning when we woke up we saw so many people. Mr. and Mrs. Jacobovich had twelve children, and they were all lined up to meet us. It was hard to remember the names.

We learned that we were living on a street called Kasho Drive.

35

On Monday, January 30, Belgian authorities formally requested the extradition of Chaim Yarden. Mr. Flament, an official at the Belgian Consulate in New York City, agreed to attend the extradition hearing, indicating by his presence that Belgian authorities were interested in the case.

My father and I spent the day at the ICTS offices near Fifty-sixth Street, awaiting news of the children. We sat for hours, hoping that something would happen. Each time the phone rang we jumped.

Some of the ICTS people pressured my father to pay the promised thirty thousand dollars to Abraham, but Papa resisted, arguing that the agreement called for him to pay the fee in return for the children. We had Chaim, but we did not yet have the children. Abraham would receive nothing, he declared. I agreed with him, but I was surprised at the vehemence in his voice. I realized that, for two years, he had devoted his life to this search. Now, he was emotionally, financially, and physically drained. Yet he still had to carry on. The hunt was not over, but the hunter was exhausted. I worried about his health.

Chaim would not give any helpful information to the police, so our best hope was to get more information from Judas. But he called the ICTS office, crying in fear. "Don't ever contact me," he pleaded. "I don't want to know anything. It will bring me nothing but trouble." We realized now that the marshals, as well as Arad, had made a critical error in judgment. At the moment of Chaim's arrest, the marshals had merely pushed Judas aside, when they could have made a show of "arresting" him too. To compound the error, Arad had shoved an envelope of money at the informant. Word quickly spread throughout the Hasidic community: Judas had betrayed a Jew to a non-Jew. He was branded as a turncoat, useless to us for any more undercover work.

We learned disturbing news. At the police station one day, an officer sought us out and remarked in an offhand manner that, very soon after Chaim's arrest, two men claiming to be rebbes had come into the precinct house. Speaking with the desk officer, they offered to turn over the children in exchange for Chaim's release. Unfortunately, the desk officer knew nothing of the Yarden case. He told the two men that the officer in charge of the case was not in and asked them to come back later. He dismissed them without even getting their names, and they never returned. It was an opportunity lost.

Papa and I were extremely frustrated. And I wondered: What kind of people are we dealing with, who want to trade children for a man?

My father rented a car. Accompanied by Arad, we drove to Monsey and snooped around, attempting to speak with people who knew Chaim. The Hasidim were very cold to us, and I realized why the surveillance had failed to find the children. The Hasidic neighborhood of Monsey is such a closed community that the presence of a strange car is sure to raise an immediate alarm. Perhaps the children had, indeed, been inside the house at Eight Maple Terrace but had been spirited away under cover of darkness. We did not know, but we decided to try to find out.

Papa parked in front of Eight Maple Terrace, the split-level residence of the man we knew as Y. Borochov. We knocked on the door and waited. A Hasidic man, perhaps in his sixties, answered. Arad identified us and asked for Mr. Borochov.

"I am Borochov," the man answered.

Arad asked if we could come in.

"*You* may," Borochov said, indicating Arad and my father. "*She* may not."

I returned to the car to wait. It was painful, knowing that the men were inside talking about my children, and I—the mother—was banished. I wondered: Why am I so obedient? Why do I so easily do what I'm told, like a trained puppy?

With Arad and my father, Borochov was surprisingly talkative. He worked in the diamond business, he said. He admitted that he knew Chaim very well. In fact, Iris Buttel had lived in this house with Borochov's family before she married Chaim. He said that the two of them, Chaim and Iris, had spent Shabbat with him six days before Chaim's arrest. He acknowledged that the children had, for a time, lived in his home, and he even took his visitors to a room on the ground floor. Pointing to the four beds, he said to my father, "This is where your grandchildren and Chaim had been sleeping."

But Borochov insisted that he had no idea the children had been kidnapped. Arad pointed out the seriousness of the situation. From the moment of Chaim's arrest, the case of the three missing youngsters became far more than a parental kidnapping. Somewhere, certain of Chaim's allies in the Hasidic community, people were now participating in what was legally a stranger abduction, and they could face serious penalties.

Borochov grew solemn. He vowed that now that he knew the truth of the situation, he would help us locate the children.

They arranged a second meeting, and this time Rebbe Tauber would be there as well.

We spent more frustrating days at the ICTS office, waiting for something to happen. This was, as we say in French, *les temps morts* (dead time). Sometimes I took long walks along Broadway, from Times Square toward downtown.

In the evenings Papa and I sat in our hotel suite, desperate for the telephone to ring. Once or twice we tried to relieve the stress by going to a movie, but neither of us could concentrate.

We existed on our strange separate schedules. Papa went to bed by 8:00 P.M., leaving me alone to fill the void of the night. I spent hours working on a variety of intricate jigsaw puzzles. As I prowled the claustrophobic rooms of our suite, my early feelings of giddiness gave way to anxiety and apprehension. Always my mind buzzed with questions: What will it be like? Will they run to me and throw their arms around me? Will they be scared? Will they remember me? What have they been told? Will we have to get to know one another all over again?

In the mornings, when I rose about 8:00 A.M., I knew that I would find Papa across the street in a coffee shop, where he lingered after breakfast, waiting for me.

For the second meeting with Borochov I dressed conservatively. I wore a plain green knee-length skirt with thick tights to cover my legs. My pale-pink sweater came up to my neck. I wore a small jacket, matching my skirt, that covered my arms.

Still, Borochov refused to let me in. He used the excuse that I was a woman, but it was clear that he did not wish to be confronted directly with the mother of the children.

It was dark and cold in the car, and I shivered with apprehension. I was alone, in a community of people who viewed me as an enemy. I saw a middle-aged Hasid approach the house, and I realized that he must be Rebbe Tauber. His eyes stared through me as if I did not exist.

We knew from Chaim's papers that Tauber was intimately involved in the conspiracy to keep my children away from me, and now, in conversation with Arad and my father, he was wary. He acknowledged that he had written the letter of recommendation for Chaim and had signed it. Like Borochov, he claimed that he did not know where the children were but he did have certain contacts who might point us in the proper direction. First, he needed assurance. He told my father that he wanted a promise in writing that we would not sue him, Borochov, or anyone else who had been involved with my children. Then he would make discreet inquiries.

This development energized my father. He checked with our New York lawyer, Franklyn H. Snitow, who advised that such a document would not be binding, since it was executed under duress. In other words, we could promise not to sue, then get the children back and sue anyway. Our interest was not to recover money but to maintain legal leverage over Tauber and his friends. Knowing this, my father agreed. Snitow prepared the document. We signed it and took it to Tauber, along with a file of official papers showing that I had legal custody of the children in Belgium and that the old Haifa court decision, granting custody to Chaim, had been canceled. Tauber stepped from his office onto the porch and took the papers from me but refused to speak.

More nervous days followed as we lingered at the ICTS office. Tauber did not call.

That weekend, unable to wait any longer, my father phoned Rebbe Tauber to see what had been done and if there was any news.

Yes, Tauber replied, he had been able to contact some people. Then he said, "Okay, I will do everything that's possible for the kids to be back within a few days."

"That's it!" my father said as he hung up the phone. "We've got the children." He wanted to drink a toast.

My reaction was hostile and spontaneous. "We don't have them!" I barked. "We don't have them until we have them." I remembered my disappointment over the little girl in London, whom I thought was Moriah, and I would not allow my hopes to build.

"Patsy," my father shot back, "nothing is ever good enough for you. Whatever we do for you, it is never good enough!"

We argued sharply. Both of us were ready to explode.

My suspicions were correct. Rebbe Tauber was quick with promises, but his actions seemed to be simple stalling tactics.

When my father next spoke to him, the rebbe added another condition: Chaim claimed that, long ago, I had converted to Judaism. That meant the children were Jews. Tauber said that if I could prove I had never converted, then the children were not Jewish and the community would have no further interest in them.

That was his assignment to me: Patsy, prove that you are not a Jew.

Three weeks after Chaim's arrest, we still had no trace of the children. My father had been in New York for a full month, and it was time to go home. We would allow the police and the private detectives to do their work. Then, we would return for Chaim's extradition hearing.

As the airplane took off from JFK International Airport, through blurry eyes I looked down at the endless rows of tenements and town houses. In my mind, I spoke to Marina, Simon, and Moriah: I have to leave you, at least for now. I'm sorry.

I wanted to cry. But I forced back the tears.

I thought about the man at my side. I was extremely grateful for everything that Papa and Maman had done. They had spent a small fortune to search for their grandchildren. More important, they had been available for any task, regardless of the physical and emotional cost. Now they were spent.

Papa slept.

When I finally arrived home in Brussels, I unpacked slowly, suffering from a severe case of depression aggravated by jet lag. I came upon the toys that my father had bought for the children and placed them in a corner.

I found myself constantly watching the clock, subtracting six hours from the time and thinking: The kids are waking up now; they are probably going to school; eating lunch. On Friday night, six hours after sundown in Belgium, I said to myself: Shabbat begins for them now.

It was difficult to concentrate on my work. My body was in

Brussels, but my heart was in New York. My boss understood this and tried to make allowances, but I could sense his frustration.

Hearing that I was planning a return trip to New York, a friend told me about her former secretary, Sabine Tarter, who was married to a man with dual Belgian-American citizenship. Sabine lived in Beacon, New York, almost midway between Albany and Manhattan—and less than one hour's drive from Monsey. This woman had told Sabine of my situation, and Sabine had said that I was welcome to stay with her when I came back to the States. I assumed that I would stay in a hotel suite with my father. Nevertheless, I copied Sabine's number into my notebook. This was a kind and generous offer from a total stranger.

Back in New York for Chaim's extradition hearing, Papa and I were both dismayed to hear Chaim's lawyer, Richard Finkle, contend that the crime was not severe enough to warrant extradition. He argued that, under a new U.S.–Belgian treaty, Chaim would have to face a sentence of *more* than one year before the U.S. government could extradite him. In Belgium, Chaim had been convicted *in absentia* and sentenced to *exactly* one year in jail—one day short of the minimum requirement. This raised the very real possibility that we would not be able to force him back to Belgium to serve his sentence. And in America he had been convicted of nothing. He could go free. Our link to the children would be lost.

It would take time and additional hearings to resolve the matter. We were extremely concerned that, yielding to community pressure, the judge might set bail. And no matter what amount the judge determined, the wealthy Hasidic community could, and undoubtedly would, raise it immediately.

But, to our relief, the judge denied bail on the grounds that Chaim was not an American citizen and had already exhibited a tendency to flee. He would remain in a cell at the Manhattan Correctional Center until the courts decided what to do with him.

These developments were extremely frustrating. There was such a simple solution. All Chaim had to do was give the children back and we would drop the charges. With much trepidation, I decided that I had to confront him face to face.

My father and I rode a subway to a downtown plaza dominated by the large, modern, brown building known as the Manhattan Correctional Center. Presenting papers that identified me as Mrs. Chaim Yarden, I asked to visit my husband. We waited for more than an hour before I was allowed upstairs with other waiting visitors. My father remained downstairs. I was taken to a large, open room where other visitors chatted with inmates. Everyone moved freely about the room, between the metal-and-plastic institutional furniture and the vending machines that lined one wall.

I composed my words: Okay, Chaim, you took the kids and you got away with it for two years. But we caught you and now you are in jail. Just tell me where the children are, and we can all get on with our lives.

Much time passed before a guard approached and asked tentatively, "Mrs. Yarden?"

"Yes."

"Your husband refuses to see you."

"Can't you persuade him?" I asked. "I came especially from Belgium for this visit. It's very important."

The guard disappeared for many minutes. When he returned he reported, "No. He refuses."

I looked about. All visitors were supposed to stay for a designated time. Then we were to be escorted out together. "Listen," I said to the guard, "I'm not going to stay here with everybody. I want to go."

He tried to refuse, but I persisted until he phoned for a special escort. I felt very silly as I left, knowing that the guards must be laughing at me and thinking: What kind of wife is she, who comes all the way from Belgium and her husband refuses to see her?

Father could not stay in the States very long on this trip. He made his return-flight reservation, but I kept my ticket open. I was determined to remain, at least for a while. There were several people I wanted to visit.

One of those meetings would take place in a few days. Arad had arranged for me to speak with the Brooklyn police investigator who was handling the case, and he told me how to reach the office by subway from Grand Central Station. He gave me the man's business card, which identified him as Det. Shirripa of the Sixty-sixth Precinct. *Det?* I thought. I had never before heard of this unusual first name, but I knew that my English needed polishing. Arad explained that he was the man who interrogated Chaim immediately after his arrest. It was important that I remain in New York for this meeting.

But I did not wish to stay in a hotel by myself, so I finally called Sabine Tarter. On the telephone, I found her to be very gracious. In a warm voice, she repeated the invitation for me to stay with herself and her family. The thought of being surrounded by a French-speaking Belgian family, rather than by the bleak walls of an empty hotel room, was appealing. I accepted.

At the appointed time, I met Paul Tarter at Grand Central Station. He had thinning black hair and a beard. An obviously brilliant man, he specialized in the field of satellite communications. During the ninety-minute train ride, he tried to explain his work to me, but it was difficult to understand. He asked a few questions about my search for the children, and he proved to be a good listener.

It was blustery and snowy outside when we arrived in Beacon, but Sabine's friendly French greeting and her outgoing personality instantly warmed me. She was about my age and a bit taller. She had prepared a wonderful dinner of Japanese food, and she wore a kimono, completing the outfit with long needles in her dark hair. It was her way of saying: relax, be at home, have some fun.

Sabine and Paul had three children. The eldest was a girl named Marjorie, about Marina's age; I studied her carefully and thought: I wonder what Marina looks like now. The youngest was barely four months old and caused me to think wistfully about babies. It was nice to be around youngsters again. Sabine missed her family and friends in Belgium, and we passed the time sharing news and getting acquainted.

The morning of the scheduled meeting with Det. Shirripa, I found myself running late. After a brisk twenty-minute hike from Sabine's house to the station, I arrived to see the train pulling away. The next train would not leave for another hour. Concerned that I might upset the police investigator, I found a pay telephone and dialed the number on his business card. To my dismay, I heard strange electrical tones, followed by a recorded message advising me: "Your call cannot be completed as dialed. Please check the number and dial again." I tried once more, but I heard another strange tone and another frustrating message. When I dialed the operator, she mumbled something about coins, but I could not understand. I rushed back to Sabine's home for help.

"What number did you dial?" Sabine asked. I pulled out the business card and showed her. Sabine thought for a moment and asked, "Did you dial *one* first?"

"No."

"That's the problem. When you call long distance, you have to dial *one* first."

"Oh." This was a very confusing country.

Sabine placed the call for me and informed Det. Shirripa that I would be late.

I hurried back to the train station and hoped that Det. Shirripa would not be upset at my late arrival.

My anxiety increased during the long train ride into the city and the subway trip to the office in Brooklyn. The moment I arrived, I apologized for being late. "I'm sorry, Det.," I said.

The man looked puzzled. He asked, "Why do you call me 'Det.'?"

"Oh, I'm sorry, Mr. Shirripa. I should not use your first name?"

He studied his own business card and grinned. " 'Det.' is not my first name," he explained. "It's an abbreviation. It's short for 'Detective.'"

I felt my face grow warm. I felt like an idiot.

We spoke for some time about the case and about how we might pressure Chaim to deliver the children. I briefed the investigator on the information delivered so mysteriously to my father, and I also supplied him with several photographs of the children. He promised that he would study the details of the case and scheduled another meeting with me.

When I left the office I felt extremely proud of myself. At last, I had accomplished something on my own.

Sabine and Paul allowed me to use their telephone freely; I kept a record of all my calls so that I could reimburse them. Now that I knew the procedure, I made call after call to Rebbe Tauber, Borochov, and anyone else who might be able to help. With a Monsey telephone book in front of me, I called everyone who had the word *rebbe* in front of his name. Most of the time I left messages on answering machines. Few called me back. No one offered real help.

It helped to know that a warm meal and friendly French conversation waited for me at the end of every long day. As a young mother herself, Sabine felt great empathy for my problems, and she also knew that I needed some relief from the pressure. When I had a bit of free time, she took me shopping and she introduced me to her hobby of making crafts. Sitting together, working with our hands to create little trinkets, we got to know much about one another. Like Walter, Sabine seemed to know when I wanted to talk and when I needed to be silent. She never intruded on my thoughts or my privacy, yet she was always there when I needed her.

I knew that I had to return to my job in Belgium, but I planned to come back to America soon. Whether or not my presence was legally required, I was determined to be there for the next extradition proceeding, to demonstrate to the court that I was a concerned mother.

Sabine and Paul extended their invitation for me to stay with them whenever I needed to come back to New York.

Once again, as the airplane took off, I apologized silently to Marina, Simon, and Moriah. I'm sorry for leaving you, I said. I'll be back soon. Next time I will find you.

I was in an agitated state during the entire flight to Brussels; I found it impossible to sleep during the seven-hour, overnight journey. For some reason, I was haunted by thoughts of the little girl in London whom I had mistakenly identified as Moriah. I wondered how I could possibly have allowed myself to be taken back to Belgium as we awaited the DNA test results. Despite the judge's restraining order, how could I have left London at such a time? Why didn't I camp out near the apartment to keep an eye on the family, just in case they tried to run? How could I have been so passive?

Patsy, I berated myself, if you really loved your children you would have slept in the street in front of that house to make sure nobody tried to get away. My head knew that I could not have done this, but my heart told me I should have.

Like a slap in the face, I was struck by the realization that I had been totally passive during the entire two-year ordeal. Whenever the ICTS detectives—or anyone else—uncovered information concerning the children, they reported directly to my father. He, in turn, filtered the information to me. When my father and I were together in a meeting, police officers, attorneys, and private detectives spoke to him and ignored me. I knew that everyone was trying to shelter me from additional stress or disappointment, but they seemed to forget that we were talking about *my* children. This was mostly my fault. I had allowed everyone to lead me through the past two years as if I were a helpless child instead of an angry and determined mother. Increasingly, I bristled whenever my father—with the best of intentions—attempted to overprotect his little girl.

I reminded myself: You are twenty-eight years old. *You* are the mother of these children, and it is *your* responsibility to find them.

36

"We have a problem," my father said.

Dominique Buysschaert listened carefully, growing increasingly interested as he learned the details of our dilemma. A smooth, cultured advocate, Buysschaert was a partner in the prestigious Brussels law firm of DeBacker & Associés. My father knew him as a specialist in commercial law; but now we sought his help on a criminal matter. Buysschaert was immediately interested, for his son had been a schoolmate of Simon's at Sint Jozef's. He had followed news reports concerning the case.

My father explained the contention of Chaim's lawyer that the one-year sentence was too short—by a single day—to warrant extradition.

Buysschaert agreed to represent us in the case, viewing it as a new and intriguing challenge. "I am amazed that you were able to obtain his arrest without real judicial and legal assistance in Belgium," he said. Buysschaert would oversee the case, and he enlisted the aid of attorney Patrick Mandoux, a specialist in criminal law and assistant professor at Université Libre de Bruxelles, to assist him. As Chaim's lawyer asserted, they determined that U.S. and Belgian officials had negotiated a new extradition treaty which did indeed require a sentence of more than one year. *But that treaty had not yet been ratified.*

Paul Jenard, an employee of the Foreign Ministry, obtained a copy of the existing treaty, the 1902 extradition convention between the U.S. and Belgium. As Buysschaert and Mandoux studied it, their analysis revealed that it did not establish a length-of-sentence requirement; rather, the extradition convention was based upon categories of crimes. The most recent revision of the convention, on November 14, 1966, added kidnapping to the categories of covered crimes. The lawyers were confident that this convention was the one currently in force and that we could persuade the U.S. to extradite Chaim. But they knew the process would be lengthy, involving several court appearances in New York.

In Brussels, the case was now assigned to prosecutor Nadia De Vroede, a brilliant specialist in children's law who enjoyed a reputation for tenacity. She began to study the details of the case but knew that she could not become actively involved until—and unless—Chaim was returned to Belgium.

Private detectives were too expensive, and I reasoned that I could remain in contact with the Hasidim as effectively as they. I decided that I would become like the persistent little bug that will not go away. I resolved: I'm going to speak to so many people that maybe someday I'll speak to the right person, the one who will agree to help me. Maybe there was only a small chance that this strategy would work, but I had to take that chance. I purchased a thick green notebook with the intention of keeping a written record of contacts, telephone numbers, addresses, and everything that I did to search for the children.

I calculated that if I was careful to take advantage of special air fares, I could afford to fly to the U.S. once every month or six weeks. This would allow me to attend Chaim's court hearings and to continue to seek information about my children.

I found a helpful travel agent who arranged for a low-priced airline ticket. She explained that I could save one hundred dollars by flying from Luxembourg instead of Brussels. The aircraft would stop in Iceland before continuing on to New York, but that inconvenience was worth a hundred dollars to me. The travel agent suggested that I leave on a Saturday, so that I would have a full day to recover from the journey before I began my activities on Monday. My father saw an additional benefit in this plan. "By traveling on Saturday," he said, "you can be sure that no Hasids will be on the plane."

I called Sabine to let her know that I was coming and told her of my plans. My first priority was to be present in court, but I would also visit with Detective Shirripa to check on the progress of the case. I would contact the National Center for Missing and Exploited Children to see what help they could provide, and I would somehow get the necessary documentation to prove to Rebbe Tauber that I had never converted to Judaism.

I was reluctant to approach Père Albert at St. Paul's. As I anticipated, when I asked him for written verification of my Roman Catholic baptism he provided it, but he also scolded me for my lack of church attendance. I sidestepped the issue with the disclaimer that I spent most of my weekends searching for the children or relaxing in Nassogne. Père Albert also provided baptismal certificates for the children, showing that all three of them had been christened as Roman Catholics after I had left Chaim.

I also visited the religious Jew who had circumcised Simon and asked him to verify, in writing, that the simple surgical procedure had not been a religious ritual. He was reluctant to do so, but I drew his wife aside and asked her to intervene. "There is nothing bad about saying the truth," I argued. She finally agreed and persuaded her husband to sign the document.

I wrote an affidavit declaring that I had never converted to Judaism and swore to its authenticity in the presence of a notary.

Armed with my documentation, I was confident I could prove to Rebbe Tauber that I had never converted and, thus, the children were not Jewish. If I were a Jew, I would have insisted upon a religious circumcision. If I were a Jew, why would I have had the children baptized as Christians *after* I left Chaim? Jewish law states clearly that the children are of the mother's religion.

My spirits rose whenever I contemplated the possibility of locating the children, but they plummeted when I realized the enormity of the task. I happened to be in a surly mood when, a few days before my trip, I answered a knock on the door to find two women whom I did not know. One of them, a bright-faced woman carrying a stuffed suitcase, introduced herself. "Hi," she said cheerily, "I'm Danielle Willeput, Sabine's sister."

"Hi," I responded without enthusiasm. I knew that the suitcase was filled with gifts to be delivered to Sabine and her family—chocolates, cheeses, hams. I thought: What am I, a donkey, that I have to carry all this stuff?

Danielle said, "I'm bringing—"

"Okay," I interrupted. I dragged the heavy suitcase inside and shut the door in her face.

Within minutes I was overcome with shame. My own troubles were no excuse for such rude behavior. I searched for the scrap of paper where I had scrawled Danielle's number, called her, and apologized. She was very gracious; she said that she understood the pressure I was under. We spoke long enough for me to know that she shared her sister's compassion as well as her sense of humor. Their maiden name was Ryons, which means, "Let's laugh." It fit their personalities.

By the time I hung up the phone, I knew that my bad manners had been forgiven and that I had a new friend and ally in Brussels.

I sustained myself throughout the long flights with the thought that the closer I got to the States, the closer I got to my children. Each time I hoped this would be the time I would find them.

From JFK International Airport, I took a bus to Grand Central Station and a train to the suburbs.

By the time I arrived at Sabine's home, it was late Saturday afternoon for her but approaching midnight in Belgium. I was truly exhausted. Sabine was in the midst of cooking dinner. She greeted me warmly but announced with mock severity that she planned to keep me awake throughout the evening, so that I would get a good night's sleep and begin to adjust to the time change. She was excited about the suitcase full of treats from Danielle.

After dinner we sat at the kitchen table and talked as Sabine painted small, intricate wooden figures. Her easygoing personality helped relax me as I prepared for the week ahead. I had many places to go, many people to see.

Rebbe Tauber had two telephone numbers. One was for his shul and the other was for his living quarters. Both were located in the same building.

The rebbe proved very elusive. I called him from Sabine's home and left a polite message on his answering machine, informing him that I was back in the States and had proof that neither I nor my children were Jewish. I waited impatiently for him to return the call, but nothing happened. His wife answered my next call. I repeated my message, and she promised to tell her husband.

Frustrating days passed. I called back several times, sometimes speaking to the answering machine, sometimes speaking to his wife or one of the children. With each call, I grew more insistent and abrasive, until finally, with obvious great reluctance, he spoke with me.

Over the phone I described the evidence I had assembled: baptismal certificates from the Roman Catholic church, a signed statement declaring that Simon's circumcision was not a spiritual ritual, and my sworn affidavit.

Tauber quickly dismissed all of my effort with the statement, "You converted *after* all of this."

"I did not," I argued. "Prove to me that I did convert."

He responded, "Chaim said so."

"He lied to you."

"No, he's a Jew." The rebbe closed the conversation in a

whiny, heavily accented voice, saying, "I have promised I would help you. Now stop calling me. I cannot help you if you are bothering me all the time."

So there it was. "He's a Jew" were the rebbe's code words meaning: He's a good religious man who follows all the rules of the Satmar teachings—and you do not. Tauber would accept Chaim's story at face value simply because he wore the proper clothing and knew the correct words. I could prove that I and the children were baptized Roman Catholics, but how could I establish that we had *never* converted to Judaism? It was impossible to prove a negative. It was like trying to prove to Chaim that I was a virgin *after* I slept with him. I suspected that the rebbe had set me on this task simply as a stalling tactic. I had wasted time, effort, and money, and, in the meantime, the children's trail had grown colder.

As the days passed, I attempted to develop leads. I checked in with Detective Shirripa, but he had no new information. I doubted that his office was either willing or able to give much effort to the case.

In the New York area there were at least fifty different offices for Jewish Legal Services. Each one I contacted sent me in another direction. I felt like a beanbag being passed from one person to the next. I was caught in a dizzying circle. The Hasidic Jews refused to help, and the non-Hasidic Jews, the people who were willing to help, were ineffective because they had no influence on the Satmar community. The circle continued to spin.

I tried to locate our informant, Judas, to see if the offer of additional money might lure more information from him. But he had moved from his house in Monsey and had left no trace of his whereabouts. I knew that he was afraid.

I realized that Chaim's arrest, instead of leading me to the children, had actually impeded the search. An adult on the run leaves a trail that investigators can follow: cashed checks, credit-card receipts, telephone records, airline reservations, visa applications, and other bits of traceable information. But children are much more difficult to follow. We did not even know what names to use in our search. We knew that they had been given Jewish names during their "conversion" ritual in London, but there was nothing to stop Chaim and others from giving them additional identities. The children I knew as Marina, Simon, and Moriah were like wisps of smoke that had disappeared into the atmosphere.

With each failure my spirits plunged. I was so close to the children that I could almost hear them crying out to me. They had to be hidden in one of these secretive communities. And yet I was so far from them too.

In the bleakest of times, I started to think that perhaps I should let Chaim go free. Then, at least, the children would have one parent.

I waited nervously. A man named Jim Stanco was due at Sabine's house momentarily. He was from the Albany Clearinghouse of the National Center for Missing and Exploited Children. I was desperate for his help but not looking forward to telling my story once again from the beginning.

Sabine had prepared a small buffet of sandwiches, cakes, and cookies for our meeting. Right on time, a car pulled into the drive and a man approached the front door.

I liked Stanco immediately. In his forties, with thinning black hair and a round, jovial shape, he had a warm, vibrant personality and listened intently to all the details of the case. He asked many questions. Stanco pledged his full support in such a sincere manner that I almost wanted to throw my arms about him in sheer joy. At last I had found someone committed to action.

When I complained that Detective Shirripa seemed to be going nowhere with his investigation, Stanco suggested, "Why don't you visit the D.A.'s office?"

"What is that?" I asked.

Realizing that I knew little about the U.S. criminal justice system, he gave me a basic explanation. In Belgium, there is a national police force, and each community has a local police force.

But in America there are various police organizations for the fed-eral government, the states, counties, cities, townships, boroughs, and villages. It was all very confusing. Stanco explained that each jurisdiction also has its own prosecuting arm. I had been dealing with a precinct detective. But the district attorney's office would also have assigned one or more people to monitor the case. These people would know a great deal about the Hasidic community, since the Brooklyn neighborhoods of Williamsburg and Borough Park contain such concentrated populations of religious Jews. Stanco strongly advised me to introduce myself to officials at the Brooklyn D.A.'s office. Then they would see me as a real person, rather than as an abstract Belgian woman whom they knew only from the court record.

"I'll do it," I said.

Stanco took copies of my photographs and explained that he would create posters prominently featuring the images of Marina, Simon, and Moriah. These would be displayed in and around Hasidic neighborhoods. We hoped that there were some Hasids who would side with us, at least quietly. Perhaps these posters would induce someone to call the center's toll-free, confidential tele-phone number with information that would lead us to the children.

Finally, Stanco suggested that I call him after every meeting I had with anyone—a police officer, a lawyer, a rebbe, a reporter. We would discuss what I had learned and where I should go next.

Stanco's visit filled me with enthusiasm and hope. He was the first person I had met from any sort of official organization who seemed ready to take charge of the case. When he left, I stood at Sabine's front door and stared out the small window after him, like a movie heroine watching her hero depart.

37

Sarah's Story

Each time we moved, there were new rules to learn. The people were different. Even the prayers were different.

Mr. and Mrs. Jacobovich were very strict. We were not allowed to speak any English, but sometimes we sneaked downstairs and spoke to each other anyway.

They sent us to school right away. The girls' school was in very bad shape. The top floor was dangerous and could not be used. Once, a man came from a newspaper and took some pictures. The paper printed a story about the school, and my picture was in the paper.

We almost didn't learn anything. School wasn't as important for the girls as it was for the boys. Our teachers were not paid and sometimes they didn't even come to school. When that happened, we just played.

Rachel should have been in the first grade, but they put her in a class with all third-graders. She hated her school and her teacher.

After school, Josef had to study, but Rachel and I had chores to do. Rachel had to clean the toilets and she hated it. I had to do the dishes all the time. At first there was a dishwasher, and it was easier. But then the dishwasher broke and Mrs. Jacobovich said she didn't have to get it fixed. I guess that was because I was the new dishwasher. It was very hard because I was so short and the sink was so high. Sometimes I could use the small kitchen stool, but if somebody else needed it, I had to let them have it. There were a lot of dishes and pots and pans to feed seventeen people every meal.

Every night I had to vacuum the downstairs. It was a big house and it took me an hour to finish.

38

My boss at Display Point said, "Listen, Patsy, I'm sorry, but you have to make a choice. You have to choose between your work and your kids."

I understood completely. He could not count on me to be around. We were losing track of the inventory. The small office was in a state of confusion. He was not being unkind, merely realistic. And he nodded with sympathy when I said, "I choose my kids."

Before I left for my next trip to the States, Walter suggested that, rather than keep notes on all my conversations, it would be far more efficient and reliable to record my interviews.

I bought a voice-activated tape recorder, small and slender like a cigarette case. I could slip it into my purse and turn it on prior to any important appointment, with or without the knowledge of the person with whom I spoke.

Back in New York, I visited the Brooklyn District Attorney's office and was received cordially by a chief investigator, who assigned Detective Allen Presser to work with me. Presser had very friendly, bright blue eyes and thinning white-blond hair. In a soft, warm voice, he explained that he had been raised as a religious Jew and thus could understand and appreciate what was happening to my children. I decided that I really liked this man.

Together we went through the packet of information that was delivered so mysteriously to my father on the night after Chaim's arrest. Presser was interested, and he suggested that I visit him whenever I was in Brooklyn, so that we could compare notes and share information.

When I told him of my plans to search the Hasidic neighborhoods, he instructed me on survival skills in the big city: wear your purse strap around your neck, not merely over one shoulder; walk close to the curb so that it is more difficult for someone to force you against, or into, a building; never look around as if you are lost or confused—especially on the subway. Presser glanced at my diamond ring and said, "You're crazy to wear that in the city." He advised that I check in with him first, before I went into the neighborhoods; he wanted to keep track of me.

The Hasidim are generally not violent people, but they can be, when they are cornered. One of Presser's colleagues advised me, "Be careful. Don't go alone. You never know what can happen." But I was determined to go. Perhaps my real motivation was to develop a better understanding of this unfamiliar world. Somewhere, Marina, Simon, and Moriah were living as "good little Jews." The Hasidic culture was alien to me, and I desperately sought to understand it.

From my base at Sabine's house in Beacon, I made the long daily journey into the city, culminating with a subway ride to Brooklyn, which took another hour. Whenever possible I walked, so as not to waste money on a taxi.

I became such a regular visitor to the Brooklyn D.A.'s office that the receptionist at the security desk always greeted me with a cheery, "Hi, how are you?" and immediately wrote my name in the visitors' ledger. From there, I frequently headed to Williamsburg or Borough Park.

The Williamsburg enclave consisted of aging one-, two-, and three-story houses that had been converted into apartments.

These were often sandwiched between kosher restaurants and small kosher groceries. Many of these residences had baby carriages chained to their stoops. On average, a Hasidic woman gives birth every two years throughout her childbearing years. It was not unusual for a family of ten to be crammed into a small apartment.

Men in long black coats walked the sidewalks with their heads bowed low, concentrating upon their prayers as a defense against viewing the temptations of the world. I knew that many of these men went straight from their jobs to hours of scriptural study classes.

The scene was much the same in Borough Park, although this was primarily a residential community. To me, both communities were islands of the past set in the sea of the modern world.

Trudging slowly through the streets, my eyes darting quickly to the face of any child who appeared, my mouth ready to respond instantly to anyone willing to talk, I felt very conspicuous. No one volunteered information.

I could not differentiate between Satmars and other Hasidim. There were subtle differences in dress and demeanor that even the Jews could not explain. Perhaps the quiet signals were in the eyes, but I could not read them.

If I saw a Hasidic man on the street, I would try to approach and ask, "Are you a Satmar?" If the answer was yes, I displayed photos and asked if he knew anything about my children. Invariably, while avoiding my eyes, the man would reply that he knew about the case but he did not know where my children were. Then he would hurry away, often muttering, "Ah, but I'm not really a Satmar."

I appeared unannounced at the homes and offices of influential rebbes, attempting to talk my way inside; most of the time I was not granted entry, but occasionally someone listened as I poured out my story.

In the evenings, I called Jim Stanco of the National Center's Albany Clearinghouse to report on the day's activity. He was eternally optimistic, cheering me with comments such as, "You did well. Just keep on."

My eyes quickly spotted every snippet of information in a magazine article or newspaper story relating to the Hasidim. My ears were attuned to any mention of religious Jews. I asked people to recommend books that would teach me more. Someone gave me a small handbook and I read through it several times, underlining passages that interested me.

Over the years, the Hasidim have been able to concentrate their power in Williamsburg. They vote as a bloc and thus gain the attention of local politicians, who, in turn, provide a disproportionate percentage of local services. The Hasidim in Brooklyn have used their resources to exploit the real-estate market, aggressively getting city monies for renovating homes, sometimes making cash purchases at top-of-the-market prices, pressuring neighboring non-Hasidic homeowners to sell. Those who fail to sell gradually find themselves surrounded by more and more families of extremely religious Jews, who multiply their numbers and expand their parochial borders.

The Hasidim take care of and regulate their own. Government agencies that routinely investigate such things as suspected child abuse, domestic violence, and vandalism are impotent in a community that enforces its own value system. The rabbinical court is the final authority. There is even a quasi police force, known as *Shomrim* (Guardian) consisting of volunteers who carry walkie-talkies and cruise the streets in their own cars.

The children are sometimes sent to small, unlicensed schools, where the quality of education—by secular standards—is extremely poor. It is not unusual to find a twelve-year-old Hasidic boy who has only the math skills of a typical second-grade student. Aside from religious writings, he is allowed to read little else but accounts of Jewish history and its defining tragedy, the Holocaust.

The name Satmar is derived from the town of Sztmar, Hungary, where, in the prewar years, Grand Rebbe Joel Teitelbaum led a movement that was vigorously opposed to

Zionism. The grounds for this position were scriptural passages prophesying that the Jews would be dispersed throughout the world until the coming of the Messiah; thus, any attempt to create a Jewish state was premature and antiscriptural. During the various Arab-Israeli wars, the Satmars actually prayed for Israel's defeat.

Most of the Satmar faithful were sent to the gas chambers at Auschwitz when Hitler sentenced Hungarian Jews in 1944. But Rebbe Teitelbaum and the few others who survived migrated to Brooklyn in 1945. Today, nearly every Satmar in Williamsburg is a concentration-camp survivor—or the descendant of one. Some experts believe that most members of the Williamsburg sect suffer from Post-Holocaust Stress Syndrome.

The Holocaust is a subtext to almost every conversation. Schoolchildren study the subject in detail, although the information is limited to stories of Nazi atrocities against the six million Jewish victims; they know nothing of the additional five million non-Jewish Holocaust victims. The Satmar believe that the Holocaust was a punishment for Zionism.

The Satmar use the "Nazi" defense as a convenient argument against anyone with whom they disagree. Often, when I announced to a Hasid that I was looking for my children, stolen away by my husband, I faced a hostile stare. Who was I to disturb their world? Frequently I heard the comment, "Oh, you are the lady who makes very bad publicity for us."

"No," I countered. "You took the children. You made it necessary for me to make the publicity. Is it bad publicity to ask about your children?"

Sometimes a Hasid would call me "Hitler's daughter!" and walk away.

Intertwined with my reconnaissance tours, I met and spoke with a variety of characters who had contact with the Satmar community. Some of these encounters were encouraging, some devastating. Some were even comic. But all carried the potential to swing my mood rapidly between the extremes of hope and despair.

On several occasions I met with a certain Rebbe Greenberg, a polite man who worked for a rabbinical court that handled matters of concern to religious Jews both in the U.S. and Canada. His small office was in lower Manhattan, near Chinatown. He dressed in the typically stern style of the Hasidim, but he seemed more open-minded and accessible than some.

Rebbe Greenberg believed that a person should temper his religious behavior somewhat, to conform to the realities of modern life. He told me the story of a woman who had come to him with another problem that involved the Jewish and Christian cultures. The woman was a Jewish convert whose parents were Christian. Her mother suffered from a serious illness, and the woman wanted to move back with her parents for a time, to help out during the crisis. Her question was: How could she maintain a kosher lifestyle in her mother's house? The rebbe's common-sense advice was: "It's your mother. You cannot reject her. She's not Jewish, so she doesn't have to have a kosher kitchen. You try to do your best, but if it's not one-hundred-percent kosher, God will forgive you, because you do something good."

Rebbe Greenberg brought the same sensible attitude to my case. He listened to my story and asked careful questions. After consulting books on Jewish law, he declared to me, "No, the kids are not Jewish. If they were converted, it was not a good conversion, because if the mother is a non-Jew, she has to give her agreement. By the law, you have a right to your children because they are not Jewish."

This was heartening to hear. It was a weapon that I could use in future discussions. But the victory was theoretical rather than practical. Rebbe Greenberg was not a Satmar, and he admitted that the Satmars held to their own interpretation of the law.

He gave me a very thoughtful piece of advice concerning our use of ICTS. I complained that the expensive Jewish security agents seemed to have had difficulty gaining the cooperation of the Hasidim. Rebbe Greenberg shrugged and said, "What do you expect when Jewish people come to our community—and they are not religious?"

This comment strengthened my resolve to do my own detective work.

Finally, Rebbe Greenberg noted that the mainstream press had covered aspects of my story, but he suggested that much of the coverage would have no impact upon the Jewish community. Perhaps I would have more success if I dealt directly with the Jewish press. He gave me a name to contact: Chaim Shaulson. Perhaps I could place an ad in his newspaper or pay to have an article written.

Shaulson was a native Israeli whose father had been deputy mayor of Jerusalem. He was editor of *Panim Chadachot* (New Faces), a controversial newspaper published in both Hebrew and Yiddish editions. He had published a series of articles detailing strife within the New York Satmar community and thus had created bitter enemies. One local Hasidic leader described the newspaper as "the Hebrew language *National Enquirer.*" The previous May, when a computer repairman attempted to drive away from Shaulson's office at 12:30 A.M., his car was cut off by two others. A man with a hammer smashed his windshield and others dragged him from the car as he screamed, "I'm not Shaulson! I'm not Shaulson!" The Hasidic thugs—as many as a dozen—ignored his protestations and dragged him into one of their cars, where he was beaten, stabbed, and dumped onto the pavement four blocks away; police openly theorized that the attackers had mistaken the computer repairman for the hated editor.

Shaulson's newspaper office was in the basement of his Brooklyn home. The dirty, cramped room was cluttered with floor-to-ceiling stacks of papers. As I attempted to speak with Shaulson, the phone rang constantly. People meandered in and out. It was sheer chaos.

I was extremely nervous. What should I say? What should I do?

To my relief, Shaulson was warm and welcoming, reminiscent of many of the Israelis I had met and liked. The fifty-three-year-old Orthodox Jew was more dark-skinned than light. He dressed in the normal "religious" style but his *peiyot* were short. He had dark, bright, expressive eyes and appeared to be full of nervous energy. Our communication was somewhat strained in the beginning. As we got to know one another, we spoke more freely, half the time in English and half the time in Hebrew. He often emphasized his points by flailing his hands in the air.

Shaulson bragged that his experience as a journalist within the religious community, and the fact that he was Orthodox but not a Satmar, gave him access to information that was impossible for others to find. He hinted that he could use his contacts to help me find the children. But it was clear that he wanted money up front.

By now I was used to this request and wary of it. I gave him my standard reply: "I don't have money, forget about it. If you come up with something real, then I might give you money. I would find a way to borrow it from the bank."

With a thoughtful stare, Shaulson said that he would consider my words.

Shortly thereafter he called me at Sabine's home and asked for a second meeting, saying enigmatically, "Maybe we could find another way."

When I arrived for this discussion, Shaulson shook my hand eagerly. He cleared the office of other people, which was very surprising. Normally it would be forbidden for us to meet alone. Suddenly I realized that, as we say in French, he was "eating me with his eyes."

"I found a way of helping you," he declared. His plan emerged very slowly as he spoke in both English and Hebrew, choosing his words carefully. From what I could understand, he professed to be quite successful in the extortion business. He explained that whenever he suspected an influential Hasidim of cheating on his wife—or sometimes the other way around—he followed the adulterer, generally at night, and gathered the necessary evidence. Then he demanded payment. "If they don't pay," he boasted, "I put it in the newspaper."

I could not believe what I was hearing. When Shaulson paused and left the room for a few moments, I casually reached into my purse for a tissue. My fingers found the switch to my tape recorder, and I turned it on.

When he returned, Shaulson continued to speak haltingly, taking his proposal one small step at a time. As he spoke, he found subtle ways to brush his fingers against mine or place a hand on my shoulder. I struggled to grasp the meaning of his words. It sounded as if he was suggesting that he would pay for me to live in a small basement apartment nearby, where I would serve as his mistress in exchange for any information he might uncover. Justifying his lust, he demurred, "We are men, you know, like all men. We have certain needs."

"How can you ask me that?" I said. "I am looking for my children and you ask me to do this?"

He pinched his thumb against the first two fingers of his hand and shook his fist back and forth, as if to say: Wait a minute. Listen to me. Let me explain. "But you are a shiksa," he said. "There is nothing bad for you to sleep with men. All of you shiksas are doing it and you may do it, and that's it, it's nothing. Every day you can change from man to man, and nothing bad. Our wives may not, but you may."

A vulgar phrase that I had heard in Israel came to mind: *It's a mitzvah to f—— a shiksa.* I was so taken aback by his proposition that I cast my eyes downward and mumbled, "It is not always like that. We are not all like that."

"Well, you don't have so many rules to keep. It's not so important for you."

I suppose I should have slapped Shaulson and stormed out of his office. But, as shocked as I was, I did not immediately turn him down. I wanted all the information I could get from this man, even if he was repulsive. So I said nothing, tacitly giving him permission to detail his scheme further.

After he had personally schooled me in the art of being a

Hasidic mistress, he explained, I would be placed into a Satmar home—a rebbe's house would be best—as a cleaning lady. He said that I would be introduced as a Polish girl who did not understand Hebrew or Yiddish. I should not speak, lest a French accent betray me. Shaulson continued, "And I will teach you how to seduce a Hasidic man—because you don't seduce a Hasidic man the same way you seduce a Christian one—by making small things when the wife is not there. And then, when you are sure that the man has found that you want to seduce him, you will go to bed with him and, after a while, you will try to take him to bed in another place, and we will have a video there. And we will put everything on the video and we will blackmail him. And then," Shaulson ended with a satisfied flourish, "you will get your children!"

This sleazy proposal was absurd, of course, but, as far as Shaulson was concerned, I remained noncommittal. I told him that I would consider his offer and meet with him again to discuss it further.

During the train ride back to Sabine's home, I tried to convince myself that I had misunderstood some of Shaulson's words. No, Patsy, I said to myself, you must be mistaken. You must have lost your grasp of Hebrew.

Sabine and I listened to the tape recording that I had made. She was as astonished as I was, both by Shaulson's statements in English and my translations of his Hebrew. "No, no," she said, "you are not wrong. You are right."

Working at Sabine's house, I suffered through the tedious job of transcribing the dual-language interview onto paper. I knew that Walter was right in urging me to document my activities, but I realized that the exhausting and time-consuming task of transcribing interviews would bog me down in paperwork and limit my energies. I simply could not do this with every encounter, so I decided to keep the tape recorder with me but only use it to document especially important discussions. For most meetings, I would continue to rely upon handwritten notes.

When the transcript was finally finished, I turned it over to

Allen Presser in the Brooklyn D.A.'s office, hoping that he might be able to pressure Shaulson to cooperate. Presser took me to a lab in the building and copied my microcassette onto a large tape. He also copied my transcription, since I had translated the Hebrew portions. He said, "Well, we can do something with this. This is blackmail."

When he reached me by phone at Sabine's house, a man who identified himself as Rebbe Moreino announced in a cool, somewhat sinister tone, "I want to speak to you. I have something important to say to you." He refused to go into detail on the phone and insisted upon scheduling a meeting.

I was apprehensive but also excited. This was the first time that a Hasidic rebbe had approached me. I immediately informed Jim Stanco and Allen Presser.

"You could try to get information out of that man," Presser suggested. "Maybe he will say something that we can use against him." Worried that the rebbe was setting some sort of trap, Presser convinced me to wear a wire, a small, hidden microphone contained in a belt worn underneath my clothing, so that he could monitor the conversation from a surveillance car outside.

On the day of the meeting, I arrived at the Brooklyn D.A.'s office early. A technician took me into a lab, installed the wire, and laughed when he had difficulty adjusting the belt on my size-five body—skinny from stress. Wires were stretched around my back. I felt like a character in a spy movie.

Presser and another detective would accompany me. They instructed me that if at any point during the meeting I felt I was in danger, I was to use a code word—we decided on the number *eighteen*—in the midst of a sentence, and they would rush inside to my rescue.

Their caution made me nervous. Am I really in danger? I wondered.

On the way to the appointment I suddenly felt self-conscious in my knee-length skirt. Worried that the sight of my legs would offend Rebbe Moreino, I persuaded the detectives to stop at a small boutique. I bought a floor-length beige skirt and explained to Presser that it was so I wouldn't shock the rebbe. "I don't want him to be able to say, 'Look, she doesn't respect me.'"

Rebbe Moreino was very old, very religious, and very careful. He and his wife met me at their home in Borough Park, close to the Forty-third Street apartment where Chaim had been living with Iris Buttel. They led me to a square room with a large table and several chairs. It was closed off from the next room, not by a door, but by a curtain. I assumed this was a precaution so that if the rebbe had to be alone with a woman, the privacy would be minimal.

"I don't trust you," the rebbe said, taking my purse and placing it on a table outside of his office. "Your bag stays outside. We don't know if you are recording."

The rebbe sat across from me at a desk piled high with books. His wife, obviously acting the role of chaperone but saying nothing, assumed a defensive posture at the far side of the room. The rebbe picked up one of his books and, now apparently oblivious to my presence, began to intone prayers. In a voice quivering with anxiety, I attempted to start a conversation, but he held up his right hand with the index finger pointing upward, indicating that I should wait. His ritual continued for many minutes.

I was extremely nervous knowing that two detectives were parked around the corner in an unmarked car, listening to every word as it was spoken. Silently I said to myself, Patsy, don't say anything stupid.

Finally, in what Rebbe Moreino assumed was the privacy of his office, he said, "My wife understands your position perfectly well. She was taken by a Catholic family to protect her from the Nazis. So she understands you, and she is more on your side. But she's not going to speak to you."

I remarked about how lucky she was and glanced at her, but she did not return my gaze. She said nothing.

To my surprise the rebbe declared, "It would have been better if she had died in Auschwitz or Treblinka than to have been with the Christians." I was shocked. I could not believe that he was serious; perhaps he was simply trying to emphasize his antipathy toward Christians. Once more, his wife gave no indication of a response.

Following this absurd preamble, the rebbe slowly, in a soft, gentle voice, indicated the "something important" that he wanted to discuss. His conversational style was to suggest, rather than to declare. He asked questions that were disguised to convey information, rather than elicit it. In a long and rambling but careful discourse, he slowly allowed me to realize the solution he offered. He asked, "Did you ever consider that if you became a Jew, maybe it would help?" Here was a tacit admission that the Hasidic community was aware I had never converted to Judaism, despite Chaim's claim to the contrary. This plain fact meant that the children were not Jewish, and the realization disturbed them. If I converted, their problem was solved. He added, "Of course, I'm not talking about modern Judaism. Did you ever consider becoming a real Jew?"—meaning a religious Jew.

I knew that this would involve years of study and I would have to pass difficult examinations. I remembered speaking once with a young woman who had converted from Christianity to Judaism. "You will flunk your exam two times for sure," she had said. "They make it difficult on purpose. They really want to make sure you are serious."

Rebbe Moreino's voice drew me back to the present conversation. "We can come and check on you," he said. After a period of time that he defined as "a while," the Hasidic community would decide whether I converted simply because I wanted my children back or if I really believed in the Jewish faith.

I could picture a group of solemn-featured rebbes attempting to discern my religious motivations. The scene was absurd, yet I wanted to hear more. Where would Moreino take this discussion? Would he say something that would lead me closer to my children? I wished that he would speak more directly.

He had planned my life for me. "And you will marry a good

Jew," he said in a matter-of-fact tone. "And you would have children with him, of course."

That would put me neatly into a Hasidic trap. I would certainly love the children and would be unable to leave them.

Finally, after all of this, Rebbe Moreino indicated that *if* the Hasidic elders decided I was a true believer, they *might* put me in contact with my children.

It was a ridiculous proposition, of course, designed both to ease the consciences of my children's kidnappers and, at the same time, silence me. But once again I did not refuse it immediately, because I did not wish to stifle further discussion. "How long?" I asked.

He answered, "One week, two weeks, five years." He shrugged.

In truth, if I really thought that this tactic would bring back my children, I would have attempted to at least appear sincere. I was willing to work at the deception for five long years and even endure marriage to a Hasidic man—if the effort would pay off. But my mind raced through to the likely outcome: The conversion process alone might take five years. Then, having married a good Hasidic Jew, borne his children, and waited perhaps another five years, someone like Rebbe Moreino would declare that my conversion was insincere and I had done it all just to get my children back and refuse to hand them over. By then they would be nearly grown anyway. I would be trapped among my enemies. I raised this possibility.

Rebbe Moreino declared with a shrug, "You take your own risk."

What did the detectives think about all this? I wondered nervously, remembering that they were listening.

I made eye contact with the rebbe's silent wife. Her expression seemed to say, "I'm sorry."

I did not say yes, but I still did not say no. Keep the door open, I advised myself, at least for a time. Rebbe Moreino knew something about the whereabouts of my children, and I did not want to close off any leads. Maybe, in the context of discussing this insane plan, I would learn something valuable.

By now, I had been with the rebbe for nearly two hours. I was drained. I told him that I would consider his suggestion and return to him on my next visit to the States to give him an answer. I knew I could never adopt Moreino's plan, yet, once again, as with Chaim Shaulson, I felt guilty about rejecting any suggestion that might reunite me with my children.

When the meeting finally ended, I was anxious to learn what the D.A.'s office might be able to do with this new knowledge. Rebbe Moreino's statements seemed to indicate that he was withholding information concerning my children, and I believed we could bring legal action against him. If he did not know where the children were, he certainly knew how to find out. But when I walked around the block to the surveillance car, I found the two detectives in an agitated state. The police transmitter had malfunctioned. The detectives had been unable to listen in on the conversation and were very concerned that I might be in danger. The meeting had lasted far longer than we had predicted.

In the car, as we drove back to the D.A.'s office, a deep depression settled over me. I thought: If a simple thing like listening to a conversation will not work properly, then nothing will go right. It suddenly seemed so futile to believe that I would ever see my kids again.

Several people advised me to take my case before a rabbinical court, and I spent a great deal of time considering this possibility. But the more I thought about it, the riskier it seemed. First, as a shiksa appearing in a rabbinical court, I would have to find a religious Jew who would agree to act as my lawyer, and I had not yet found one of them whom I could trust. I did not even know if I would be allowed to be present and, at any rate, the proceedings would be conducted in Yiddish, so I would not understand what anyone was saying.

And what could I expect afterward? By now I was learning how some of the Hasidic minds worked. They present a unified appearance to the outside world. But internally they are split into a multitude of small groups—cults, sects, cells—that squabble over seemingly minor interpretations of the Torah. The groups tend to cluster around the personality of a particular rebbe. Thus, if a rabbinical court found in my favor and decreed that the children should be returned to me, people such as Rebbe Tauber or Rebbe Moreino might say something like, "It's not a good decision, because you didn't go to *our* court." But if any rabbinical court ruled against me, my children's captors were sure to pronounce it a good decision. My opponents had a very convenient sense of justice.

It will come to nothing, I reasoned. I will not do it. It's much too dangerous. But maybe in the future, if I find people I can trust, I will consider it.

Jim Stanco gave me the name of a woman whom I will call Sarah, a mother of twelve, who claimed that her nine oldest children had been kidnapped by the Satmars. I thought: Certainly this woman will understand my situation and perhaps she will be willing to help. From Sabine's house I phoned her at her Brooklyn apartment, asking permission to visit. Sarah agreed to see me, complaining, "They stole my kids." But she set strict conditions. "You come to my house, but you come dressed with respect. No perfumes. My man is not allowed to smell the perfume of another lady, and he may smell some perfume on me only when I'm available." I knew that she was referring to two weeks after her period, the time of the month when she was likely to conceive—the only time when sex was permissible. "Even if he would come in the house after you leave, there must be no trace of perfume," she warned.

I assured her that I would respect her wishes.

Sarah lived in a small, three-room apartment on the third floor of a very old building. Elevated railroad tracks were situated near the front of the building. Periodically during my visit, trains roared by, drowning conversation, shaking the building. The atmosphere was musty and oppressive. Furniture was piled high in front of all the windows, effectively eliminating sunlight and fresh air. I felt claustrophobic, as if I were stuck in an elevator. A girl, four or five years old, struggled to change a baby's diaper. A two-year-old toddler mumbled a childish prayer. The children had a sickly white pallor, like flowers that had been hidden from the sun.

"Do you have a minute?" Sarah asked. "I have a rat in the kitchen and the baby sleeps there, so I'm trying to catch the rat." I watched quietly as she lumbered from the room. Twelve pregnancies had left her thick and stocky. Huge, pendulous breasts threatened to escape from beneath her stained brown dress.

Our conversation, when it began, was stilted, although she spoke English quite well. Sarah explained that these three younger children were from her current marriage. She had nine children by her first husband before a rabbinical court had decreed a divorce, and those were the children who were taken away.

To my extreme discomfort, she wanted to speak about sex. She spoke of it only in a negative sense, but with obvious, intense interest. It seemed that her first husband was, in her mind, a sexual pervert. She complained that he wanted to have sex in ways other than the traditional "missionary" position. "He wanted—like dogs," she explained. When she refused, he took up with another woman and came home to detail the lurid specifics to Sarah. I did not wish to hear any of this and could only assume that in a society where so much is forbidden, sexual matters take on extreme importance.

Our discussion was interrupted when Sarah's current husband arrived home. Seeing me, he immediately retreated to a corner where, like an errant schoolboy, he stood facing the wall. Sarah quickly explained to me that he was ten years younger than she was, and a bit simple-minded, but no one else would have her.

I felt as if I had arrived on another planet. How can people live like this? I wondered.

Sarah had nothing of value to tell me, and I realized that her nine older children had not been kidnapped in the same manner as mine. In truth, they had been taken away by the internal welfare system of the Hasids. The children had been trapped in the apartment, never allowed to venture into the sinful outside world, even for school. In Sarah's mind, the Hasidic schools were not religious enough. The rabbinical court had decided that her children were suffering from neglect and had removed them from her care, placing them for adoption in various families. It was an action with which I tended to agree.

The encounter left me anxious and depressed. Were my children living in such an environment? If a two year old was already spending his days trying to recite prayers, what were the hours like for Marina, Simon, and Moriah? Was their daylight shut out by shrouded windows or, worse, by closed and rigid minds?

39

Josef's Story

I had to share a room with Mr. and Mrs. Jacobovich's son Yoely and I didn't like him at all. We fought about everything, and Mrs. Jacobovich always took his side.

In the summertime it was very hot. We had a small fan in our room and Yoely always aimed it at his bed. When I tried to turn it, he wouldn't let me have any of the cool air.

He was twelve years old, and still, every night, he made pee-pee in his bed.

I made a friend at school. His name was Yoely too. We played like we were the police of all the other children. Everybody wanted to be our friend.

Playing with matches and fire was forbidden, but some of the small boys liked to sneak into the woods around Kasho Drive and start fires. They liked to do things that were forbidden. Yoely and I used to spy on them. We would say, "Aha! I saw you!" and then we threatened to tell the grown-ups what they were doing. Sometimes we did tell. We were like the chiefs of the kids, and it was fun.

There was no school for the boys in Kasho so we studied in a nearby village. We went to school six days a week. There were about a hundred and ten boys in the school. My class had twenty-five students. One hour each day we studied English, but it was just for the math problems. All of the time, we spoke Yiddish. Mostly we studied the Bible and prayed.

Sometimes we repeated after our teacher:

"We will not change our way of life!"
"We will reject this society!"
"We will keep on living like our grandparents did!"

I thought that maybe, when I grew up, I'd become a rebbe.

40

A question haunted me that I kept hidden from everyone, including Walter. Could Rebbe Moreino's plan work? If I converted to Judaism, married a "good Jew," and agreed to bear his children, would the community eventually return Marina, Simon, and Moriah to me? Could I refuse to take the chance, no matter how slim?

One part of me argued: Be reasonable, Patsy. It will not work. They are playing games with you. They are cheating you.

But another part responded: Patsy, whatever it takes, you have to do your best for your kids.

Walter was very quiet when I finally confided what the rebbe had suggested. "Would you do it?" he asked.

"Yes," I answered quickly. "But only if I were sure. Believe me, when I have the children, I wouldn't stay with the Hasidic people. It would be a way to get the children, not a way to become like the Hasidic people. It's a question of time. If I have to do it until I find the kids, you will wait for me. And I'll come back and we'll live like nothing happened."

"But if you created another family, your love for the children would trap you," Walter pointed out.

"No, no. I would agree to it, but I would keep the IUD. They would never know," I reasoned.

At any rate, Walter's question was theoretical. So was my answer, but I could see in his eyes that my blunt honesty had caused him pain.

"For me, it would mean nothing," I reassured him. "I would not love him; it's a way to get the kids back. It is just that, for me, the end would justify the means."

Walter was even more distressed when I told him that the newspaper publisher Chaim Shaulson had suggested I seduce and blackmail a rebbe. "I wouldn't be able to do it," I insisted.

But, as time passed, the episode with Shaulson led me into even more melancholy moments of internal debate. If I was sure—*if I was one-hundred-percent sure*—that such a distasteful act would actually reunite me with my children, would I do it? I began to suspect that the answer was yes.

I concluded that it was best to keep a lot of these issues to myself. Sharing them with Walter, when I could not give him the answers that he wanted to hear, was too cruel.

We went on a ten-day camping trip to Sweden for a much-needed holiday. Although Walter had been there before, it was my first visit. I found the country to be breathtaking and the people warm and friendly. In the evenings we set up camp on the shores of one of Sweden's many beautiful, clear lakes. The nights were cold and crisp and we awoke to the incredible scene of sparkling ice crystals reflecting in the sun, with mist rising from the lake. It was like a shimmering fairyland, and the sheer beauty of it left me breathless.

During our drives through the countryside, pictures of the children were propped up in the car where I could always see them. I said to Walter, "The kids would like this."

"You always say things like that," Walter said.

"That's because I don't spend one day without thinking: they are not here," I responded.

By now Walter knew Marina, Simon, and Moriah almost as well as I did. We had been together for two and a half years, and even though he had never met them, they were our constant companions.

Many times Walter and I had spoken about the possibility of having a child of our own, and I was more than willing, but Walter had been wary. He wanted a child but cautioned, "One child cannot replace another. We have to be sure we do it for the right reason." There was no way that I would ever—could ever—stop searching. But amid the beauty and tranquility of Sweden we acknowledged that life had to go on. I could not let go of the past, but it was unhealthy to live in it constantly. Walter and I needed to shape a future as well. We decided that the time was right. We would have a child of our own.

I wondered if the arrival of a new child would lessen my resolve to find Marina, Simon, and Moriah. I also worried that there might not be enough room in my heart to unreservedly love a new child. Would I be too hard on the baby, comparing him or her to Marina, Simon, and Moriah, who, in my mind, were perfect?

Walter encouraged me to read as much as I could about the world in which my children now found themselves. He counseled, "You'll want to know, because when they come home it will be helpful to you, and to them."

I obtained a copy of a book by Marek Aalter that detailed Jewish religious life and the education of children, and reaffirmed many of the points I had already learned from the Duchess's book. In Hasidic schools, imagination and curiosity are simply not tolerated. One passage told a story that illustrated the proper way for a parent or teacher to answer a child's common questions. A child asked, "Why does the sun rise?" and "Why does the sun set?" The answer to both questions was the same. "Because it is written in the Bible. Don't question it." As I read, I transposed Marina, Simon, and Moriah into these scenes.

I could not bring myself to continue reading and was unable to vocalize my fears, frustration, and anger, even to Walter. I threw the book onto the floor, climbed into the car, and drove for hours, aimlessly. Walter instinctively knew what had happened. He picked up the book and read it from cover to cover, so that he too would better understand the lives of these three children whom he did not know and yet, somehow, had come to love.

More and more, whenever I encountered a Hasidic Jew in a train station or on a plane, I could barely control my anger. I wanted to spit in his face and shout out a curse. But, of course, venting my anger so crudely could only hurt my case. Sometimes I had to bite my tongue hard to force it to behave. I knew that if I was ever assigned an airplane seat next to one of them, I would have to move. It was not because of their religious beliefs; it was because of what a few of them were doing to my children.

I planned my next trip to the States to coincide with a court hearing on Chaim's extradition. On July 26, I met with FBI agents and attempted to involve them in our search. The request was denied because Marina, Simon, and Moriah were not U.S. citizens.

In between my visits to the Brooklyn D.A.'s office and my exhausting trips through Williamsburg and Borough Park, I met with Jim Stanco, and he proudly displayed his handiwork. He had used the photos of the children that we had received from Zvi Armoni in Amsterdam to fashion posters and managed to find someone to translate the text into Yiddish. The word MISSING was emblazoned across the top, written in English, repeated in Yiddish. My children's faces stared at me from the eleven-by-fourteen, bright-yellow poster. Underneath each child's photo was basic information, also appearing in both English and Yiddish:

Name..Simon Yarden
Born ....January 2, 1981
Height ....4'9" (approx.)
Weight..................................80 pounds (approx.)
Eyes ....Dark Brown
Hair...Black
Languages....................................Multilingual

Name ....Moriah Yarden
Born...June 7, 1982
Height ....4'4" (approx.)
Weight...............................80 pounds (approx.)
Eyes ....Dark Brown
Hair ....Dark Brown
Languages..Multilingual

Name: ....Marina Yarden
Born ....October 19, 1979
Height ....4'6" (approx.)
Weight...............................80 pounds (approx.)
Eyes..Light Brown
Hair ....Brown
Languages..Multilingual

The children were abducted on 12/11/86 by their noncusto-
dial father, Chaim Yarden (AKA Edwar & Jarden) who has
been in custody since 1/89 awaiting extradition to Belgium
on kidnapping charges.

New York State Missing and Exploited Children Clearinghouse.
Sightings in New York State may be reported on our toll-free
hotline: 1-800-FIND KID (1-800-346-3543)
Sightings outside of New York State may be reported to:
1-800-843-5678

Stanco told me that he would distribute the posters as widely
as possible in and around Hasidic neighborhoods. Whenever he
traveled, whether on business or vacation, he would take a supply
of posters with him. He would make sure to place copies at highway tollbooths leading to the Catskill Mountains, where many
Jewish people, including Hasidim, vacation.

Stanco theorized that we would never be able to infiltrate the
community. Our break would come only when we found someone like Judas, who lived within the Hasidic culture but was in

trouble with the police or was so desperate for money that he would sell out his religious brothers.

The authorities and I discussed Stanco's prediction that our break would not come until we found a Hasidic informant. Several police officers told me that they were aware of numerous incidents among the Hasidim involving incest, wife-beating, and sexual abuse of children. But such issues were dealt with almost exclusively by the rabbinical courts, thus shielding the community from unwanted publicity. One officer lamented, "We have almost nothing on them. We know these things happen, but we don't have anyone whom we can pressure to help us."

On August 14, 1989, after nearly seven months of legal wrangling and more than a half-dozen hearings, a U.S. court ordered Chaim's immediate extradition. Chaim resisted physically, and Tony Crook and another U.S. marshal had to force him into a car and take him to JFK International Airport. They accompanied him on the flight.

The move was a surprise to everyone. I was still in the States that day, but from across the ocean I made sure that the media was alerted. Walter and others contacted those reporters who had covered the story in the past, and the Brussels airport was jammed with reporters and cameramen, who captured the moment when Chaim was turned over to the Belgian police. He shuffled along with his eyes downcast and his head held low.

Belgian authorities interviewed Chaim, pressing him for information regarding the whereabouts of the children. But he refused to tell them anything.

Walter and I worked long hours to prepare for Chaim's appearance in a Belgian court. We wrote a detailed summary of the history of the case and gathered statements from various sources attesting that, contrary to Chaim's assertions, the children were happy and thriving when they were living with me. The students at Mater Dei wrote a sweet, simple letter to the Satmar community, which read:

Dear Gentlemen:
We are the friends of Moriah. We were in the same kindergarten when Moriah one day didn't come back. The teacher told us something and explained us something but we didn't understand it so well. Our current teacher did re-explain it now. It must not be very funny to lose your family and all your friends at once. It would be real fun if we could play and work together again with Moriah. Can you take care of that? Thank you.

The children from Simon's class at Sint Jozef's sent a similar plea directly to Chaim, addressed to the prison:

Dear Sir,
Your son, Simon Edwar, is one of the 21 boys that on the first of September, '86, started the first year primary school in the class of Mr. Ivo Devesse. Three months later, on Dec. 11, '86, he was kidnapped together with his two sisters, in front of our school gate.
What since then happened to our classmate Simon and his two sisters, we don't know. Through newspapers, weekly reviews, and television, we learned that they must stay somewhere in N.Y., U.S., and that their mother, Patsy Heymans, and her family do desperate things to find them back and that their father stays in the prison in Vorst (Brussels).
In our class we talk very seriously about Simon. What became of him? When does he come back? Therefore, we decided to write to you, his father, and ask you this very urgent question: Dear Mr. Yarden, please bring us back Simon.
We keep on hoping that Simon will be soon back amongst us and ask you Mr. Yarden to help us with that.

In the name of all classmates.

The letter was signed with the childish scrawls of twenty young boys, along with the signatures of their teacher and director.

Walter and I prepared the bundle of documents in both French and Dutch versions and inserted photos of the children. The results were thick press kits—a yellow-covered French version and a green-covered Dutch translation—which we distributed as widely as possible.

We phoned friends and relatives, asking them to show up in court as a sign of support.

The Palais de Justice is an imposing, domed edifice that dominates a portion of Brussels' downtown business area. Inside the grand entranceway a huge, open chamber resounds with the echoes of footsteps on the marble floors. Black-robed barristers hurry about. Along the sides of the vast hall, numerous attorney-client conferences are conducted at isolated desks. Doors lead off on all sides to quiet courtrooms.

The room where Chaim was to appear—designed to seat perhaps fifty people—was jammed with more than one hundred and fifty spectators.

The business of this initial hearing was to determine whether Chaim wanted to contest his parental-kidnapping conviction and, if so, whether he should remain in jail pending trial. He had been sentenced *in absentia* to one year in jail. At the time, he had not had the opportunity to defend himself. Now that he was back in Belgium, it was his right to take a position on the judgment, whether to accept it or contest it. Chaim did not have any money, but the Hasidic community provided him with expert legal counsel.

Our attorneys, Dominique Buysschaert and Patrick Mandoux, had researched the legal aspects with precision and thoroughness. Our immediate goal was to keep Chaim locked up—not to punish him, but to maintain our link to the children. By now, he had already served more than six months at the Manhattan Correctional Center, and that time counted against his sentence in Belgium.

With only six months remaining on his jail term, we worried about an amnesty. At the will of King Baudouin I, the sentence could be commuted at any time. Belgium, partly to relieve overcrowded jails, often celebrates various occasions by declaring a general amnesty, in which case Chaim could easily go free. Clearly, he would once more disappear, and we would have no leverage to pressure for the return of the children.

District Attorney Nadia De Vroede agreed that it was critical to keep Chaim behind bars. She explained her approach to us. When it comes to legal issues involving children, she proclaimed, "There are no ordinary cases. Everything involves human pain, so any case is taken as extraordinary." But she acknowledged that our case was especially interesting from a legal point of view, because there were no precedents regarding many of the issues. Belgian law had never before grappled with an international parental kidnapping case as complicated and convoluted as this. The government had never confronted, so directly, a powerful religious community that—in the minds of some—sought to elevate its own standards above the laws of Belgium, or any other country.

In addition to her compassion, her legal skills, and her unique view of the case, De Vroede was unusually empathic. She too was the mother of three children.

Chaim was escorted into the courtroom by a police officer. He carried a small bag filled with legal papers and religious books. He also brought an apple for a snack. His physical appearance indicated that, in jail, he had become even more religious. He wore a yarmulke over a head that was shaved, and his beard and *peiyot* were longer than ever. The natural robust tan of his skin was replaced by a prison pallor. He stood in front of the judge with his shoulders hunched and his head low, refusing to make eye contact.

The judge asked a question. Keeping his head down, Chaim mumbled an incoherent answer.

"Please look at me when you're talking," the judge requested.

Chaim raised his head slightly, repeated his statement, and then quickly dropped his gaze.

Claiming a poor understanding of French, Chaim requested an English translator. I recognized this as a ploy. In fact, he was fluent in French, but his English skills were limited. Nevertheless, the law allowed him this right. The judge postponed the case for one week and sent Chaim back to jail.

During the next session, every question and answer, as well as extraneous comments, had to be translated back and forth, and little business was resolved. At one point, Chaim corrected his translator. "No," he said in English, "that word does not convey the meaning that I wanted." The judge glanced sharply at Chaim, for he had just displayed that he understood French very well.

Realizing his mistake—the judge spoke English—Chaim turned thoughtful. Within a few minutes, he complained that his English skills were insufficient. Now, he demanded a Hebrew translator. The judge saw through this easily. Chaim would be able to converse with the translator in a language the judge could not understand. But Chaim had a legal right to the translator and the judge complied. Once more the hearing was postponed.

The next week a Hebrew translator was on hand, and the laborious process began again. The judge asked a question. The translator repeated it in Hebrew. Chaim responded in Hebrew and spoke at great length—he had always seemed incapable of saying anything quickly and clearly. When the translator finished repeating the lengthy answer in French, the judge summarized the statement for the official court record. The summary then had to be translated so that Chaim could read it and agree that it was accurate. He often chose to bicker over one or two words. The process dragged on and on.

To reduce my own stress level, I made detailed notes of everything that occurred.

Whenever he was forced to refer to me, Chaim reverted to formal French. I was not his wife or his ex-wife or even Patsy. To Chaim, I was "Madame Patricia Heymans."

The Hebrew translator occasionally stumbled over words

and phrases. At times Chaim jumped in with a comment in Hebrew such as, "No, no, it was not that that I said," once again indicating a working knowledge of French. Since I understood Hebrew, I knew exactly what was going on. The almost comical sequence of translations allowed Chaim extra time to formulate his answers. I also understood the judge's reluctance to object to this procedure. Because of Chaim's contentious personality, the court had to exercise extreme patience to avoid any appearance that his rights were being violated.

Speaking about my feelings had never come easily to me. Now, verbally articulating my concerns about the children and the life that I envisioned them living was becoming impossible. Sometimes when I tried, the words tumbled around in my mind and I could not force them out. I found that coherent speech of any kind was difficult. What's happening to me? I wondered. I can say nothing that makes any sense.

My moods were also in turmoil for another reason. I had just learned that I was pregnant with Walter's child. Obviously, I was ecstatic. But at the same time, this news deepened my resolve to find Marina, Simon, and Moriah. I wanted us to be a family.

My experience with the psychiatrist immediately after the kidnapping had been counterproductive and I resisted the idea, but I knew I needed help sorting out my feelings. I desperately wanted to share my innermost thoughts, but I could not. Walter said, "It's your decision." But I knew that he wanted me to seek help.

Through a friend's referral I obtained the name of a therapist. Recognizing my tendency to run away when things became too difficult, I paid for five sessions in advance.

The first thing the therapist said to me was that she knew some of my relatives. This made me very uncomfortable.

Then she grew silent.

I waited for her to ask a question.

She waited for me to speak.

We stared at one another awkwardly.

This is ridiculous, I thought. I want someone to ask me questions, to help me speak, to draw me out. I might just as well have a tape recorder here next to me, not her.

Our second session was just as painful. I mumbled a few statements about the children, hoping to free *her* tongue, but the therapist maintained her silence.

Afterward, I felt like a failure. Nobody's going to get me there another time, I vowed. Or to anybody else. I'm through with therapists.

The frustrated judge, attempting to see if Chaim and I could work out our own differences, asked us to meet together in a small side room in the Palais de Justice, with a police officer present.

As we sat across from one another, Chaim said quietly that he wanted to tell me something—but first, I had to promise not to pass on the information to anyone. My heart leaped, hoping that I would hear news of the children. Of course I promised. Then Chaim declared, "I don't know where the kids are, but if you agree to come back with me, to marry me, we will look for the kids together and someday we will find them."

I immediately realized that he was serious. Actually, under Belgian law, we were still married, but I knew that Chaim was talking about a Hasidic ceremony. "I'm not Jewish," I answered. "How can you, a religious Jew, ask that of a Christian?"

"Everything can be fixed," he said.

"And what about Iris?"

"Everything can be fixed."

With a start, I realized he had just admitted that he did, indeed, at least know where to begin to look for the children.

After the meeting I thought: I like to keep my promises, but this is the kind of promise I don't have to keep. I immediately reported the conversation to Nadia De Vroede as well as to Buysschaert. De Vroede revealed to the judge our fresh evidence of Chaim's continuing complicity in keeping the children from me.

The incident was reported at the next court hearing. Chaim's response was arrogant and typical of his inability to take responsibility for his own actions. I could tell from the tone of his voice that he was furious with me. He asked the court: "How can you trust somebody like her, when she's promising something to me, her husband, and the first thing she does is speak to you about it?"

The judge dismissed that specious argument and ordered Chaim returned to his cell. A policewoman stepped forward, carrying handcuffs. Chaim shied away from her, unwilling to be touched by a woman. Anger flashed across the officer's face, and she demanded that Chaim obey. Hanging his head in shame, Chaim offered his wrists in embarrassing submission.

Walter asked, "Would you go back with Chaim, after all that he did, if he could bring you the kids?"

"Yes, of course," I answered honestly. But I repeated what I had said concerning Rebbe Moreino's proposal. "Only if I was one hundred percent sure. Besides, it would mean nothing. You would just wait for me."

Walter's silence made me very uneasy.

Chaim's attorneys bothered us with various motions and contentions that forced court hearings nearly every week. Knowing that each delay raised our legal bills, Chaim found numerous ways to complicate the process. Mounting legal bills were of no concern to Chaim, since his defense was being financed by the deep, diamond-lined pockets of the Hasidic community. Each ruling of the lower court was appealed to the highest level. Almost every Wednesday my parents and I were at the Palais de Justice for yet another hearing. Some sessions, known as "extraordinary hearings," lasted from 1:00 P.M. until 8:00 P.M., with few breaks. Once, the session went so late that the front entrance of the Palais de Justice was sealed for the night and the concierge had to let us out through a back door.

Chaim was still angry about the sudden implementation of

the decision to extradite him. He argued that it was illegal. But the judge lectured, "Listen, Mr. Yarden, this is past. If the U.S. decides to extradite you, well, okay, you are here now. It's not up to a Belgian court to decide whether the U.S. was right or wrong."

The day before each court hearing I phoned Buysschaert to ask, "What's going on tomorrow?"

Sometimes he was forced to answer with bitter honesty, "I don't know."

I was supremely agitated by all of this. The court endlessly debated Chaim's rights but never spoke about my children. They had forgotten the real issue. I wanted to stand up and scream: "What about the rights of Marina, Simon, and Moriah?"

When we finally reached the substance of the case, Chaim insisted that he had not kidnapped the children. He charged that it was my father who had abducted them and attempted to place the blame on his hated son-in-law.

We countered by presenting to the court all the physical evidence that had been delivered to my father: photographs, the wedding invitation to Chaim *and* the children, and the open letter to Chaim from Rebbe Tauber, which asked the members of the religious community to support Chaim in his effort to keep the children away from their harmful Christian mother.

Chaim responded by asserting, "Well, it's a stolen letter." And if it was stolen, he argued, how can anyone know whether it is real or fake?

The judge responded by pointing out that ICTS detectives had secured a signed statement from Tauber attesting that he did, indeed, write the letter.

We exhibited the photograph showing Chaim and the children in front of the White House in Washington. Chaim took one look at the photograph and declared, "It's not me. It has been falsified." He admitted that he had once traveled to Washington, where he was allowed to visit with the children briefly, but still denied the authenticity of the photo. He said that the Washington visit took place in the springtime. The judge pointed out the "Oct.

'88" notation on the back. He asked, "Do the trees in Washington have red leaves in the spring?"

Chaim replied that the seasons were different in the U.S.

At the next court session, I supplied evidence obtained from the U.S. Embassy that the seasons in Washington, D.C., corresponded to Belgian seasons. The leaves turn red in the autumn, not in the spring. I also had documents from the weather bureau.

"Who took the picture?" the judge asked.

We waited several moments as the question was translated from French to Hebrew and Chaim's answer was translated from Hebrew to French. The reply continued Chaim's attack on my father: "Well, I don't know, but Mr. Jacques Heymans has money, maybe you should ask him how he took those pictures." As the answer was translated, Chaim turned slowly and aimed a Cheshire-cat grin at the spectators, as if to say: Look what a good joke I made!

The performance was evasive and disgusting. The judge was obviously convinced of Chaim's guilt, but judgment was reserved for yet another week. As Chaim was led out of the courtroom and back to his jail cell, I felt fresh outrage at his lying and conniving. I wondered what kind of treatment he would receive from the other prisoners, once they found out what he had done. Prisoners have their own code of ethics. I knew that Chaim, as a convicted kidnapper, would not fare too well, and the vengeful side of me was tempted to spread the word about his abuse toward his wife and children.

At yet another hearing, he changed his story, admitting that the photograph of him and the children in front of the White House was genuine, and he offered this explanation: "I was walking down Fifty-sixth Street in Manhattan when somebody I had never seen before, a total stranger, stopped me. He said his name was David and said, 'If you want to see your kids, you come at a certain time in front of the White House and we'll show you the kids.' And I went and this stranger who called himself David was there with the kids, and I talked a bit to the kids and saw that they looked fine. We had a cold drink together and they seemed happy. Then I left."

The judge asked, "You didn't ask any questions about where they were living? If they wanted to stay with you? Where they went to school? You are the father! You trusted somebody you don't know?"

"No," Chaim responded. "They looked fine, and for me that was okay. Ask David, he knows better than me."

The judge appeared to be very angry over this ridiculous story.

Chaim's courtroom antics were so disruptive and disturbing that one of his own attorneys confided privately to Buysschaert, "I cannot accept the position of Mr. Yarden anymore."

Buysschaert was impressed with this admission. He told me, "It is good information that there is important opposition within the Jewish community. Some support Chaim and some want to be very distant from him. One thing we have to avoid is entering into opposition with the community as a whole. If we say one thing against the Jewish people, we give them a reason to refuse any cooperation. If there is only one door open, please don't shut it."

I certainly agreed. "I don't have anything against the religion," I said. "I still have Jewish friends."

Various people accused me of making a religious affair out of the case. My response was: "I'm sorry, I don't think it's me who made it a religious affair. For me, Chaim could be Muslim, Christian, or have no religion whatsoever. I don't care. The fact is, he took my kids." I had already met a great many Jews, religious and nonreligious, whom I trusted and respected. My argument was with Chaim and his few unreasonable allies.

Chaim's attorneys raised the issue in court, accusing me of bringing a procedure against all Jews. To counter this allegation, Buysschaert contacted Marcus Pardes, one of the most prominent and respected attorneys in Brussels, who was also a Jew. Pardes was interested in the case. Unfortunately, the timing was bad. A prominent Belgian Jew had recently been murdered, and Pardes was busy handling details of that case. However, he recommended another lawyer, a religious Jew named François Motulsky.

At the next court session, Buysschaert introduced Motulsky as his new associate counsel. "This has nothing to do with the Jewish community," Buysschaert argued. "If Chaim Yarden were a Catholic or agnostic or Buddhist, he could not be above the law."

As we waited for the court's decision on whether to reaffirm Chaim's sentence, King Baudouin I, in celebration of the fortieth year of his reign, granted a general amnesty that would reduce the sentences of most Belgian prisoners by six months. This threw us into panic. "The Kingdom of Belgium is the Land of Amnesty," Buysschaert noted wryly. "We do not have enough jails and not enough people to take care of all these prisoners."

But Nadia De Vroede assured us that, since Chaim was contesting his sentence, he was not covered by the amnesty. She also told me that she was preparing legal moves designed to keep Chaim in prison beyond the time of his original sentence.

January 20, 1990. Buysschaert placed a call to Chaim's attorney to discuss the proceedings at tomorrow's scheduled court session. Chaim's lawyer could not contain his enthusiasm. He taunted Buysschaert with the prediction, "Tomorrow in court we will do something that no one will believe. It will be like theater."

Immediately, Buysschaert and Mandoux met to discuss this new threat. What did it mean? They pored over law books, checking precedents. They studied the case record with special care. Had they missed something? Had they or the prosecutor or one of the judges committed some sort of technical violation? They could find nothing that would provide the "theater" which Chaim's attorney had predicted. Clearly, however, they faced the threat that Chaim would, somehow, walk freely out of the courtroom the following day.

Buysschaert called De Vroede, relayed his conversation with

Chaim's lawyer, and suggested, "You must be ready to issue a new complaint against Yarden." The prosecutor agreed that she would prepare a case, based on a novel concept of the law.

Meanwhile, Mandoux phoned the airport and the train station. He carefully copied the departure times of all flights and international train departures and secured the cooperation of security personnel. Tomorrow, if Chaim was somehow allowed to go free—and if De Vroede was successful in filing new charges—we needed to be able to arrest him once more before he fled the country.

January 21. Chaim's attorney, obviously proud of his clever maneuver, announced that his client was withdrawing his opposition to his conviction. Throughout the courtroom there were expressions of surprise.

Buysschaert and Mandoux stared at one another in surprise. This was one possibility they had not considered, but the reasoning was immediately obvious: If Chaim had not contested his conviction, he would be free now, thanks to the amnesty. In any event, he had served nine months of his one-year jail term already. He concluded that if he confessed his guilt and accepted the original sentence, he would either be freed immediately under the terms of the amnesty or would merely face another three months in jail.

The judge asked Chaim if, by withdrawing his opposition, he realized that he was admitting to parental kidnapping. Chaim said, "No, I don't recognize that I kidnapped the kids, I just withdrew it in order to be let out of jail."

The reporters in the courtroom had a field day. It was the first time they could remember that a prisoner withdrew his opposition—effectively pleading guilty—yet still maintained his innocence!

The judge looked to De Vroede for her response. The prosecutor was prepared. Instantly, she filed a new charge, retroactive to August 14, 1989, the day that Chaim was extradited, claiming that he was guilty of the "continuing offense" of kidnapping. This was a concept that had been discussed in legal journals but never applied in Belgium in this sort of case—but Chaim had now opened the door to this charge by acknowledging, if only by default, that he was guilty of the original kidnapping. De Vroede argued that, when Chaim arrived in Brussels on August 14 and refused to give the authorities any information concerning the children, he had compounded the original crime. He had committed the continuing offense of keeping them away from their legal custodian. Thus, he was subject to an additional prison term, up to two years, retroactive to August 14. In fact, she argued, each and every day that he refused to cooperate in finding the children, he was guilty of a continuing offense.

Perhaps the trickiest aspect of the case was that it was not based on anything Chaim did or said, but on what he did *not* do or say. Chaim's lawyer argued that his client had a right to remain silent and could not be prosecuted simply because he did not provide information.

Buysschaert acknowledged that Chaim did have a right to silence but that, within narrow limits, his refusal to answer direct questions concerning the whereabouts of the children placed obstacles in the way of law enforcement authorities who were attempting to locate them. This, he declared, was an obstruction of justice. The rights of the children, the mother, and the state had to be weighed against the rights of the defendant. Privately, Buysschaert admitted to me, "It is very delicate."

But the judge saw the issues clearly. For the first time under Belgian law, the court ruled that a defendant's silence, under special circumstances, could incriminate him. The judge decreed that Chaim was, indeed, guilty of a continuing offense. He sentenced Chaim to an additional two years in prison, retroactive to August 14.

De Vroede had won her precedent-setting decision.

41

Despite my frustration with Chaim, he was still my best link to the children, and I was determined to speak with him again, to see if I could, somehow, win his cooperation. There were two types of jail visits—either through a glass partition, where the prisoner and the visitor speak by telephone, or in a larger, open room filled with tables and chairs. I would have preferred the former arrangement because it was more impersonal and because, if I became exasperated with Chaim, I could hang up the telephone and leave. The latter type of visit, known in prison parlance as *visite de table*, was strictly regulated to sixty minutes, no more, no less. Chaim responded to my request by insisting on a *visite de table*.

Okay, I said to myself, I will go. It's for the children.

The Saint Gilles jail was built for about three hundred prisoners but now held twice that number. The facilities can only accommodate twenty-five visitors at any one time, and the privilege is granted on a first-come, first-served basis. Wearing loose-fitting clothes to disguise my pregnancy, I arrived at 7:00 A.M. and waited outside on Avenue Ducpetiaux for more than an hour before I was allowed through the heavy wooden door and into the fortresslike building. During a cumbersome ritual of security checks, where I had to relinquish my ID card for the duration of the visit, I was surprised to realize that several of the prison workers recognized me as a result of news coverage.

"It's wonderful what you do for your kids," one man said.

"Keep going," another encouraged me.

Finally I was escorted through several metal detectors and into the visiting area. The large room held twenty-five separate tables, each with two or three chairs. The room filled quickly. I felt totally lost among all these people and very conspicuous sitting there with curious eyes glancing in my direction. Everyone seemed to know everyone else—except me. They greeted one another easily and shared laughter.

Chaim strode in confidently, nodding and smiling at other prisoners. In the crowded room, he stood out as the only Hasidic prisoner. All wore identical gray shirts and pants, but Chaim's shaved head and *peiyot* set him apart. He joked casually with the two guards. He did not seem anything like the docile, oppressed prisoner who appeared in court.

Casually he took a seat across the table from me. With his head cocked to one side, he began to chat as if I were simply an old friend whom he had not seen in years. He asked about my family. "What are you doing?" he asked. "What kind of job do you have?"

I had no interest in small talk. I was extremely nervous, and I sat stiff as a statue as he attempted to speak about any subject other than the children. As he chattered on I realized that I had lost every trace of feeling for him. Almost in wonder I thought: I don't love him, but I don't hate him either. It was hard to believe that I had once loved this pathetic man.

Still, he manipulated me. He would, as we say in French, "turn around the pot," change the subject to avoid what I really wanted to talk about. He was a fish I could not catch. He concocted stories about our past that were not true and continued to deny the reality. "I never beat you," he said, "or if I did, maybe it was a small smack, but never like you claimed." I suddenly felt weak and a bit ill, perhaps the result of my early stage of pregnancy.

Several times I asked, "Where are the children? Do you know anything about the kids?" Each time he veered the conversation to other subjects. I tried other tactics, asking, "Do you remember when Marina was small? . . ."

Nothing worked.

Then the soft, syrupy voice became sharp and cutting. He pointed a finger at me and accused, "It's your father who forces you to do all this. I didn't take the kids. Ask your father. Jacques Heymans took the kids so that he could accuse me and I could sit in jail."

By the end of the visit my head was spinning. I was totally confused. I knew intellectually that Chaim had abused and beaten me during the years of our marriage, but he had twisted the memories so that my heart began to wonder if things had been as bad as I remembered them.

It took me three days to recover emotionally from the one-hour visit.

I returned to the Saint Gilles jail five times within a very short period, for additional hours of difficult and exasperating conversations with Chaim. I gathered from his descriptions that he received a measure of special treatment. He had a freshly painted cell to himself, outfitted with new furniture, whereas most inmates had to share with three, four, or even five other prisoners. He did not have to work. His laundry was done for him. He did not turn off his lights at curfew time. He had won over the prison social worker, who allowed him unlimited access to the office telephone. He could obtain all the religious books he wanted. A social-services agency provided kosher food for Jewish prisoners, but this was not good enough for Chaim. A journalist told us that a kosher restaurant in Antwerp delivered Chaim a weekly supply of meals and billed the offices of the Satmar community. Nadia De Vroede told me that many of the jailers resented Chaim because of his constant use of his religion to seek special privileges. For example, he claimed that he needed a thicker mattress for his bed because, in his religion, "it is written" that he must have such a mattress. The jailers were kept in turmoil because they could not risk any action that would hint at a bias against Judaism. Prisoners had to clean their toilets on Saturday; but Chaim was the first prisoner ever given permission to clean his toilet on Friday. We were told that he regularly received a substantial sum of money to buy various items from the canteen and to bribe prison employees for special comforts.

In some ways, this was the kind of life that Chaim had always wanted. His needs were supplied, and he did not have to work. Others catered to many of his small whims. Nevertheless, he complained to me during one visit, "Living here is very hard."

"Why?" I asked.

He shrugged and, with a self-satisfied smirk, answered, "Because at ten in the morning I start telling myself, you have to get up, and finally at one in the afternoon I succeed in standing up."

During each visit, he attempted to confuse me further. He asked for news of my father, and when I responded to the question, he declared that he could not believe I made my own decision to end our marriage. "It's your father who forced you to leave me," he said. "You couldn't leave me, because you love me."

Chaim clearly enjoyed these visits. First, they provided a break from his normal day. Second, they gave him an opportunity to play his favorite game of cat-and-mouse.

He was late for my sixth visit to the jail. Other prisoners all had to enter the visiting room at the same time, but Chaim came sauntering in twenty-five minutes after everyone else. When I asked why he was late, he replied, "Oh, I couldn't get up from my bed, so they waited for me."

During our conversation, when I once more pushed for information about the children, he growled, "I gave them up to people who I know will take care of them. I don't know where they are and I don't want to know. They are not with you. That's what's important."

I said to myself: It's over. I cannot stand this torture anymore. I rose quickly from my chair. Although five minutes remained in the visiting session, I demanded that a guard escort me out immediately.

It was my last visit with Chaim.

As my pregnancy began to show, well-meaning people occasionally approached me with comments such as: "Good, at last you have decided to forget about the past," or "The children are settled into their new lives by now—you turn a page."

"No, it has nothing to do with that," I responded. I explained that I knew it was unwise to live only in the past, but I could never give up my efforts to find Marina, Simon, and Moriah. That would be like throwing them out of my life. My pregnancy only meant that Walter and I had decided it was vital to look forward also, to blend the past with the future.

At times, particularly when the case was profiled in the press, crank calls and letters plagued us and impeded our search. My father and I wasted time and a bit of money on one of Chaim's fellow prisoners, whom we dubbed "Source." Through an intermediary, Source hinted that he was willing to befriend Chaim and channel information to us. But Source proved to be a typical prison "con," who accepted several small cash payments from us, yet gave no useful information in return.

On another occasion, three rough-looking Palestinians arrived at Buysschaert's office and demanded a private discussion. One of them declared, "We are able to find the children."

Buysschaert questioned them carefully. They wanted money, of course. After much discussion, Buysschaert asked, "Can you guarantee to bring the children back—alive?"

One of the mysterious visitors replied, "Well, no."

Buysschaert ended the meeting immediately.

Another lead surfaced. Tamar Golan, an Israeli reporter stationed in Paris, put my father in contact with two men who edited a small Jewish newspaper. They were the sons of a rebbe who served the Petakh-Tikva area in Israel, where Iris Buttel was living. Shortly after my father met with them, one of them traveled to Israel and returned with the news that his father was willing to speak to us. Papa flew to Israel to speak to him in person. Knowing that a "good Jew" may not lie to his or her rebbe, Papa persuaded him to ask Iris about the children. Some time passed before the rebbe reported back to us that Iris denied knowing anything about the whereabouts of the children. Still, the rebbe felt that she knew more than she was willing to say.

We asked the Israeli police to interview her. Through their report, as well as other information that we developed, we were able to assemble a dossier: Iris's marriage to Chaim had been arranged by none other than our old friend the Duchess, who supposedly had worked for us. The children were not present at the wedding; nor were they told when it took place. On the day of Chaim's arrest, Iris had used a telephone credit card to call Rebbe Tauber in Monsey. Obviously her question to him was, "What should I do?" and the rebbe's just-as-obvious advice was to leave the country immediately. Iris fled to Canada. Eventually she returned to her home country of Israel to live with her parents, her sister, and brother-in-law in a tiny apartment. This must have been difficult, since she was religious and the other family members were not.

I copied her address into my book.

During frequent, sometimes heated sessions, Walter and I discussed names for the baby. I felt instinctively that it was a girl, although I refused available confirmation of that fact. Walter favored what, to me, were harsh-sounding Germanic names. I preferred softer, more melodic ones. More disturbing was the fact that, since I was still legally married to Chaim, whatever name we chose would be followed by the surname Edwar.

We finally came to agreement on the name Noélie if, indeed, the child was a girl.

The baby was due on Monday, June 18, 1990, but by Thursday we were still waiting. I remained cooped up in the house, concerned that labor would begin or my water might break when I was in a public place.

The phone rang. An anonymous voice with a thick Yiddish accent said, "I have information about your children." He spoke in a roundabout manner, only gradually coming to the point. Eventually he said that my son, Josef—the name given to Simon when he was supposedly converted—would undergo open-heart surgery on July 9. I knew that Simon had no history of heart problems and tried to convince myself that this call was merely another cruel hoax, but the seed of worry was planted in my mind. "I cannot tell you anything over the telephone," the caller said. "I want to meet you on Monday. I will call back on Monday around two o'clock."

Something in the man's tone was ominous and threatening, but I had to assume that he might truly have news of the children—and I had to question him more closely about Simon. I agreed to the meeting.

Then the man's voice grew more sinister. He hinted that he had connections to the Mossad and warned, "If you call the police, I have a weapon and I know very well how to use it. I know where you live. Don't call the police." He repeated this threat several times. He indicated that I was under surveillance and that he knew exactly what I was doing.

"Okay, okay, okay," I replied nervously. I was terrified.

The moment I hung up I ran to my neighbor's house and used her telephone—just in case the caller, or someone else, had tapped my line. I reported to the Belgian police officer assigned to my case. He may have been unsure whether I was hallucinating or whether the threat was real, but he prepared to tap my phone to record the conversation on Monday.

Next, I called my parents. Back home, after my nerves had settled a bit, I phoned my obstetrician and asked him to make arrangements to induce labor immediately, so I would be assured that I could keep the critical Monday appointment. My doctor refused, since there was no valid medical reason to induce labor, but he said, "I promise you one thing: Even if you have to go in an ambulance, you will be there for the meeting, unless you give birth at that very second."

The police instructed me to keep them informed.

I felt the first mild contraction on Sunday, about 9:00 A.M. That's it, no doubt about it, I thought. It might be later in the day or sometime tonight.

We were supposed to spend this day at my parents' country home, where they planned one of their traditional sheep roasts for about thirty guests. I knew that my father was already preparing the animal on the spit. I'd been looking forward to the gathering as a welcome respite from the traumas of the past few days and saw no reason to allow a few contractions to prevent me from going. Nor did I bother to alert Walter. This was my fourth child, and my fifth pregnancy. I knew there was plenty of time; these were preliminary twinges, not strong contractions.

The party was already under way when we arrived in Nassogne. My sister-in-law Caroline, Eric's wife, grew suspicious because I asked often, "What time is it?" so that I could gauge the frequency of my contractions. They came about every fifteen minutes. Walter, too, grew suspicious when he saw me grimace in pain occasionally. By mid-afternoon I told him that I was in labor.

"You want to go?" he asked.

"No, we still have time."

We left at 5:00 P.M. for the drive back to Brussels. Since neither of us was wearing a watch, Walter drove at a steady pace of seventy-five miles per hour, enabling us to time the pains by studying the odometer. By the time we arrived home the contractions were only five minutes apart, but they were not yet the strong, gripping pains of late-stage labor. "Let's wait a bit," I said.

I finished work on some curtains that I was sewing. Walter mentioned that he was hungry, and I wanted to keep busy, so I fixed spaghetti. My water broke as I carried his plate to the table.

Walter cleaned up the mess and asked, "Do you want to go right away?"

"No, we'll wait a bit."

I tucked my ever-present photograph of Marina, Simon, and

Moriah into my bag. I wanted my older children to share this experience with us. Soon it was time to leave for the hospital.

Only when I was in the labor room did I realize how nervous I was—perhaps the past few days had left me in shock. I was given an injection to help me relax.

This was Walter's first child, but I had experienced labor and delivery three times. I gave him specific instructions: "You sit in a chair in the corner, read, do whatever you want, but don't speak to me and bother me with stupid questions. Don't ask me, 'Does it hurt?' Of course it hurts."

In the labor room, Walter did as I asked, saying very little but occasionally refreshing me by dabbing my brow with a cool, damp cloth. The nurse was not as accommodating. Her constant chatter and hovering drove me crazy.

After three hours, when I had dilated almost seven centimeters, the nurse prepared to take me to the delivery room. As I was wheeled down the hallway, lying on my side, I experienced an intense contraction. Walking beside me, Walter saw the baby's elongated, bluish head emerge from the birth canal. The attending nurse became confused and lost her composure. A swirl of activity encompassed me. Suddenly I was in the delivery room and the baby was born within minutes. Unlike her three dark-haired half-siblings, Noélie was fair and blond, resembling me as a newborn.

Walter, struck speechless, was permitted to carry his newborn daughter to the nursery.

Walter and I were, of course, overjoyed that Noélie had arrived, strong and healthy, but something was missing. Walter appeared in my room early the next morning, drained, even unhappy. "What's wrong?" I asked.

He spoke slowly, measuring his words: "Considering all the problems confronting us, the birth was reduced for me to an ordinary, natural act that I have seen hundreds of times on the farms in my neighborhood. What should have been such a magical experience was . . . like a cow giving birth to a calf. There was too much going on to feel the spirituality of it."

He was right. Giving birth is supposed to be a joyous experience; but there was too much stress shrouding our lives. Perhaps this was why we had both reacted with such bizarre calm to the onset of labor.

There was no time to dwell on these depressing emotions. At 7:00 A.M. I called the police to tell them where I was. At 11:00 A.M. Caroline arrived to keep watch over baby Noélie, for I was too nervous to leave her only with strangers. Walter drove me home to await the promised phone call.

Two police officers installed a recording device on my telephone and advised, "Try to keep him on the line as long as you can, so that we can trace the call."

At 1:00 P.M., a full hour early, and only minutes after the police had finished their preparations, the phone rang. With shaking hands I grasped the receiver and immediately recognized the thick Yiddish accent. The man spoke more carefully this time, instructing me to meet him at 4:00 P.M. at a small café on Rue Vanderkindere.

Police officers moved in slow motion about the room, trying not to make noise. I found it difficult to speak normally, to pretend that I was alone. I tried not to look at the police as I made the caller repeat the address, stalling for time. This seemed to alarm him and he spoke quickly, repeating some of his threatening statements to me, convincing the police that I was in real danger. The call lasted barely two minutes, but it felt much longer.

After the call, Walter and I waited nervously until the police reported on the results of their telephone surveillance. They traced the call to a public phone in a subway station and immediately sent officers to investigate, but the man had fled by the time they arrived.

Walter drove me back to the hospital so that I could nurse Noélie and rest. Meanwhile, a half-dozen undercover police officers moved immediately to stake out the café.

I felt weak. I craved sleep. I wanted to hold my baby. But all too soon it was time to leave for the rendezvous. Walter drove me to Rue Vanderkindere on the south side of Brussels and parked around the corner from the café. The day was sunny and uncomfortably hot. As I walked toward the café I wondered who among the normal assortment of people out on the street this afternoon might be an undercover officer. What about the casual shopper across the street, peering into a window? As I entered, I knew that my picture was being taken by a hidden camera, but I dared not try to spot it.

I sat alone at a small corner table on the left side of the café, terrified, weak, and nervous. I ordered a hot chocolate and studied the room. There were several patrons, and again I wondered which ones were police officers. One man sat alone at a table by the window, drinking coffee and perusing a newspaper. He glanced up momentarily, peering across the paper's banner, and we made eye contact. He seemed tense. I quickly averted my gaze and stared out the window. Was this a casual, momentary encounter or something more? I could not know.

One agonizing hour passed. Patrons came and went, except for two men at a far table—who joked casually with the proprietor and seemed in no hurry to go about their business—and the solitary man by the window. I shifted uncomfortably in my chair. My back ached and my legs felt numb. The air in the café seemed incredibly warm, and I perspired heavily.

The solitary man shuffled his newspaper and placed it next to him, as if he were finished with it. But he ordered another cup of coffee and then returned to his reading. He glanced in my direction several times, and I continued to see signs of anxiety in his features. I thought: Normally, if you are alone in a café, you look out the window, not at someone else. If this is the man, why does he not attempt to speak with me?

I ordered another hot chocolate. A second hour passed. I was exhausted, disappointed, and angry. I felt weaker with every passing moment. We waited a bit longer before the café's telephone rang. One of the two men at the far table was summoned to the phone. He spoke for a moment, then came to me, shrugged, and said, "Let's go."

Why do they do these things? I wondered, as Walter drove me back to the hospital. Why do they sound false alarms? Why didn't the man speak with me? Perhaps he had seen Walter bring me here. I was angry with myself. Why didn't I think to take a taxi?

At the hospital, I asked one of the police officers if he had noticed the man at the window table. "I suspect that *that* was the man," I said. The officer conceded that it was possible, but by now it was too late to act upon my suspicions.

Hoping that the man would call again, the police instructed me to record a message on my answering machine, referring callers to the number of a portable phone which they brought to the hospital, but he did not call again.

Only after two days did Walter and I surrender to the wonder and happiness of Noélie's birth.

I remained in the hospital for one full week, with my room under twenty-four-hour-a-day police guard—one officer during the day and two at night. They did not like it whenever I tried to leave my room. No one could enter until the police inspected and approved his ID card. Security was so tight that even Walter and my parents had difficulty getting in to see us. I felt as if I were in prison.

The police did not want me to return home right away, so Walter and I, along with baby Noélie, spent a week at my brother's home and a second week at my parents' country house.

Meanwhile, we initiated a vital inquiry. I called Jim Stanco in Albany, New York, and told him about the unconfirmed report that Simon was to undergo open-heart surgery on July 9. Stanco spent weeks inquiring at all the New York–area hospitals, to see whether a boy of Simon's age was scheduled for open-heart surgery. He found no evidence to support the report, but, of course, we could not rule it out. Maybe it was not a New York hospital. Maybe it was not open-heart surgery but something else. Inside, I tended to disbelieve the report from the threatening caller. It's too much, I thought.

Still, it was impossible to quell the nagging fear that somewhere out in the big, frightening world, my son was critically ill.

*   *   *

My worry that a new baby would lessen my feelings for the lost children, or that I would be resentful of her, quickly dissipated. I relearned a lesson that all mothers know: The capacity to love expands exponentially with the birth of each new child. In fact, now I missed Marina, Simon, and Moriah more than ever. Our small house at Nine Rue Verte continued to echo with their silence.

To make room for Noélie's crib, I replaced Marina and Moriah's twin beds with bunk beds, so that all the girls would have a place to sleep.

I renewed my vow that I would never give up. If I could not find the children, I held out the hope that, as time passed, they might find me. A child wants to know his roots. I was heartened whenever I heard about an adopted child searching for his real parents. Something told me that my children, when they were old enough, would do the same. Yet I realized that the passage of time made this increasingly unlikely. They lived in a world that educated them to believe that all contact with non-Jews was harmful. They were being brainwashed against me. The darker side of my imagination still feared that they might never forgive me for what—to them—must seem like abandonment. They might never believe, or never know, how long and how desperately I had searched.

42

Sarah's Story

I started thinking to myself: I know I was born in Belgium, and I know that Mr. and Mrs. Jacobovich are not really my parents. Although I could never speak of it, I had a picture in my mind of the house where we used to live. I remembered it as being out in the country, around the mountains, where a lot of hunters were. It was a fun place with a big garden.

I knew that I must have a mother somewhere. I didn't just fall from the sky. But I knew better than to say anything.

I tried to remember what she looked like. I tried and tried, but I couldn't see her face. All I could see was long hair.

43

Concerned that one of the many motions and appeals filed by Chaim's attorneys might succeed in getting Chaim off on a technicality—and always worried that another amnesty might free him—Nadia De Vroede and our lawyers pressed the advantage we had gained.

Theoretically, Chaim was guilty of yet another continuing offense with each passing day, so De Vroede filed the charge again, and it began to make its way through the laborious court system. This necessitated many more days at the Palais de Justice, but court pressure was our most effective weapon. My parents and I were always in attendance, to emphasize our commitment to the children.

We reasoned that the more publicity we could generate, the better chance we would have that someone would come forward with helpful information. So I called upon my allies in the media—in Belgium, England, and the U.S.—to keep as much pressure as possible on the Satmar community. Every week, we found one way or another to interest a reporter in our story. I always emphasized: "The children are not Jewish," and the press realized the drama in presenting the clash of a mother fighting for her children against a powerful sect.

To reporter after reporter I explained my position carefully: "I am not fighting because they are in the Jewish world, but because they refuse to return the kids despite the fact that the father is in jail." I respected the Satmars' right to live and worship in their own way. But even by their criterion, my children should not be kept in their cloistered world. I was not a Jew. Chaim and I had been married in a civil ceremony. From the religious Jewish perspective, since a rebbe did not officiate, our marriage was not valid. A "good Jew" should consider the children illegitimate, and they most certainly were not Jewish.

I believed that, in the beginning, the Satmar elders took Chaim at his word when he claimed that I had converted to Judaism; they never bothered to check with the rebbe who supposedly managed my conversion. Chaim must have shown them proof that the Israeli courts had granted custody to him, but he never told them that the decision was later rescinded. They may have believed his charge that I was insane and abused the children. I could understand—even if I could not agree—that, in the beginning, certain Satmar leaders might have considered it their duty to lie to the authorities in order to raise the children as "good little Jews." When Chaim demonstrated his willingness to remain in jail rather than give up the children, he must have achieved a kind of hero status with some.

But I argued that, with the passage of time, the Satmar leaders should have seen through Chaim's deceptions. By now, they must have realized that I never converted to Judaism. They had seen me and heard my side of the story. I was not insane. I had not abused my children. They knew that courts in Belgium, England, and the U.S. had granted me custody. They knew that the Israeli court decision had been canceled. Most important, I stressed, they must be convinced by now that *the children were not Jewish.* My message to the Satmar world was: "I know Chaim lied to you in the beginning. It's a pity, but now you know the truth. Do the right thing. Give Marina, Simon, and Moriah back." To others I said: "That's what I don't accept. They have been cheated—it happens to everybody. But now that they know what is really happening, they won't change their minds." For these reasons—and not because of their religion—I declared with controlled anger, I could never forgive them.

Although Hasidim are forbidden to watch television, listen to the radio, or read secular newspapers, every time a story appeared, the community appeared to be aware of it instantly. The Jewish newspaper *Belgisch Israelitisch Weekblad* and the Jewish weekly *Regards* both published stories about the case and condemned Chaim's position. Hasidic enclaves, particularly in Belgium, were shaken by the negative publicity. Diamond dealers in Antwerp lost sales to outraged customers who instead took their business to nearby exchanges owned by Indian proprietors. I sensed that the Hasidic community, in general, disapproved of the kidnapping scheme, but I knew that the Satmar sect and individual groups within it live by their own rules.

Surely, I thought, some of the Satmar leaders must hope that the problem will just go away and be forgotten.

One Wednesday, during yet another of the interminable hearings at the Palais de Justice, a man wearing typical Hasidic garb appeared in the courtroom and asked to speak to the court. He identified himself as Simon Friedman, a businessman and a representative of the Satmar community in Antwerp, which had asked him to take an interest in the Chaim Yarden matter. He assured the judge, "The Satmar community has nothing to do with this case. The Heymans family is confused." But he tempered his comments, declaring, "I am really sorry for this woman. I will do my best to help." He added, "I don't want to see anything of Chaim Yarden. What he did is not okay."

After the court session, as we stood outside the Palais de Justice discussing matters with our attorneys, Friedman spoke quietly with my brother Eric. Friedman claimed that someone had placed several telephone calls to him—anonymously—and asked him to help find a solution to this delicate problem. He said that he had agreed to act as an intermediary and quietly pleaded with Eric to persuade the family to cooperate with him in order to end this drama in an amicable manner.

At first, Eric was interested in what the man had to say. But the longer they spoke, the more evasive Friedman seemed to become. He said that he had received the anonymous calls "when he was traveling" or "outside of his house." No, he did not know how to contact the caller. My hot-tempered older brother decided that he disliked Friedman and did not want to continue the discussion. Afterward, as he reported the conversation to me, he called Friedman names and expressed his disgust at the community's collective plot to keep a mother's children away from her. Eric advised me, "Don't trust that man."

Buysschaert was suspicious of Friedman also.

Walter warned, "Patsy, that man is not right in his boots."

Since Friedman represented himself as a Satmar spokesman, and since he gave the impression that he knew much about the case, De Vroede asked the Police Judiciare to interview him. After the next court session, Inspector Jean Dooms took Friedman from the Palais de Justice to the nearby offices of the Police Judiciare. The two men chatted at length as they waited for Detective Bernard Humbeeck to begin the interview. Although he was not assigned to the Yarden case, Dooms found the details interesting. During the official interview, Friedman told Humbeeck that he had inserted himself into the Yarden matter in an attempt to act in the best interests of everybody. There was no evidence to detain Friedman or charge him with a crime, and Humbeeck had no choice but to send him on his way.

The persistent Friedman continued to appear in court from week to week and finally managed to draw me aside. Speaking softly, he said, "I can help you. We can make negotiations." To my surprise—Hasidic men are not supposed to touch women outside of their immediate family members—he shook my hand.

The soft-spoken Friedman was a man of medium height and weight. His short-cropped hair showed signs of graying. In appearance, he was like most Hasidim, with the notable exception that he wore no eyeglasses; he had been one of the few Hasidic boys to escape the studies of childhood with unimpaired vision. He spoke fluent French, with just a trace of a German or Yiddish accent, and was the most sophisticated Satmar I had ever met—but he was plagued by dandruff. As we spoke, he constantly flicked dry, white bits of scalp from the shoulders of his black jacket.

Who was this man, and what connection did he have with my children? I asked him what he did for a living. He searched through his pockets and emerged with several bits of crumpled tissue paper. Right there in the Palais de Justice, he unwrapped the papers to exhibit an assortment of diamonds, rubies, and emeralds. Some were mounted into rings and earrings. Friedman grinned and showed me a particularly spectacular diamond ring. "This is for my wife," he said.

I replied, "Wow! For that I would like to be your wife."

Friedman's easy chuckle in response to my joke gave me hope that I had finally found a Satmar with whom I could negotiate. To my brother Eric, who still distrusted the man, I said, "I think you are wrong. He's somebody good. He's going to help me."

Soon after this encounter, Friedman phoned and asked me to visit him at his home at Eleven Jacob Jacobs Straat in Antwerp. He said he had news of the children. He asked that we keep this and any future conversation confidential.

My search was at a low point. There were no fresh leads, and I did not know what else to do. Increasingly, I found myself thinking that I would *never* find my children. I was ready to do just about anything, if only I could see Marina, Simon, and Moriah once more. So of course I agreed to the meeting.

I drove Highway E19 from Brussels to Antwerp and entered the city through the dark, twisting Kennedy Tunnel. The wide, bumpy main thoroughfares were cluttered with cars. Dutch-speaking pedestrians scurried about, boarding ubiquitous electric trolleys.

Off to my right was Mercator Straat, and I recalled that the day Chaim took the children, he received assistance from someone who lived on this avenue.

I turned left onto Pelikans Straat. Here, within the compass of only a few square blocks near the railway station, is a small Hasidic neighborhood that controls a disproportionate share of the world's diamond trade.

The Hasidim live in a cluster of three- and four-story apartment buildings and town houses, with some of the ground-level floors given over to kosher restaurants and yeshivas. Those Hasidim who have need to walk the streets appear to do so in fear and embarrassment over contact with the outside world. They keep their heads low to avoid viewing temptation. I saw a young boy clutching his mother's hand as they moved along briskly. His head was shaved except for the *peiyot* that dangled beneath his ears. The boy wore thick eyeglasses. With a sigh, I realized that Simon probably wore such glasses too.

I located Jacob Jacobs Straat, but it was a one-way lane and I had to circle about through narrow side alleys to approach from the proper direction. On Quinten Matsys Straat I waited impatiently behind a van that blocked the way as its driver unloaded large baskets of artificial flowers. Finally the truck moved on. I turned left onto Jacob Jacobs Straat and was lucky to find a parking space almost directly across from number eleven.

The three-story, pale-yellow brick house stood out prominently as a single-family residence set among surrounding tenements. I crossed the street, approached the heavy brown door, and announced my arrival by pushing a small bell.

Friedman invited me inside and spent a few minutes on small talk, showing off his exquisite collection of miniature silver figurines. His wife wore her jewelry prominently. I was surprised to see a television set and a VCR.

We settled into easy chairs in the quiet elegance of his living room and discussed the situation. Friedman impressed me as an extremely intelligent man with a sincere interest in helping me. He knew how I felt, he said, because he had ten children of his own, and another was on the way. He also had an engaging sense of humor that he knew how to use at just the right moments. He reiterated that he was a Satmar, representing the Satmar community, but he insisted that the Satmars did not have the children. "Don't worry," he purred, "the children are fine. I don't know where they are, but I know they are being well cared for." He said his anonymous contact told him that the people who were holding Marina, Simon, and Moriah did not know that they were wrongly taken; if we could convince them that Chaim had lied to them, we could negotiate their return.

Friedman stressed that he did not know how to get in touch with his contact. If he did, he said, he would go to the man and say, "You are making a big mistake." But instead he had to wait for the man to contact him. I did not believe this, but I had no way to disprove it, and I really needed to trust him.

As promised, Friedman provided news of the children. He said, "They are having problems with Sarah, your oldest daughter."

"Oh, Marina," I said.

Friedman nodded. He said that "Sarah" had gained too much weight and looked like "a tower." This really upset me, because I had bad memories of my own teenage weight problems.

"They are having other problems," Friedman continued.

I desperately wanted to ask who "they" were, but I knew that he would not tell me. I was extremely worried, for this information concurred with what Chaim Shaulson had told me. "What kind of problems?" I asked.

"She is making trouble. Some people went to the children and told them that their mother is dead—so that they will stop asking about you. Your oldest daughter does not believe it, and she is making trouble." When I asked for more details, Friedman said, "Oh, she wouldn't speak, really, but you could see that something was wrong inside her."

These words made me shudder. This was exactly how Marina would react.

"The people want to know, what should they do?" Friedman asked.

I could scarcely believe what I had just heard. My children's captors sought advice from me—even though they claimed that I was dead—on how to control my oldest daughter and stop her from asking questions? "What kind of a question is this to ask me? Tell her the truth!" I pleaded.

In a roundabout way he communicated his response, "No, I am sorry. They cannot."

Friedman smoothly changed the subject. Together, he said, we had to see if we could settle the problem in a "nice way, not like barbarians. First, stop the press," he asked.

I agreed to stem the flood of news stories, so damaging to the image of the Satmar community, but I warned, "If nothing comes of this, we will start the stories again." Then I explained the dilemma I faced in trying to discuss the matter: I assumed that the children were alive and well, but I did not have a shred of evidence to confirm that fact. Before I did anything, I said, I had to have contact with my children.

"I agree," he said. "But it would be very difficult to convince the other people to allow this."

I pressed the point. "Tell the kids to call me."

Friedman worried aloud that I would have the police trace the call.

"Use a public phone," I suggested.

He shook his head.

"Have them send me a letter."

"It's impossible. If the kids are to do something, they are not supposed to know it's for you."

I tried another idea: "Send me a videotape of them."

Friedman pondered this and agreed that a video might be possible but would take time to produce.

We ended the meeting on that note. Friedman would check on the possibility of supplying me with a videotape; then we would speak further.

Driving home from this encounter, I was plagued by conflicting emotions. I was terribly upset, of course, that Marina was unhappy. I was incredibly angry that her captors would lie about my being dead. This was too painful to speak about, even to Walter or my family. Yet, I thought, perhaps Marina's doubts will cause her to rebel against these people. Perhaps she will try to find me! Perhaps she will pick up the phone and call the police.

Weeks passed. Sometimes Friedman called me merely to report, "Well, I don't have any news for you yet." He always had some excuse for the delay.

When I could wait no longer, I called him to ask about the videotape. Finally he admitted, "Well, no, if they give you a tape, you will see how they look."

Did this mean that the children had been subjected to plastic surgery? I wondered. I remembered the Duchess's thoughts on this subject. I was very concerned. Then I thought, if I could not see them, could I at least hear them? "How about a tape cassette?" I asked anxiously.

"Oh, that's not good," he said quickly. "They don't know if the kids will want to speak to you." He explained that they were living now in an extremely religious world, and they might choose to remain out of contact with their non-Jewish mother.

Friedman had me so confused that only later did I wonder about his explanation. How could they choose to remain out of contact with me if they had been told that I was dead?

I remained wary of Friedman, unsure of how much I could trust him but knowing that I had to maintain contact with him. At the moment, he was my only link to the children.

With the cooperation of De Vroede, Friedman obtained special visiting privileges with Chaim, which allowed them to speak in the privacy of a lawyers' room. We hoped that Friedman would be able to influence Chaim to cooperate with us.

He reported to me that he continually urged Chaim to help me find the children. He said that he advised Chaim, "You have to think about what's good for the kids."

In the privacy of his home, Friedman always greeted me with a warm handshake. He would also shake my hand when we met in the Palais de Justice, but he stressed that he would follow this custom "only, only, only if other Hasidic people are not around."

During one of our meetings, Friedman proposed what he characterized as a "gentlemen's agreement": Marina, Simon, and Moriah would remain in the Jewish world, still with a Hasidic family but less extreme than most Satmars; in return for our acquiescence to their religious upbringing, Chaim and I would both be granted generous visiting privileges. Once we worked out the details, we would take the agreement to court for full legal approval.

I was ready to agree to almost any compromise that would allow me to visit my children. If I could only see them, maybe I could get them back—no matter what I promised Friedman. The possibilities raced through my desperate mind: If I can just get to see them I will grab them back! No, I must let them get used to me. What if they disappear again? If they only see me once, at least they will know that I exist. But then I wondered how the judge would regard such an agreement. Unsure of the legal ground, I fell back upon my strategy: Don't say yes, don't say no. I responded, "I will think about it."

For his part, Friedman said that he would try to secure Chaim's approval.

Walter and I spent many hours composing an eleven-page proposal that would frame Friedman's "gentlemen's agreement" in specific terms. The key points were these:

1) The children have to come back to Belgium and stay there. They are not allowed to leave the country without the written authorization of their mother.

2) (a) The legal custody will remain with the mother.

(b) The children will be allowed to stay in a moderately religious Jewish family, living in Belgium, whom Patricia Heymans will have met before and agreed to.

(c) Patricia Heymans will be allowed to withdraw her agreement if the relationship between the family and the children is not compatible.

(d) If this family plans to move away, Patricia Heymans will have to be informed in writing at least two weeks in advance, so that new arrangements can be made for the children.

3) The cost of raising the children shall be covered by the child support that Chaim Yarden was supposed to pay. If he cannot pay, the costs should be covered by the Jewish community.

4) The children will go to a moderate Jewish school, in Belgium, for which Patricia Heymans will have to give a written agreement.

5) (a) Patricia Heymans will have the right to visit the children every day. Telephone contacts will be unlimited.

(b) If possible, Patricia Heymans will give twenty-four-hours' notice of visits.

(c) Patricia Heymans will have the opportunity to visit the children in a neutral place, without surveillance.

(d) The children must be given the opportunity to visit their mother as much as they want.

(e) Even if the children do not want to see their mother, the family and the community will have to encourage the kids to come and see their mother often.

6) All the concerned parties will respect the social, philosophical, and religious views of one another, so that the children can grow up in a bicultural environment. The parties will respect the rules and customs of the religious philosophies.

7) Grandparents and uncles have the right to visit the children once each week.

8) It is understood that the children will have the right to have their opinion taken into account regarding their education and choice of religious community. . . . As soon as the children turn sixteen, their choices will

have to be followed. The choice will have to be said freely in front of both parents, or their representatives.

9) (a) In the event the children disappear again . . . the Jewish community, represented by Mr. Friedman, guarantees to pay all the expenses of finding them, and the community will also have to help Patricia Heymans in her search.

(b) Mr. Yarden, or the community, will put one million Belgian francs into an account . . . so that their mother will be able to pay for the first costs of the search.

10) From now on, the children will be called by their real names—Marina, Simon, and Moriah.

In an attempt to be fair, we also included provisions allowing for Chaim to visit the children. We further pledged to respect the children's religious practices; none of us would attempt to visit on Shabbat or Jewish holidays.

Friedman considered our proposal carefully. "Okay, it's a good one," he announced. But then he began to barter over details. He argued about our demand for a financial guarantee, insinuating that we might be out to cheat him. He conceded that I would be allowed to see the children almost anytime, but he said that a few conditions were necessary. He was not so sure that the children could come to see me whenever they wished. For example, if there was a wedding in my family, my children would not be allowed to attend the Christian ceremony. "Very bad," he muttered. In fact, they would be banned from most family functions where men and women would be mixed together.

"Okay," I said in frustration, "these are little things we can work out later."

Our discussions continued, sometimes in person, sometimes by phone, for a long period of time. My temper simmered.

On one occasion my mother cornered Friedman outside the Palais de Justice. She asked angrily, "How would you feel if someone took three of your kids?"

Friedman replied calmly, "I'd make three new ones," as if children were like puppies.

Each step in these negotiations was painfully slow. Whenever we settled a minor point between ourselves, Friedman announced, "Okay, now I have to wait for the people to call me. Then I will have news as to whether they agree." He continued to claim that he did not know the identity of the caller.

I no longer believed or trusted him, but I had no choice other than to continue the discussions. Occasionally I had to resist the impulse to strangle him, reminding myself that he was my only hope. Often, during a phone conversation with him, I felt my insides shaking. Sometimes, when I am nervous, my vocabulary degenerates into colorful expletives. At one point I could no longer hold my tongue and ranted at Friedman, using language that would make a sailor blush. "Don't use those kinds of words with me!" he snapped.

"I apologize," I said, "but you just drive me crazy." I crashed down the receiver.

I knew that Friedman was manipulating me, but I could not stop him. I also knew that I was wasting time—losing time—but I did not know how to disengage myself from this frustrating dialogue. This was the low point, I realized, the very worst of times.

I stormed about the house, slamming doors and pounding walls, angry with everyone and everything. I had to, as we say in French, "empty my bag."

On Christmas Eve, 1990, Chaim was again found guilty of a continuing offense and sentenced to begin serving a fresh two-year term.

"This is not for revenge," Nadia De Vroede explained. "It is because Chaim Yarden is the key to finding the children."

44

January 1991. I flagged a taxi and gave the driver the address that I had copied into my notebook.

"It doesn't exist," he said.

I studied the notation and realized that it did not look right. From somewhere deep in my memory, I retrieved another address and blurted it out. The driver nodded and drove off.

The streets were busy. At first glance, it appeared to be a normal evening in Tel Aviv, but there was an undercurrent of tension visible on everyone's face. Shoppers in the grocery stores stockpiled canned foods. Every citizen had a gas mask. The bomb shelters were prepared. The subject of every conversation was: What is Saddam saying now?

I shivered, partly from the evening cold, partly from apprehension. I had just learned that I was pregnant once again, and pregnancy always heightens my emotions.

Months earlier, when I first heard that Iraqi dictator Saddam Hussein had invaded Kuwait, I did not see any immediate reason for Israel to become involved. Then, when the United Nations issued an ultimatum, and world military forces, led by the U.S., moved toward an inevitable confrontation with Iraq, and Saddam Hussein threatened to launch a hundred missiles toward Israel in retaliation for every one sent to Iraq, I began to think seriously about returning to Chaim's homeland. Despite our belief that the children were somewhere in the U.S., the possibility lingered that they might be in Israel. And I knew of someone in Tel Aviv who might be able to help me locate them.

It was about 7:00 P.M. when the taxi dropped me off at the apartment building. I stepped onto the porch and rang the bell. Within moments, a woman's voice came over the speaker system: "Yes?"

In Hebrew I asked, "Am I at Iris Buttel's house?"

"Who is it?"

"It's a friend. I'd like to speak to Iris."

"What's your name?"

I sidestepped the question. "Come on, it's cold out here," I complained. "Please, let me get in." Someone upstairs pushed the buzzer, allowing me entry into the building. I made my way up to the designated apartment and banged on the door.

A young woman answered. She was dressed in dark clothing, with long, thick socks and heavy shoes. Her head was covered in the fashion of the religious. She had a plain face and an oversized nose, a frequent characteristic of Yemenite Jews.

I announced, "Hello, I'm Chaim Yarden's first wife."

Iris appeared to be so shocked that I thought she might collapse upon the floor.

"Listen," I said quickly, "I don't have anything against you. I'm just looking for my children."

Cautiously she allowed me inside and beckoned me to sit in a chair in one corner of the room. We were both very nervous. She sat opposite me, far away in another corner. She was very reserved, and I noted tension among the members of the household. Iris's sister wore a very short skirt and her brother-in-law wore his hair in a ponytail. Obviously, there were conflicting attitudes toward religion here, and I hoped that Iris's background had left her more open-minded than some of the other Hasids. Her mother and her sister stood off to one side, staring at me curiously, listening carefully.

"I don't have anything against you," I repeated.

The conversation was slow and stilted. Her sister politely offered to serve coffee and a tray of sweets, and that allowed us a brief break.

When we resumed speaking, Iris admitted that she really wanted to have Chaim back so that she could have children of her own. She had met Chaim only once or twice prior to the marriage, and they were together for only three or four months before his arrest. During their brief time together, she had not been able to conceive.

She was shocked when I told her that Chaim and I had never legally divorced, and I could see that this news also upset her mother and sister. I said I had been told that she had married Chaim under the condition that my children would not live with them. That was when Chaim turned them over to the Satmar community, to continue to make "good little Jews" out of them.

Iris did not deny this, but she claimed, "I didn't know they were Chaim's kids."

"Listen, I don't believe you!" I snapped. "Don't expect me to believe you when you say such kind of *shtooyot* [nonsense]. It's a lie."

"Okay, okay," she admitted with a shrug.

Over the course of our two-hour conversation, we spoke mostly about Chaim and the children. Sometimes I sought to ease the tension by changing the subject. I asked what she did. She told me that she taught in a kindergarten and really enjoyed working with small children. Gradually she shifted across the room, until we were sitting very close. Several times her mother muttered something to her; I could not understand, so I assumed that they were speaking Yemenite.

Iris still contended that she did not know where my children were living. I believed her, but I also believed that she could find out. The encounter was extremely tiring, my fatigue compounded by the physical effects of my pregnancy. "Help me," I implored. "You don't have children, but you are a woman. You can understand what my feelings are." I explained that the way to get

Chaim out of prison was to return the children. "You want your husband back. I want my children. We can both have what we want. Let's help one another, okay?"

She said, "I'm married to Chaim. I have to ask permission of my husband."

I asked, "Do you want your husband back?"

"Yes."

I repeated, "And I want my children back. The only way to get them back is to change Chaim's mind. So try to get him to talk. That will serve you. That will serve me. That will serve everybody."

"Okay," she agreed. "I'm going to write him a letter. And if he calls, I will try to speak to him about it."

At the end of our visit, Iris walked me to a bus station and waited with me until I was safely aboard. I was dead tired but confident that she would at least attempt to help.

Chaim's mother, Leah, was also surprised to see me in Israel at this dangerous time. She said that she did not know where Chaim was.

I reported, "He's been in jail for two years now."

Color drained from Leah's face. Her mouth dropped open. I was afraid that she would faint. As we spoke more, I realized she did not even know that Chaim had remarried, or that his wife, Iris, was living only a few miles from her house. I wrote out Chaim's jail address on several envelopes—Leah could not write in Latin characters—so that she could contact her son. I also gave her Iris Buttel's address and phone number.

"It's because of you that Chaim is in jail," she accused angrily.

"No, Leah," I replied, "I'm sorry, but I didn't put your son in jail. He put himself in jail because of his behavior."

By long-distance phone from Belgium, I spoke with Iris three more times. During the first two calls she was friendly and repeated her promise to speak to Chaim about returning the children.

But during the third call she snarled, "You are a liar. I cannot trust you. Leave me alone. It's not my business. I don't want anything to do with it."

From this, I concluded that she had indeed spoken to Chaim.

45

Rachel's Story

When Mr. and Mrs. Jacobovich got mad, they screamed and smacked us, sometimes with a belt and sometimes with their hands. I wished we could go back to the Browns' house. They didn't smack us when we were bad.

I made a friend named Esther. On Shabbat, we played together all day. I liked it because I didn't have to clean the toilets and I didn't have to go to school. But there were so many "may nots" to remember: You may not touch anything electric. You may not write. You may not cut with scissors. You may not stick anything with tape. You may not color in a book.

I had to share a room with two small babies. Mrs. Jacobovich slept right across the hall, but she never woke up when the babies cried. I had to take care of them, and I hated it. One night Sarah slept in our room too, and when the babies cried, I pretended to stay asleep so that my older sister would have to take care of them for a change.

The Jacoboviches had a girl named Esther too. She was older than me, but she still made pee-pee in her bed all the time. I hated it when we had to sleep in the same room.

Mr. and Mrs. Jacobovich's youngest child liked to pretend that the oven was a garage. Sometimes he parked his small cars and trucks in it. One Friday evening, when Shabbat had already begun, Mrs. Jacobovich realized that she had forgotten to turn off the stove. Now, it was forbidden. But she worried that her son might play in it and burn himself. Mr. Jacobovich had to go see the rebbe to get permission to turn off the oven. The rebbe was a very smart man. He did not want the boy to burn himself, so he arranged for a non-Jew to come to the house and turn off the oven.

I decided to be very bad and cause as much trouble as I could. Sometimes I even hit my teacher. When the teacher asked me to fetch some papers, I just yelled No! I never, ever obeyed. When the teacher complained to Mr. and Mrs. Jacobovich about my bad behavior, they got very mad at me.

Lots of mornings I told Mrs. Jacobovich that I was sick so that I wouldn't have to go to school.

After a while, Mr. and Mrs. Jacobovich told us that we had to call them mammy and pappy. I said, "I don't want to."

Mrs. Jacobovich said, "Well, anyhow, you will never go back to your mother."

So I knew I had a mother somewhere.

46

Several generous people helped with donations, but my money was dwindling. I faced a difficult decision. In order to keep Chaim in jail, I had to continue to pay Dominique Buysschaert and Patrick Mandoux to work on the case. But if I paid the legal fees, I would not have the money to continue my frequent travels.

During the twenty-four months since Chaim's arrest, I had made eighteen separate trips to the U.S. Only the most important encounters were documented in my green book. So many other contacts had come and gone that I had lost track of them. Nameless and faceless police officers and attorneys had expressed initial support and interest, but as soon as I left their offices, the information that I had provided was placed in never-opened folders and stored in overflowing file cabinets. An assortment of rebbes and would-be informants had proved worthless to my cause. I had worn out several pairs of shoes walking the streets of Williamsburg and Borough Park.

Now I realized that I would have to give up either these trips or my attorneys. I desperately wanted to be in America, for I was certain that my children were there. But I realized that the one thing I could not afford was to see Chaim walk free. He would bolt. In his continuing crusade to destroy my life, he would gather the children and disappear once more, perhaps forever. Nadia De

Vroede was an effective and creative prosecutor. I knew that she would not give up, but I wondered just how long the courts would support her continuing-offense strategy. How long before the system grew tired of keeping Chaim locked up? Buysschaert and Mandoux had proven their dedication, and I needed them on my side.

Reluctantly I decided that I would have to curtail my travel schedule. Perhaps I could still afford to visit New York three or four times a year.

Before Chaim took the children, I was a child myself, unable to do anything without the aid of my parents. I knew nothing about the complex jurisdictional problems associated with international kidnapping. In Belgium, no one had addressed the issue. But since Chaim's arrest and our publicity campaign, everyone knew about it. Frequent stories about the case appeared in the press, and I went on television whenever I had the opportunity. My case set the precedents.

If I could not immediately ease my own pain, I was determined to help others. With Walter's active assistance, I formed an organization called the Missing Children International Network. Loosely patterned after the National Center for Missing and Exploited Children in the United States, it was designed to act as a Brussels-based clearinghouse to provide both general and specific information to other grieving parents. The government agreed that donations of one thousand Belgain francs or more would be tax-deductible.

In the beginning we functioned much like a fire department, responding and reacting only to emergencies. Most were phone calls from mothers, pleading, "Please help me. My child is kidnapped! What do I do?"

Gradually we were able to increase our efforts. I began writing a small book about the prevention of kidnapping. It felt good to be doing something constructive.

We wanted to educate the public about the dimensions of the problem, but statistics had never been compiled. Many parental kidnappings were not reported to the authorities. After consulting with the police and the justice ministry, we were able to document 435 active cases in Belgium. We guessed that the problem was much greater than this, but it was the only number we could justify.

To garner press coverage, we celebrated the observance of the International Day for Missing Children by launching 435 helium-filled balloons, which floated off into the sky, toward unknown destinations.

One of the interested people who attended was Police Judiciare investigator Jean Dooms, who had escorted Simon Friedman to his initial police interrogation. Dooms said he wished that he could work more directly on my case. "As a parent, I feel your pain," he commented.

Dooms tried to cheer me. He told me about a case he had been working on since 1985, concerning a missing boy who was most likely the victim of a stranger abduction. There were few leads, and it was quite likely that the boy would never be found alive. In contrast, he pointed out, there was considerable evidence that my children were alive and well, and we had at least some leads. Simon Friedman, he believed, knew exactly where they were.

We tried every possible way to find something illegal in Friedman's words and actions. If we could throw him in jail for just a single night, the police might be able to pressure him into telling us where the children were. But he was clever. Any information he provided concerning the children was tempered with the caveat that he did not know the identity of the person who gave him the information. He did nothing illegal; we had no charge against him.

As we continued to debate minor points of our proposed gentlemen's agreement, Friedman tried to reassure me that the children would live with a family that was not overly strict. "What do you think about a family as religious as mine?" he asked. "We are not too religious. Look at my daughters—they can have pink and red in their clothes."

Over the course of several conversations it became clear that Friedman was seriously considering the idea of bringing my children into his home. He said, "I spoke with my wife. Between having eleven kids and fourteen kids, there is not much difference." He responded to my amazed look by reassuring, "We know each other. We can trust one another. You know that I am on your side. We are not *too* religious." His expression said: Look what a good man I am; I accept your kids.

Friedman insisted that I would have to give up, formally, not only my custody rights but my status as the children's mother. He wanted me to allow a Hasidic family to legally adopt Marina, Simon, and Moriah. "If you do that for us," he declared, "then we can keep them in a Hasidic family and we know there will not be any more problems. Look, this way there will be no trouble. There will be no change in their lives. We are doing it for their sake."

I screamed to myself: Are you crazy? You want me to give up my kids to you, to anyone? No! But to Friedman I said, "I'll think about it."

In court, Chaim suddenly changed his strategy. He declared that, although he did not know where the children were, he was prepared to cooperate in helping to find them. The judge gave him two weeks to prove his good intentions.

That evening my phone rang constantly as reporters called me for comment. To all of them I said, "Let's wait and see. I hope it will be true." But to a few reporters whom I had learned to trust, I added, off the record, "I doubt it."

Buysschaert devised a bold strategy to test Chaim's intentions. He suggested that we prepare a letter for both Chaim and me to sign, pleading for the return of the children. We would advertise the letter in newspapers all over the world, with a particular emphasis on Jewish publications.

The key to success, of course, was to persuade Chaim to sign the letter, but the maneuver carried great risk. If Chaim signed and any resulting information proved useless, he could argue in court that, since he had cooperated in a serious attempt to locate the children, he was no longer guilty of a continuing offense. But we felt that the potential impact of the letter outweighed the risk, and Buysschaert composed a draft:

TO WHOM IT MAY CONCERN

We the undersigned, Patricia HEYMANS and Chaim YARDEN (also called Chaim EDWAR) . . . are the mother and father of
    —Marina EDWAR, born on October 18, 1979,
    —Simon EDWAR, born on January 2, 1981, and
    —Moriah EDWAR (YARDEN), born on June 7, 1982
who disappeared from their Belgian hometown, Brussels, on December 11, 1986 . . .
    We together request any person having recent or less-recent information, or any person being or having been in contact with either one or all three children, or anybody having information that could help to locate the children, to call immediately, even anonymously, one of the here-below indicated phone numbers:

We then listed telephone numbers for the Belgian police, Buysschaert, and De Vroede, as well as for Chaim's current attorney, Guy San Bartolome Sarrey. Finally we listed the toll-free number in the U.S. for the National Center for Missing and Exploited Children: 1-800-FIND KID.
    Buysschaert's draft of the letter continued:

The undersigned Chaim YARDEN authorizes, out of his free will and without restraint, all people and institutions that have or had the children—Marina, Simon, and Moriah—or one of them in charge, either upon my request or upon request from people speaking in my name, to provide all information in their possession to either one of the above-mentioned phone numbers.
    We ask you to copy this message to any other person

you know who might be able to provide the information requested above.

I signed the letter immediately. The next move was up to Chaim.

Chaim refused to sign our letter. Instead, he countered with a proposal of his own, which he presented in court: 1) Chaim and I would agree to look for the children together; 2) neither of us would do anything to impede the other's ability to search.

That's totally crazy, I thought. And the judge agreed. He immediately indicated that if I accepted point number two, I would have to drop the charges so as not to impede Chaim's ability to search.

Simon Friedman backed away from his proposal that my children live with him and now suggested that they would live with a Hasidic family in the United Kingdom.

"I might do it," I said, leading him on. "But I want to see the kids at least six times before I agree. I want to see them at least six times before Chaim gets out of jail." I had to make sure that the children knew me before Chaim had a chance to steal them away again.

Friedman refused. I had to do things his way; then, I *might* be allowed to see the children.

Frustrated, I once again raised the issue of proof. How did I know that Friedman could really produce the children? How did I know that the children really were alive and well? "I don't have a clue that the kids are still alive," I pointed out.

Friedman shrugged and reassured me, "Oh, the kids are fine." Realizing his lapse, he added rapidly, "It's the anonymous person who told me that."

"Yeah, but that's not sufficient proof for me. I want tangible proof." I knew that he would not comply, but I had to ask.

Friedman offered, "When the person calls me, I will tell him to call you, to let you speak to the children. In two weeks I am going to the States. I will be able to arrange it."

For many weeks afterward, I leaped for the phone whenever it rang. But the children never called.

Nadia De Vroede was promoted to a higher position, but she requested that she be allowed to continue working on our case. She remained ready to help us as much as possible.

Friedman and I arranged a meeting with her to discuss the "gentlemen's agreement" that we had been negotiating for so long. But I arrived early, so that the prosecutor and I could discuss the issue privately. I asked De Vroede if the court would accept such an agreement.

"No," she answered quickly. She noted that this was not a simple civil custody case where the parents might come to some private arrangement. This was a case of criminal kidnapping. "If the court starts playing that kind of game, where will it end? It's not up to Friedman to tell the court how Patricia Heymans has to see her kids."

"Thank you," I said, "now I can tell Friedman that I would have agreed, but the court will not allow it."

The prosecutor nodded her approval.

When Friedman arrived, he began a discussion of some of the specific points of the contract. He explained that I would have the right to visit my children within a Hasidic household, but I would not have the right to take them out, because he did not want them exposed to the outside world. De Vroede asked, "Do you do that with all of your kids, shield them from contact with the regular world?"

"Yes," Friedman replied.

"Oh, so what you're telling me is that you're not really sure you're educating your kids in the best way. You have to keep them locked in your world so that they will not see the rest of the world. It's not the natural way."

Friedman, as smart and glib as he was, did not know how to respond to this comment.

After Friedman left, I told De Vroede, "You really made a point that I hadn't thought about. They are not so sure that their way of education is good."

Life in Brussels was simply too expensive. When my lease at Nine Rue Verte expired at the end of July 1991, I reluctantly agreed to move. Walter and I wanted to raise Noélie, and the baby we were expecting, in a quieter, country environment. My parents offered to let us stay at the country home in Nassogne until we found a place of our own.

Before we moved, I scrubbed the walls and floors of Nine Rue Verte. As I worked, I sensed that my past and future lives were on a collision course. Giving up the town house made me feel as if I were giving up Marina, Simon, and Moriah. I wrote letters to the owner and the new tenant, instructing them to contact me immediately if there was any news of my children.

The baby was due on September 12. Since I had a history of late deliveries I viewed the date with skepticism, but because I also had a history of giving birth quickly once labor began, my doctor advised that we leave Nassogne and come back to Brussels to be closer to the hospital.

On September 11, Walter and I packed the car and, along with fifteen-month-old Noélie, drove to my parents' house in Brussels. This had been my most difficult and uncomfortable pregnancy. The baby was positioned low, on my right side, creating a lot of pressure. Poor circulation and varicose veins caused my legs to swell and ache. By the time we reached Brussels, all I could do was sit in a chair, like an inflated balloon, and wait.

My mother had an appointment in Nassogne the following day and left shortly after we arrived. Papa remained behind to care for Noélie if need be. Before she left, Maman gave me some embroidery to keep my hands busy and my mind occupied.

That night, as Walter snored contentedly at my side, I was jolted by my first contraction. I glanced at the clock. It was 1:00 A.M. With my other labors, contractions started slowly, gradually building in intensity, but this was a major, full-fledged arc of pain. Fifteen minutes later, I was hit by another bolt of pain.

Walter awoke as I was twisting around, trying to ride through the severe contraction. We roused my sleeping father and asked him to care for Noélie.

The streets of Brussels were quiet and empty as we made the fifteen-minute drive. Now, the contractions seemed to radiate from my hardened stomach to the small of my back, where they shot up and down my spine with agonizing intensity. Never before had I experienced such pain.

As we turned a corner and approached the hospital, we were confronted by a barricade of flashing lights and sirens. A house fire, on the same street as the hospital, had brought traffic to a standstill.

"If they don't let us through," I moaned to Walter, "we'll have to detour. We won't be able to pull up to the emergency room, and I just can't walk." Fortunately, a policeman waved us on. We were the last car to get through.

Once inside the hospital, I was immediately placed in a wheelchair. Walter and I filled out the necessary paperwork. Within minutes we were escorted to a labor room.

As a nurse helped remove my leggings, she noticed that they were bloodstained. In a quiet, calm voice she assured me that it was nothing to be concerned about, but she wanted the doctor to examine me. Remembering how quickly Noélie had appeared, I told her that she had better do it fast.

By the time the doctor arrived I was bleeding quite heavily. His examination revealed that the placenta was separating and the baby was not in an optimal birthing position. I would be watched closely, but the birth was not imminent. I was rolled over on my side and felt the sting of the needle as a relaxant was administered. A belt was placed across my stomach and attached to a monitor to gauge the progress of labor. The weight of the belt crushed against my belly, and I wanted to rip it off.

Just leave me alone, I thought. Please, just let me be.

Hours passed in a painful, surreal blur. The injection rendered me light-headed and disoriented. In the corner of the room I saw three Walters, sitting in three chairs, reading three books. All around me, doctors hovered in duplicate or triplicate.

By 4:00 A.M. I was fully dilated but felt no need to push. At 5:00 A.M. a pediatrician was summoned to my room. Concern for me, and the baby, was written on every face.

With each contraction I attempted to focus my eyes on a small, oddly shaped letter on a box of sterile gloves that rested on a nearby table. My vision blurred. I started counting to myself: *une, deux, trois,* . . . but I could not remember what came after *dix,* so I started over again.

Doctors prepared for an emergency C-section.

Several more hours passed. Finally, at 9:30 in the morning, I was taken to the delivery room. The obstetrician's hands were inside of me, trying to manipulate the baby into the proper position. Fifteen minutes later, the doctor placed a small suction cup on the baby's head and tried to coax the infant out of my body and into the world. I felt as though an entire army had marched inside of me.

At three minutes before 10:00 A.M., the baby finally arrived. As a precaution, the full-term infant was taken immediately to the preemie unit.

The labor had been extremely difficult and I had lost a great deal of blood. I could barely lift my head as I whispered to Walter, "I know it's a boy. It's Gautier."

47

When Gautier was four months old, Walter and I found a rustic, comfortable stone house in a picturesque village not far from my parents' country house. Through the kitchen window I could see cows grazing. Birds soared above. I loved the area. This was the perfect place to raise our two new children.

And yet, I longed to have my three older children living together with us in this wonderful home. Caring for Noélie and Gautier caused dormant memories to come bubbling to the surface—memories of Marina, Simon, and Moriah as the babies I had borne and nurtured years before.

The mind and the body are linked in ways that I did not understand. Now, my body began to scream at me. I felt extremely tired. Pulling myself out of bed in the morning became an almost insurmountable task. I could not concentrate. I would begin the laundry, become distracted, start some unrelated chore, and then forget what I was doing. My blood pressure plummeted. Frequent asthma attacks left me breathless and wheezing. My skin itched and burned from eczema. My eyesight blurred.

Walter said, "Patsy, you could pack all your clothing to go on vacation in the bags you have under your eyes."

Characteristically, my quick temper targeted those with

whom I felt the safest. I would fix upon some real or imagined minor grievance and hammer away at it endlessly. Once my mouth opened I was like an express train at full throttle—with no brakes. Walter's legendary patience was tested severely. He understood that emotional frustration and physical exhaustion were behind the outbursts, but he also knew that our relationship would not survive without limits. "Don't go too far, Patsy," he cautioned.

On occasion I did go very far and we fought bitterly. But, despite his warning, Walter was able to recover and forgive quickly. His personality was such a welcome contrast to Chaim, whose anger festered for days, weeks, months, and years.

People asked, "Patsy, why do you go on? After so many false leads, dashed hopes, and slammed doors, why do you do it?"

My answer was always the same: "I am knocking my head against the wall, hoping that someday one brick will fall down and that brick will make a small opening in the wall and I'll be able to walk through it."

And I never forgot that I had three individual reasons for continuing the fight. They were Marina, Simon, and Moriah.

This nightmare had now been going on for five long years. I still went to sleep every night thinking about the children; I still woke every morning thinking about them.

Simon Friedman called Dominique Buysschaert and arranged a Sunday meeting at Buysschaert's office in Brussels.

"It is very complicated for Chaim in that jail," Friedman complained to my attorney. He noted that Chaim received a weekly delivery of food from a kosher restaurant in Antwerp, but did not have the facilities to prepare the meals. Friedman bemoaned, "He has to warm his kosher food with candles." Then he asked, "Is it not possible to have him at the prison in Antwerp? It would be easier to bring him his meals. In Antwerp, we could go every day with his food."

Buysschaert was not very sympathetic, but he promised that

he would discuss the matter with Nadia De Vroede. After the meeting, he dismissed the issue from his mind.

More than a month later, Friedman phoned Buysschaert again and thanked him for his cooperation, noting, "He is in Antwerp."

Buysschaert had absolutely nothing to do with the move but quickly decided to use the circumstance to our advantage. He mumbled a white lie: "I tried to do something for you. Now it's your turn."

After Friedman hung up, Buysschaert immediately called De Vroede to find out why Chaim had been transferred to the Antwerp prison. De Vroede was incensed. She was the one who was supposed to sign the paper authorizing any such move, but she knew nothing about it.

Chaim was supposed to be housed in one of the two large jails that were situated across from one another on Avenue Ducpetiaux in Brussels, because they were convenient to the Palais de Justice. But upon investigation, De Vroede discovered that Chaim had been in the Antwerp prison for the past month. She arranged for his immediate return to Brussels.

Here was further evidence of the lobbying power of the small, closed community of the Hasidim. Their influence extended even into the prison system. This incident also made us wonder how much influence the Hasidim wielded in other areas of the government.

Court hearings and special sessions were a way of life. Chaim appealed every decision at every level. But always, in the end, we won our points. On June 18, 1992, Chaim once again appeared in court to face another charge of committing a continuing offense. This time he chose to act as his own attorney, effectively proving the old saying that a man who acts as his own lawyer has a fool for a client. He rambled for hours, testing everyone's patience.

At times, when the judge explained provisions of the law,

Chaim interrupted: "No, no, no. That's not how it is. Go and look at" such-and-such a case.

When the judge asked Chaim where the children were and if he had attempted to find them, Chaim answered with a brittle response: "Go and look for them yourself!"

The judge glowered at him.

In the end, Chaim was again found guilty and returned to prison to begin a new two-year sentence.

I maintained a posture of cooperation toward Simon Friedman, unwilling to burn whatever bridge existed between him and my children. We continued to meet frequently or speak by phone. "I'm doing this from my heart," he assured me, "because I'm deeply concerned about what you are going through."

When I was with him or even on the phone, he was often able to convince me of his sincerity. It was only after each encounter, when I mulled over the subtleties of his words and actions, that my doubts grew.

On one occasion when I visited in his home, he said, "You know, we really have to get your children away from these people. I'm a Satmar and I'm very religious, and I think it is very bad for your children to be in such a religious world. They should be with less religious people." He reminded me that Jews consider the child's religion to come through the mother. Everyone in the Satmar community knew that I was not Jewish; therefore, they were prejudiced against my children. The more religious the community, the more bias there would be against my children, especially the girls. Friedman continued, "When it comes time to marry your daughters, they will never find them okay husbands, because the mother is the one who gives the religion to the children. They will have to find them old or simple-minded men." Simon, he contended, would fare better because he was male, but he too would never be fully accepted.

These comments hurt me deeply, but I did not want Friedman to see my pain. I was not sure if he was purposely trying to hurt me or if he was trying to show me how good he was, by helping a non-Jewish mother save her children from such a fate.

October 19, 1992. It was Marina's thirteenth birthday. If you get her back now, I thought, she will be a teenager, no longer a child. I tried to force myself to envision her and my other children as they must appear now, but they were frozen in my memory at ages seven, five, and four. A sudden thought came to me: Oh, my, Marina must have had her first period by now.

I was plagued by a recurring fear. For years my children had been lied to and deceived. When they came back to me, how could I gain their trust? How could I expect them to believe me, when their entire lives had been based on deceit? Would they ever be able to trust anyone?

Friedman, under the guise of imparting information, told me a story relayed to him by his contact: at Marina's bas mitzvah, the husband of the family she was living with had presented her with a traditional pair of earrings. Marina had refused them, saying that her father must present them, and nobody else.

For days afterward, Friedman's statements continued to haunt me. I worried constantly about Marina and Moriah's marital prospects. Time was running out for them. I knew that the Satmars married their children off at a very young age. What fate awaited Marina?

By now I had a reasonably good idea of what life was like for a Satmar wife under the best of circumstances. Her primary task was to bring as many children into the world as possible. (The Hasidim have a saying: "Over ten, don't count anymore.") She was to keep the house kosher and to monitor every word and action of the children. She had to make sure that the children spoke Yiddish in the home, rather than English or any other language that was, as they would say darkly, "not Jewish." She had to make sure that they prayed properly before biting into a biscuit or drinking a drop of water. Once her daughter reached the age of three, the Satmar mother had to make sure that she covered herself properly with long sleeves, long skirts, and thick, high socks.

Underneath, a girl had to wear a thick white jumper, to prevent the glare of sunshine from revealing the silhouette of her body. Summer and winter, she had to dress the same. A Satmar mother's daily conversations with her children were characterized by the questions: "Did you do this?" "Did you do that?" and the warnings, "You may not do this," "You may not do that." And, of course, she had to attend to her own religious duties and rituals.

Scenes played through my mind constantly. I knew that Marina and Moriah were not allowed to ride a bicycle or swing on a swing, lest their skirts swirl. I assumed that Simon, like so many other Hasidic boys, already wore thick eyeglasses. I knew that he had long, curly *peiyot*. I knew that each of the three was encouraged to spy on the others and to report even the most modest violations of obscure rules.

In particular, the story about Marina and the earrings was like a slap in the face. It sounded as if Marina had truly been indoctrinated. Too much time had passed. I thought: When I have my children back, they will have bonded completely with their father and his style of life. My work with Missing Children International had familiarized me with the phenomenon known as the "Stockholm Syndrome," wherein a hostage, over time, comes to view his captor as his savior. Had this already happened to my children? Was I the stranger they had come to hate, the one who abandoned them and did not come for them sooner?

I could say little of this out loud. I casually told Walter the story of the earrings, as if it did not affect me. To put my deeper thoughts into words would give them a kind of validity with which I could not deal.

In Brussels, I presented a two-hour speech at a conference on missing children. Because the meeting was conducted in Dutch, Walter accompanied me and answered questions. I was surprised to hear him tell a story about an unnamed girl who had refused a gift of earrings because they were not from her father— the very person who had kidnapped her. He discussed the Stockholm Syndrome and how it is an ever-present fear for any parent who is searching for her kidnapped children.

Walter never named the child, or the mother. And after the meeting, we did not discuss his speech. But his message was clear: "Patsy, I understand what you're feeling; I understand that it's hard for you to speak about it." I loved him for this, but I could not bring myself to tell him so.

Soon after the conference, we attended the thirtieth birthday of a friend. One moment I was dancing, and the next I was on the floor. Someone carried me to an adjoining private room, where I cried hysterically and babbled about Marina and the rejected earrings. Walter and my best friend, Marie-Anne, tried to calm me, but I was oblivious to their presence.

I woke at home the next morning. The mirror told me that I had been crying, but I had no memory of when or why.

48

We still believed that our best chance of finding the children was to develop an informant. Dominique Buysschaert learned that another Hasidic man was incarcerated at Saint Gilles jail. His name was Chaim Baum. Desperate for any fresh leads, Buysschaert decided to pay him a visit and try to enlist his cooperation on our behalf; perhaps he might gain Chaim Yarden's confidence or at least overhear some information that would be useful to us.

Buysschaert arrived at the prison and asked to see Chaim Baum. Waiting in the attorney's visiting room, Buysschaert was surprised—and horrified—when a guard appeared with Chaim Yarden. Prison officials had obviously misunderstood his request. Buysschaert knew immediately that this was an incredibly sensitive situation. First, any contact between my attorney and Chaim was highly unethical. Second, Buysschaert did not want *this* Chaim to realize that he was speaking with the *other* Chaim. My attorney immediately complained to the authorities, and Chaim was taken back to his cell.

After much delay, Chaim Baum was brought into the room, but he proved to be very uncooperative. After the briefest of conversations, he adamantly refused to help us.

*   *   *

Simon Friedman greeted me with his usual civility at the door of his house. Once we were inside, he shook my hand.

After a few minutes of chatting, he grew solemn. He stared at the ceiling for a moment, shifted in his seat, and flicked dry white specks of dandruff from his shoulder. What he had to say contradicted many of the things he had indicated throughout the nearly two years of our negotiations. He said with a sense of finality, "The problem, you see, is that the kids are Jewish. So we may not return them."

I pointed out that if the children had been converted, it was done without my permission and on the basis of Chaim's lies.

Friedman conceded that there were irregularities. The mother's permission is supposedly necessary. Without that permission, children are not usually converted until they are old enough to make an informed decision. "It was an in-between conversion," he admitted.

I retorted, "But they are not Jews, because the conversion was illegal—"

"Yes, but wait," Friedman interrupted. "When they will be eighteen, we will ask them if they want to remain Jewish, and if they say no, we will let them go free."

"But they will not want to be Christian when you tell them all the time that Christians are bad people."

Friedman had an answer for everything. "No, no," he said. "I remember once, a while back, there was a case of a Christian child taken by his father and put—like your kids—into the community. He was one of the best students we had for religious matters. He was so good. But when he was eighteen, we asked him, 'Do you want to remain Jewish or do you want to go back with your Christian mother?' He said he wanted to go back with his Christian mother, so we let him go."

How was I supposed to respond to this? Did Friedman expect me to sit back, wait for my children, one by one, to reach legal adulthood, and then rely upon the judgment and understanding of certain Satmar leaders to decide whether they would release them? It was absurd. I held my tongue, afraid of the words that might come out of my mouth if I allowed myself to speak.

Friedman said that the nebulous people who had contacted him now balked at moving the children either to Belgium or the U.K.; they decreed that the children—my children—would remain in the U.S.

No matter what solution Friedman came up with, one thing remained constant: I would have to relinquish my parental rights. Over and over again he reminded me that I would never be able to locate my children if the Hasids who held them did not accept our "gentlemen's agreement."

I wondered where this man got his audacity, but I tried to answer calmly. I played Nadia De Vroede's trump card, pointing out, "First of all, it's not for me to decide. The youth court will not accept it." I allowed this point to sink in. Then I added, "Second, I refuse anyway. Because, if Chaim gets out of jail, where do I have the slightest guarantee that I will see the kids again?" And even if I was to agree and was granted visitation rights, I asked, "How am I going to see them?"

"You just go to the States," Friedman replied, as if such a trip were like jumping into the car to drive to the market. "This way, the kids will stay around the people they know. It's easier for them. There will be no change."

My anger boiled over and I snapped, "It's not so that they can stay in the States. I'll tell you why it is: It's because you want me to be far away from the kids."

He did not answer. He just stared at me with his mouth open.

"Did you ever think that I might go to live in the States, just to see my kids? What are you going to do then, send them to Australia?"

Once again he had no answer.

I said to myself: That's it.

Jailhouse records revealed that Friedman had been visiting Chaim much more frequently than he had claimed. And since those discussions occurred in a lawyer's private room, we had no idea what they said to one another.

Only after our discussion did I realize the full absurdity of some of Friedman's statements. Regardless of the details of a youthful conversion, once a boy finishes his bar mitzvah ritual, he is considered Jewish. As for the girls, if we waited until they were eighteen, they would probably be engaged or already married; they might even have children of their own.

The next time Friedman attempted to visit Chaim in jail, he discovered that De Vroede had revoked his privileges.

49

"It is in relation to the case of the Yarden children," the caller said. The receptionist at DeBacker & Associés knew what that meant. She had been instructed to route any calls regarding the Yarden case to Dominique Buysschaert—immediately. Buysschaert found the caller's voice raspy and difficult to hear; the tone reminded him of sandpaper scraping across rough wood. "I have contacts in Antwerp," the man said. "And I can get information for you regarding the Yarden children. Are you interested?"

So many calls had come in the past—to Buysschaert, to my father, to me. Was this yet another empty offer from someone seeking money? Or was this another diversionary tactic—another Friedman? Buysschaert could not know. Neither could he ignore the man. "Yes, I'm interested," he responded quickly.

The caller would not discuss details over the phone. He suggested a private discussion at a kosher restaurant in Antwerp's diamond district.

"How will I know you?" Buysschaert asked.

"I'll know you," the stranger replied.

Buysschaert is an attorney, not a private detective. His daily schedule normally does not include a clandestine meeting with a secretive stranger. He would go, but he would be careful. He immediately called Nadia De Vroede to inform her of this new development. Together, they decided that they would not yet report to the police; they would wait to see if the man provided any useful information.

Buysschaert drove his gray BMW 525 to Antwerp along wide, busy Mercator Straat. Following directions, he turned through a series of crowded, narrow, one-way streets. He realized that he was not far from Simon Friedman's home. He drove past the restaurant several times searching for a parking spot, and finally found a place to leave the car, several blocks away. He walked hurriedly, glancing at his watch; he was fifteen minutes late.

He pulled open the door and stepped into the restaurant. The first section housed a food-preparation and take-out catering area. Behind it was a long, oblong room with two rows of tables. A partition was available for separating the room into two distinct areas, for men and for women. Each area had a sink attached to the wall so that patrons could wash their hands between courses or after handling bread.

Feeling rather conspicuous in his light-gray suit, Buysschaert lowered his six-two frame into a chair behind one of the empty tables. He surveyed the customers, wondering who was friend, who was foe.

Within seconds, Buysschaert was joined by a middle-aged Hasidic man, short and wiry, wearing an ill-fitting black suit. Buysschaert recognized the gravelly voice immediately. The man spoke slowly, mixing Dutch and French, as he attempted to come to his point.

He said that he had special contacts with certain officials in the Satmar community who were aiding Chaim's efforts to keep the children hidden. Some time ago he had decided that the entire affair was a liability to the community; it would be better for his people if these Christian children were returned to their mother. "I'm not doing this for you," he said. "I'm not doing this for Mrs. Heymans. I'm doing it because the Yarden children are not Jews. They are of no value to us."

Buysschaert asked, "Why do you not go to the police?"

"I have," the man admitted. "I contacted the police two, three times. They do not seem to be interested."

Buysschaert nodded. He too was concerned that the Belgian detective assigned to the case was not very enthusiastic about it. He asked directly, "Do you know where the children are?"

The man paused in order to consider his response carefully. Finally he said, "No, not yet, but I know people who do."

Buysschaert pushed for something concrete. "Several people have phoned us and said they are able to find the children," he stated. "But nothing has come of it. We will have to verify your information."

The man nodded in agreement, then turned the discussion to the matter of his own security. If others found out that he was working secretly with the Heymanses' side of this dispute, his family would be shunned and he might become a victim of violent retaliation. Buysschaert assured him that his identity would be protected. He gave the man his home phone number and beeper code.

Any future meetings within Antwerp's diamond district would be too risky, so they set up a procedure to meet at the Brussels airport: Buysschaert was to wait at the airport bookstore. The informant would walk past, without acknowledging him. Buysschaert would follow discreetly until they reached the man's car in the multilevel parking garage. The man promised that he would call Buysschaert whenever he had news.

Finally Buysschaert asked a key question: "And what do you want in return for this information?"

"Nothing. I told you. The children are of no value to us. I will tell you what I know, when I know it."

After he returned from the meeting, Buysschaert briefed De Vroede, and, together, they told me of this new development. We were concerned about the man's claim that he was ignored by the police, so we determined, at least for the time being, to keep this new relationship quiet. We decided to refer to the informant by the code name "Echo."

50

Sarah's Story

Mrs. Jacobovich let me go to a summer camp in the Catskills for four weeks. I liked the games very much, but I liked it even better because of the freedom.

After I came back, Rachel got to go for the second session, late in the summer.

51

"Come. It is urgent," the raspy voice on the telephone said. It was a Wednesday morning near the end of August 1992.

Dominique Buysschaert immediately drove to the Brussels airport. He waited nervously at the bookstore for nearly a half hour, pretending to peruse magazines and newspapers, before Echo walked past. To an observer, Echo would appear to be another of the faceless Hasidim diamond couriers who are always coming to and going from Belgium.

Trying to appear nonchalant, the lawyer followed the informant into the parking garage and stepped into the elevator just before the door closed. The two men were alone in the small cab, but Echo did not speak or even meet Buysschaert's gaze. After exiting the elevator, Echo walked up a set of stairs to the next parking level. Buysschaert followed slowly as Echo moved past a long line of parked cars. Echo turned abruptly toward an aging, pale-blue Peugeot. He unlocked the door and slid into the driver's seat. Buysschaert checked over his shoulder. He saw no one following. With what he hoped was a casual air, he slipped into the front passenger seat of the Peugeot.

Once again, there was no small talk. The informant said, "The kids are in a camp in the Catskills, New York." He said that they would be there until Sunday. "In the camp, they have been placed with a family called Goldberg." He noted a small village called South Fallsburg. "You go to the end of the village, and the road splits to go on two sides. The camp is around there someplace."

Buysschaert reported to me immediately. As yet, we had no way to judge the accuracy of this man's word. But Buysschaert believed him to be credible, and his report was very specific. If the information was correct and I did not act upon it, I could never forgive myself. We had four precious days to search.

I called Sabine and Paul and told them I was coming. I asked, and they agreed to drive to South Fallsburg prior to my arrival and look around. Walter and my mother quickly agreed to share the duties of caring for Noélie and Gautier.

As my travel agent scurried to book an airline seat to New York, I called Jim Stanco in Albany, told him that I was arriving the following morning, and explained the situation. "I don't want to work with the local police," I said, remembering the treachery we had encountered in Monsey. Also, I knew that if I appeared in a police station unannounced, detailing my story once again to a new and uninformed audience would cost me precious time. Stanco agreed to brief the New York State Troopers.

As the airplane took off for New York, I tried to focus my thoughts on the task ahead. I did not want to allow my hopes to rise, but it was impossible to fight off a growing sense of optimism. Could this be the time I really did find them? I wondered. Will there be enough time? What is this place with the funny name—Catskills?

When I arrived at Sabine and Paul's home on Thursday evening, they reported that they had driven around the area of South Fallsburg and that it was full of Hasidic families. This *might* be the time! I thought.

Only a short time after I arrived, I received a telephone call from a New York State Trooper, who asked me to come to the station house near Monsey the next morning. Obviously Stanco had done his best to pave my way.

On Friday, Sabine drove me to the station house. There, investigators questioned me carefully concerning Echo's information. "The kids are in the Catskills," I said.

One trooper rolled his eyes and commented, "You don't realize how big the Catskills are."

"But I have the name of a village," I said. "South Fallsburg. You go to the end of the road and the camp is around there. They are staying with a family called Goldberg."

The troopers' interrogation lasted for several hours and left me nervous and exhausted. Finally they agreed that the information justified a search. It was too late to start that day, but we had the weekend ahead of us. According to Echo, we had two more days to find the children.

Sabine and I were both excited as we drove away. Once more I thought: This *might* be the time! Sabine drove me to the Newburgh airport, where I rented a car. That way, if the troopers gave up the search, I would still be able to look on my own.

Paul agreed to come with me the following day, since he was already somewhat familiar with the area.

Throughout the evening, Sabine kept me very busy. We took her children to McDonald's. Later, we attacked a craft project— decorative wood-painting—with high energy. We avoided any mention of the next day's search.

On Saturday morning, Paul and I drove back to the state troopers' office. We followed an unmarked police car to a place where I could park for the day. After a short briefing, we were ushered into the rear of a surveillance van with smoky, tinted windows so that we could see out but nobody could see in. The van's interior was a mobile command center containing a periscope and audio and video monitoring equipment so sophisticated that they could print out a photograph of any portion of the videotape. There was even a small toilet area.

The driver sported a long ponytail and an earring. He wore

a baggy leather jacket. But the other officer epitomized the image of the clean-shaven, close-cropped, starched and polished policeman.

We headed for the upstate New York resort area known as the Catskills. The ride seemed to take forever.

Finally we reached the village of South Fallsburg and followed the road until it ended at a T-shaped intersection. So far, Echo's description was correct! Now all we had to do was find the camp, and the family called Goldberg.

Unfortunately, numerous camps covered the area. We would have to check them one by one.

The man I thought of as "Officer Ponytail" came into the back of the van with me, and the conservatively dressed officer took the wheel. Paul moved up front to sit with him. Slowly, we drove toward the entrance to one of the campgrounds.

The van stopped at the gate. The driver and Paul sought out the manager and asked about rental rates and reservations. As they spoke, their eyes darted about. Almost immediately, we realized that we had a problem. The Hasidim keep to themselves, even when they are on holiday. They bring their own kosher food with them, and they refuse to associate with Jews who are "less religious" than themselves. The presence of any stranger was suspicious. What were they to make of these two obviously non-Hasidic men, driving a van through their private camp? Worse, it was Shabbat.

I remained in the van with my eyes riveted to the periscope lens. I was terrified that the periscope apparatus would be noticed by someone, so I moved it very slowly. I tried to peer at every small face and compare it to the photographs that I held in my lap.

"Just take your time," Officer Ponytail advised softly, lest someone close to the van overhear. "Don't rush."

I was afraid that I might miss something or make a mistake, and the veins in my head pounded from the tension.

After many nerve-wracking minutes, Paul and the officer returned to the van and we moved on, toward another camp.

On and on we went, from one camp to the next.

Suddenly, at one camp, my attention was drawn to a group of three young girls. I studied them carefully through the van's periscope and then peeked around the edge of a curtain and through a tinted window. My eyes looked down at a photograph, then moved back to the periscope. Could the girl on the left, the small one with the stocky build, be Marina? She had brown hair and an adorable smile. There was something about her behavior that set her apart from the others. She moved about more freely in her play, not worried that someone might see a forbidden glimpse of leg. Maybe it's her, I thought.

Once more, Officer Ponytail counseled, "Take your time."

I looked down at the photograph again, then back outside. The eyes were not right. The chin was shaped differently. Perhaps the strongest evidence was that my heart did not recognize her. "No," I whispered sadly. "I guess that's not her."

Our agonizing search continued all day long. By the time we finished our tour of the camps, my head pounded.

That evening, after Shabbat was over, the van left the area and headed for a designated parking spot, where we linked up with a captain. In an unmarked car, the captain drove me to a local amusement park, where we walked about, staring at the faces of children. Once again we were conspicuous as the only non-Hasidim in sight. There was no sign of Marina, Simon, or Moriah.

When the captain and I had returned to his car, the police radio crackled to life. Someone had spotted a vehicle speeding away from the area. According to the radio report, the driver was a man. A young girl sat beside him up front and a smaller, brown-haired girl was alone in the backseat. Why was a Hasidim driving away so fast with two young children? Had we aroused suspicion? Were Marina and Moriah being spirited away from us once again?

The captain radioed back. Other troopers were to keep the car in sight and report on its position. We were on our way.

We sped off in pursuit. The captain was a skillful driver, and he knew the area. By cutting across side roads, he maneuvered his car into a position to overtake the fleeing vehicle. Then another radio message came in. Troopers had called in the license plate number, and the computer reported that the car was registered to a man named Goldberg!

The captain devised a plan. We would link up with a trooper's cruiser, stop the car, and tell the driver that his vehicle fit the description of one involved in a hit-and-run accident. I was to play the part of a witness. I would pretend to inspect the car, but I would really study the children.

We located the car and pulled alongside, lights flashing. A trooper gestured to the driver to pull over. As the troopers stalled by checking the driver's license and registration, I walked slowly around the car, twice, as if I were inspecting the vehicle. I glanced quickly at the two girls in the car, then looked at them more carefully. Disappointment flooded through me. These girls were not Marina and Moriah.

I shook my head. The troopers apologized to the driver, and we left.

Deeply shaken, I tried to sift through the events of the day. We had no sure evidence that the children were anywhere in the Catskills—yet I could feel their presence. And Echo's information seemed to be accurate. The troopers were encouraged by this, so we made plans to continue the search the following day, Sunday. It would be our last chance.

Exhausted, more emotionally than physically, Paul and I drove back to Sabine's house. I told her briefly about my day, but she knew intuitively not to press for details.

On Sunday, with the cooperation of local police, the state troopers set up a roadblock on the main road leading from the Catskills back to New York City. The troopers would conduct a routine check of driver's licenses and auto registrations, but we would all be alert for signs of the children. They considered dressing me in a police uniform, but they lacked the necessary permission. Without proper authorization, I would be guilty of impersonating a police officer. So, instead, they gave me a fistful of flyers on drug-abuse prevention to hand out while they made their routine inspections.

For six hours, the police stopped every car traveling in both directions. Many unsuspecting motorists were cited for expired licenses or tags, missing stickers, faulty seat belts, and other violations. I felt a twinge of guilt that so many traffic tickets were issued because of me. But, admittedly, I also saw some humor in the situation.

As the day progressed, the traffic grew heavier. I ran from one side of the road to the other, trying to peer into the face of every Hasidic child. Whenever we found a Hasidic car with tinted windows, I wanted to find some way to open the door and look inside. Worst of all were the buses filled with Hasidic children. There was no way I could study every face.

Late in the afternoon a car approached the roadblock. One of the troopers raised his hand, signaling for the driver to stop. The car paused but then moved forward, past the checkpoint. Troopers called out angrily after it. The confused driver stopped and claimed that he had simply misunderstood the policeman's signal. There were no children in the car.

After six frustrating hours in the August heat, I returned to Sabine's house exhausted and drained. All I had to show for my effort was a nasty sunburn.

52

One month later, Inspector Jean Dooms of the Police Judiciare—the man who had expressed his sympathies during our observance of the International Day for Missing Children—took over the case. He considered the matter to be very important, partly because of all the publicity it had generated and partly because of his own parental empathy.

He began his work by reviewing the file, then he interviewed Dominique Buysschaert and Nadia De Vroede. He spoke at length with my father and me. A lean and muscular man who enjoyed long-distance running, Dooms appeared to be in very good shape for a man with two grown children. His energy and intensity were balanced by a quick smile and easy humor. I liked and trusted him immediately.

As Dooms continued his review of past events, covering nearly six years, he grew concerned. Certain information about the case had been blocked from disclosure, as if someone in an elevated government position did not wish to disturb sensitive relations with the Hasidic community. He was also puzzled to realize that an informant from Antwerp had contacted the Police Judiciare several times—but no one had followed up. At least for the time being, he decided to keep a low profile and work quietly.

Dooms is a man of intense curiosity. As part of his case review, he devoured a private library of books about Judaism in general and the Hasidim in particular. He decided not to interview Chaim—for this would announce his presence on the case—but he believed that he was developing a good understanding of the man responsible for creating all this turmoil.

Meanwhile, Buysschaert met once more with Echo in the airport parking lot. We had failed to locate the children in the Catskills, and now the informant was pressured to offer some way to prove the value of his information. He responded that he had news that Buysschaert could verify. "Very recently, Yarden was visited in prison by a division of rebbes," he disclosed. "They discussed his religious divorce from Iris Buttel."

On the surface, the information did not seem too helpful, but Buysschaert found the report interesting. In court, Chaim consistently refused to acknowledge that he had married Iris. Nevertheless, we knew that the marriage had occurred.

Immediately after the meeting, Buysschaert called Dooms to report that he had been in contact with an informant from Antwerp. Dooms pricked up his ears; was this the man who had attempted to approach the police but had been spurned? Dooms listened carefully as Buysschaert relayed Echo's report on the visitation by the rebbes. If it was true, only someone close to the situation would know about it. The detective said that he would check the prison visitation records.

Soon, Dooms called Buysschaert back to say, "That's the man! His information is really tip-top."

Buysschaert continued to have sporadic contacts with Echo and was able to persuade him to meet with Dooms. During their first encounter, the two men tested the intentions of one another. Then Echo declared, "The children are in New York."

Dooms pressed for details, but Echo could not be more specific. Was it New York City or New York State?

Echo did not know.

*   *   *

Early in November 1992, Dooms flew to the U.S. to run in the New York City Marathon. His wife, Malou, accompanied him. He used the trip as an opportunity to make unofficial inquiries about the Yarden case and learned a particularly interesting fact: The children's Israeli ID cards contained coded numbers that identified them as *non-Jews*. Anyone who was knowledgeable about the ID cards—and that would include any Satmar rebbe—could easily discern the same information. Thus, Rebbe Tauber's demand shortly after Chaim's arrest, that I provide proof that the children were not Jewish, had been pointless.

Dooms was visited in his room at a Ramada Inn by U.S. marshals Tony Crook and Mike Hollander, the two who had participated in Chaim's arrest. Although Dooms spoke very limited English, his wife was fluent and served as translator. Her linguistic expertise, as well as her genuine interest in the case, was invaluable. Crook and Hollander shared Dooms's suspicion that the Hasidic community had long arms that stretched into many of the local police departments. The most reliable help would have to come from somewhere higher.

When he returned to Belgium, Dooms said to me, "We have to find police who are beyond the Hasidic influence. Why don't we try the FBI?"

I told him of my thwarted efforts several years earlier to gain FBI cooperation. I had visited with agents in New York, who told me that they could not work on the case because the children were not U.S. citizens. Even at the time, I suspected that this was a false excuse. "But you went as a private citizen," Dooms pointed out. "Perhaps we should try the official route."

Armed with a briefcase full of legal documents, Dooms and De Vroede paid a visit to the two special agents stationed in Brussels who handled FBI matters throughout Benelux (Belgium, the Netherlands, and Luxembourg). Malou Dooms, now thoroughly involved and interested, accompanied them and again served as translator. After considerable discussion, the FBI agents agreed to cooperate, but Dooms felt that the response was half-hearted and he asked probing questions to discover why. As he listened, he realized that these American agents had followed the details of the case over the years and had concluded that the Heymans family did not need the FBI's help. They assumed that my father's influence and wealth had enabled us to manipulate the press and the Belgian government into focusing on the case. They knew that my father had paid private detectives to search for the children, and they resented the contacts he had made in the States on his own. "Jacques Heymans will try to control the investigation," one of the men said. "He will try to tell us what to do." They presumed that I was nothing more than a poor little rich girl, spoiled and overindulged.

Dooms knew that there was little substance to these charges. He assured the men that he was not acting under my father's influence. In fact, he pointed out, Jacques and Mizou Heymans had exhausted their resources. My father now suffered from the effects of a heart condition and no longer took as active a role in the case.

As he left the meeting, Dooms knew that he had to find some way to win the active support of the FBI agents. But how?

Ordinarily, Dooms preferred not to become involved with informants. Experience had shown him that they are often of dubious character and always expect something in return for their cooperation. Now, however, information came to him on a case— unrelated to mine—that he saw as an opportunity to prove his worth to the reluctant FBI agents.

Meticulously, Dooms studied the informant's report and conducted his own background investigation. The subject's name was Eduard Lorenz. He was forty-five years old. Although he was born in Endicott, New York, he spoke German and was rumored to have Nazi sympathies; he even attempted to look like Adolf Hitler. In 1987, he was convicted in Stuttgart, Germany, of raping his twelve-year-old daughter. After a brief prison term, he was deported to the U.S. in November 1988. Now he was living, illegally, in a trailer park in Eupen, Belgium, close to the German border.

According to the informant, Lorenz claimed that, in April 1989, while living at the Central Motel in Richmond, Virginia, he had killed his three-year-old daughter, Eva, and successfully covered up the crime.

Dooms felt that if he could deliver this man into the hands of the FBI, they, in turn, might become more actively involved in my case. He discussed this strategy with De Vroede, and she agreed.

Dooms assigned a surveillance team to watch Lorenz and told the two FBI agents about the case.

Since Eupen is outside of Dooms's judicial jurisdication, he had to wait for Lorenz to travel to Brussels, as he regularly did. Shortly thereafter, when Lorenz came to the capital, he was arrested by inspectors Speltens, Humbeeck, and Alleman. That same day, Dooms interrogated him about the fact that he was living illegally in Belgium. He also broached the subject of the death of his daughter. Lorenz responded that Eva had died of natural causes, and he offered the name of a cemetery where she was buried.

Dooms had Lorenz jailed as an illegal alien and asked the FBI agents to verify his story of his daughter's death and burial.

Within forty-eight hours, the FBI reported that Lorenz's information was false; there was no record of Eva's death and no grave where he had said it was.

Meanwhile, in Richmond, Virginia, south of Washington, D.C., detectives searched for a case that matched the informant's account. Investigator Gregory C. Auditore of Henrico County reopened the case file of a three-year-old mystery. In January 1990, hunters had found a child's skull in the woods close to a cemetery, behind First Bethel Baptist Church near the town of Varina. Death resulted from multiple skull fractures caused by a blow to the head or neck. The Virginia State Bureau of Forensic Science had used the skull to fashion a clay model of the child's likeness. Police had circulated a photograph of the model among law enforcement agencies, but, at the time, no one had been able to identify the victim.

Now, armed with Dooms's information, U.S. detectives traced the whereabouts of Lorenz's estranged wife, Pamela. When they showed her the photo of the facial re-creation, she said, "That's Eva."

Dooms could keep Lorenz incarcerated for only twenty days on the illegal-alien charge. Quickly, Belgian authorities made an administrative decision to expel him from the country. They could have sent Lorenz to the Netherlands, France, or almost anywhere, but because he was an American citizen they sent him back to the United States.

Upon Lorenz's arrival in the U.S., he was arrested and ordered to stand trial for the murder of his daughter.*

Dooms's strategy worked. Now, the FBI agents in Belgium were very willing to refer the Yarden case to the appropriate office in the U.S.

January 1993. Special Agent Hilda Kogut sat at her desk in the Newburgh, New York, FBI office, reviewing the files sent to her by Inspector Jean Dooms of Belgium's Police Judiciare. The Yarden case was assigned to her partly because she was very familiar with the Rockland County area, where many of the Satmar communities were located, and partly because she was a veteran investigator in cases of sexual exploitation and child abuse. For several months she had been working with Special Agent Jerry Savnik on a similar case. Thirteen-year-old Shai Fhima had been sent to a Borough Park yeshiva to prepare for his bar mitzvah. In April 1992 he had disappeared, and his mother claimed that a Hasidic rebbe had refused to send him home, declaring, "If you do not let your son be religious, I have the right to take him away from you!" Shai had disappeared, and it was Savnik's assignment to find him.

As Kogut studied the file on the Yarden case, she noted that some of the information it contained seemed rather stale.

---

* On October 8, 1993, Lorenz was convicted of second-degree murder and subsequently sentenced to twenty years in prison.

The last known location for the children was Monsey, but that was about five years earlier. If the Belgian informant's information was correct—that the children had been in the Catskills the previous summer—then it was very likely they were still living somewhere in the New York area. But where?

Dooms had sent a long list of names and addresses of individuals who had been involved, directly or indirectly. These included Tauber and Borochov from Monsey, as well as many of the people with whom I had met and spoken over the years. There were many leads, but they were all vague.

Kogut arranged an interview with U.S. marshals Tony Crook and Mike Hollander and reviewed the events surrounding Chaim's arrest four years earlier. They briefed her on how they had located Chaim through an informant, and told her of their disappointment in not recovering the children at that time.

Okay, Kogut thought, now it is time to meet the mother.

I sat at a large conference table, fielding questions from Special Agent Hilda Kogut and several New York State Troopers. I was overcome by a paralyzing stage fright, wanting this stern-faced panel of investigators to like me but not knowing what to say or how to say it. Before I left Belgium, Jean Dooms had given me advice, and his voice echoed in my head now: *Patsy, you have to motivate them. You have to motivate them.* The memory of his words was so strong that it was difficult for me to think clearly.

I will tell the truth, I decided. That's all I can do. "I don't know how you will feel about this," I said, "but I'll tell you what I think happened earlier." I told them of my suspicions that police officials in Monsey had warned Chaim that we were looking for him. To my relief, Kogut was not surprised at this news. Monsey is a small town, and the Hasidic Jews have great influence there.

For her part, Kogut felt a great deal of pressure. She knew that six years had gone by. We had tried everything else. She was our last hope.

She copied my photographs of the children and said that she

would contact the National Center for Missing and Exploited Children, to see if they would prepare enhancements that would portray the children as they might appear now.

After we spoke for several hours, Kogut suggested that I accompany her on a sightseeing trip to Monsey. Although I dreaded the prospect of revisiting Monsey, I reluctantly agreed to go. Perhaps this was her way of assessing me.

As we walked to her car, I had difficulty keeping up with Kogut's long, purposeful strides. She wore jeans and a brown-leather jacket that had been worn to a soft, comfortable-looking sheen.

At first, during our drive together, I was tongue-tied and uncomfortable. Dooms's voice kept sounding in my ears: "motivate . . . motivate . . . motivate . . ." I wanted to be natural but felt like I was auditioning.

Kogut drove with authority and quite fast—more like a European driver—deftly weaving the car through heavy traffic. She pointed out various Hasidic schools and homes in the Monsey community. "I grew up here," she revealed. Until that time I did not realize she was Jewish.

She drove me past a Satmar school and pointed. "I went to that school," she said. "It used to be Monsey Elementary School, but now it's called Beth Rochel. We believe your two girls went there."

I found myself beginning to relax and I shared some of my experiences. Kogut had a quick, easy laugh.

She told me what she could about the Shai Fhima case. Agents had arrested a rebbe and his wife in Monsey on suspicion of involvement in Shai's kidnapping. But when the agents had attempted to take their prisoners away from the apartment, they found the streets blocked by angry Hasidim. The agents drew their guns and there was a tense, angry standoff. The rebbe's wife shielded herself with her three-week-old baby. Fortunately, no one was hurt in the incident, but it had warned the FBI of how militant the Hasidim could be when outsiders intruded into their insular world.

By the end of the day, Kogut and I were becoming friends. When she left me at Sabine's house, she promised, "I will do everything I can."

As I waited to hear more from Hilda, Sabine seemed unusually busy. "Why are you painting that now?" I asked. We usually waited for evening to work on our crafts. She continued to concentrate on the small figurine. It was a cow, and she was trying to get the black-and-white pattern just right.

"I'm in a hurry to finish it," she said.

I was distracted. I paid little attention to her as she called a few friends and invited them over. She ran off for a time and returned with colorful helium-filled balloons. Still, I did not realize what she was doing.

That evening, when the guests arrived, they all shouted, "Happy Birthday!"

I had forgotten the date. I was thirty-two years old.

Sabine gave me the painted cow as a present, and I was deeply touched by her thoughtfulness.

But there were only three presents that I really wanted.

January 23. In Brussels, Echo told Dooms: "In three days, at ten o'clock in the morning, Yarden will be visited at the jail by a certain man. It is very important." Was this the man who had the children? Echo was not sure, but he predicted, "He is the key to the whereabouts of the children."

Dooms checked with prison officials, who reported that a man named Jacobovich had been cleared to visit Chaim at 10:00 A.M., three days hence. Who was this Jacobovich? Was it his real name or did he have a false identity? What did he want to tell Chaim? Would he lead us to the children?

January 26. Shortly before 10:00 A.M., a taxi stopped along Avenue Ducpetiaux and deposited a Hasidic man at the entrance to the Saint Gilles jail. He entered, announced that he was Mr. Jacobovich, and presented his passport to the guard in the enclosed cubicle in the main lobby. He was unaware that Dooms stood behind the guard, off to one side. As Jacobovich was escorted to the prison visiting area, Dooms studied the passport. The only useful information it offered was the man's first name: Aaron. No address was listed. Dooms made a photocopy.

At the conclusion of the visit, Aaron Jacobovich retrieved his passport and stepped back out onto Avenue Ducpetiaux. He walked off at a brisk pace, unknowingly passing Dooms on the street. A hidden camera snapped photographs.

A surveillance team followed Jacobovich to his hotel and continued to watch. Dooms hoped that the subject would visit Simon Friedman in Antwerp and thereby incriminate the smooth-talking Satmar businessman. But Jacobovich kept to himself.

About 6:00 P.M., Jacobovich checked out of his hotel, flagged a taxi, and headed for the train station. Several unmarked police cars followed, rotating their positions. Jacobovich bought a train ticket to Amsterdam. Police officers followed him onto the train but had to discontinue their surveillance once the train crossed the border into the Netherlands.

From hotel records, Dooms learned that Aaron Jacobovich had placed one phone call, to Amsterdam, to a high-priced attorney with a questionable reputation.

FBI Special Agent Hilda Kogut began a systematic check of the names and addresses on her list of contacts. She spoke to local law enforcement officials to see if they had any means of identifying the children.

Impatient with the National Center, she turned the children's photographs over to FBI artists, who created their own enhancements. They broadened the faces and made them look more mature. They added *peiyot* to Simon.

Armed with these likenesses, Kogut drove her burgundy-colored 1990 Oldsmobile through the cloistered Satmar communities, scrutinizing the children she passed. She soon found herself frustrated because all the children were dressed alike and resembled one another. How could she distinguish my three children from the others?

The difficulty of her task was compounded by the fact of her gender. These were communities where the presence of an independent woman was viewed with open hostility and suspicion.

53

After six years of false leads and dashed hopes, the fates turned in our direction. Another informant came forward. Known to us by the code name "Samaritan," the man lived and worked on Kasho Drive, in the community of Bedford Hills, in Westchester County. The people who lived here had broken from the main Satmar sect to form their own community. The Kashos considered themselves to be "more religious" than other Satmars.

Samaritan was a non-Jew who did odd jobs and kitchen chores in return for bed, board, and a small salary. One day he heard a radio broadcast by the mother of Shai Fhima, pleading for information concerning her son. He had seen a boy answering Shai's description while coming into the community by taxi, and he immediately contacted the FBI with his suspicions. He spoke with Special Agent Jerry Savnik.

The interview did not lead Savnik to Shai Fhima, but during the conversation, Samaritan mentioned that he was aware of three other children in the community—two girls and one boy—who were not from the United States. They were living in the household of Herschel and Rachel Jacobovich, who had eleven children of their own. Samaritan said the boy had indicated that his father was in jail in Belgium.

Savnik contacted Kogut, who was immediately interested. Comparing notes with Jean Dooms, she determined that Herschel Jacobovich was the brother of Chaim's mysterious prison visitor.

Kogut had never heard of the Kasho Drive community, and she went to investigate. It was about thirty minutes from Monsey. She noted that there was only a single entrance to the compound, making it difficult for anyone to enter or leave unnoticed. She drove her Oldsmobile forward slowly and tried to assume an expression of confusion.

Kasho Drive was originally built as part of President Franklin D. Roosevelt's Works Progress Administration. It was comprised of large old dormitories that had been converted into homes and apartments. Kogut tried to locate the Jacobovich house, but she was stopped by a stern-looking Hasid who asked what she wanted.

"I got lost," Kogut lied. "I'm looking for, uh—" She mumbled a fictitious address.

The man said that she was in the wrong place and directed her out.

Weeks passed as Kogut, Savnik, and other agents considered various investigative techniques. They were confident that they could arrange a raid of Kasho Drive, but they still had no proof that the children were there.

Finally, they asked Samaritan if he would be able to take photographs of the three children in question.

"Don't worry," Dooms said to me. "It's moving. I can't tell you everything, but things are happening. They found somebody who may know about the kids."

My mind told me that we were very close, but my heart would not allow me to believe it. I was not sure that I could survive another disappointment.

Yet, Dooms's words to me were more than simple encouragement; they were also a warning for Walter and me to prepare ourselves to integrate Marina, Simon, and Morah into a family that now included Noélie and Gautier. "At the end of this month, I'm going to get an IUD put in again," I told Walter. "This is not the time to get pregnant."

But when I visited the doctor, he informed me that a new baby was due the following December.

54

The Children's Stories

APRIL 15, 1993.

Rachel

I had been sick with a fever the day before, so I went to my friend Esther's house to see what I needed to study. She showed me the parts in the prayer book that I had to learn. When I left Esther's house to walk across the parking lot to our house, I turned to smile at her. That's when the man took the picture.

Mrs. Jacobovich always said, "You should never let anyone take pictures of you," but this man said that he wanted to show his parents where he worked. I didn't care.

Josef

I was in the yeshiva with my friend Yoely. This was where he would have his bar mitzvah the next week. The cleaning man came in and said that he was taking pictures for his mother, because she was very sick. I kept my hands in my pockets, but Yoely and I both smiled.

When Mr. Jacobovich found out, he said, "You may never do that."

April 20, 1993.

Sarah

Mrs. Jacobovich told me to go to the yeshiva to help get ready for Yoely's bar mitzvah. I was to help set the tables and sweep the whole area. I had a broom in my hand when the man came in and said he wanted to take a picture of Yoely. I stood off to one side, near a window, and tried not to get into the picture, but I guess I did.

55

Samaritan's color photographs were amazingly similar to the FBI artist's enhancement of my old pictures. Along with Samaritan's statements that the three children were Belgian, the FBI had probable cause for action, but they wanted to delay activity in the hope that they would also locate Shai Fhima in the Kasho Drive community.

When Jean Dooms heard this, he rushed to the U.S. Embassy in Brussels and pressed the case for immediate movement. "Each day we delay, we risk having the Yarden children vanish again," he warned. "They will relocate them like they did every time before. Do it," he said, "and do it now."

56

Sarah's Story

The Jewish newspapers said that some people called the FBI were causing many troubles. They were looking for a boy named Shai, and the people were very angry. I was afraid of this FBI.

One night I had a scary dream filled with all kinds of crazy things. The FBI was coming in and pulling at me, and laughing at me. The dream made me very nervous.

A few nights later, I had the same dream again, and then I was really scared, because someone told me that if you dream the same thing more than once, it will come true.

57

Wednesday, May 5, 1993. Late in the afternoon, I tended to Noélie and Gautier and wandered through the house, tired but unable to relax. The discomforts of early pregnancy plagued me. My legs were swollen. I suffered bouts of nausea, and the medication to counteract this left me thirsty and nervous.

The telephone rang. I picked up the receiver, but the connection was so poor that I could not hear who was on the other end of the line. I hung up and wondered what to do. The noise on the line sounded like it could have been caused by a faulty overseas connection. Was someone trying to contact me from America? Intuitively, I placed a call to Hilda Kogut at the FBI office in Newburgh, New York.

"Did you just try to reach me?" I asked.

"Yes," she replied, "thank goodness you called. Patsy, we have very good news for you." Excitement bubbled in her voice. "It's very, very good news. We have located your children."

I felt my knees go weak and immediately sat down on the couch. I needed a few moments to compose myself. I said, "Hilda, I will hang up and I will call you back in a few minutes." Jean Dooms had told me that we were close, but I was still wary. I would not allow myself to believe that we had found the children until they were actually with me.

My fingers were still shaking when I redialed the telephone. There were so many emotions churning inside of me that I found it difficult to speak.

"We're going to have to act very quickly," Hilda said. "You have to put aside everything and be here within the next twenty-four hours." She asked if I could come this very day.

After twenty-five transatlantic flights, I knew the airline schedules by heart. "Today, no," I told her.

"Tomorrow morning?"

"No, tomorrow afternoon." The earliest flights from Brussels would not reach New York until then.

Kogut said that she was also contacting Dooms; he would need to be present as an official representative of the Belgian police. She said that court proceedings could take time and I should be prepared to stay in America for two or three weeks. Finally, she made me promise not to say anything to *anybody*, not even to members of my own family.

"I have to tell Walter," I said. "He's got to live with it."

"Okay," Kogut agreed. "But nobody else. Not even your parents."

The warning was unnecessary. Something could go wrong. If I did not bring the children back, I did not want to have to explain why, and I was also afraid to raise the hopes of everyone, including my parents, only to see them plummet once again. What's more, the people who held the children had demonstrated an uncanny ability to second-guess our every move, and I would not give them the chance to do so this time by risking an information leak. Also, I knew that if Papa learned the children had been located, he would expect to travel with me. But this was something I wanted to do—had to do—alone.

Dooms called from his office in downtown Brussels. We decided to book passage on tomorrow's noon flight to New York.

It was already past 4:00 P.M. There was so much to do and so little time to do it. I needed cash, but the bank was closed. I had to find a place for Noélie and Gautier to stay. I had to pack their belongings and prepare my own suitcase. Our clothes dryer was not working, so I had to wash clothes and take them to my friend Marie-Anne's house to dry them.

Each time I set my mind to one small task, another diverted my attention. Walter arrived home that evening to find me in a state of chaos. "I have to go to the States tomorrow," I blurted out. "I had a phone call from the FBI, and no one else can know about it."

Walter pulled me to the sofa and forced me to relax for several minutes. With calm questions, he drew the details from me. Then he turned the chaos into order. As he tended to Noélie and Gautier, he spoke to me in a quiet and steady voice, helping me schedule a logical sequence of activities.

Jean Dooms called back and told me he was having difficulty assembling the paperwork that would allow him to accompany me on the trip. Normally it took a full week to obtain the necessary travel documents. He thought that he could get the required signatures on an emergency basis, but it might take him several hours in the morning before he was ready to go. "This kind of paper has to be signed by the minister himself," he explained. "It has to go quite high." So we decided to take Thursday's last plane to the States. Dooms said he would try his best to get everything done in time but could make no promises. If he was ready to go, he would meet me at the airport. If not, I would have to travel alone and he would join me as soon as possible.

I checked with my travel agent. The last plane was a 1:00 P.M. flight from Brussels to Chicago's O'Hare Airport. Once I reached Chicago I would have to take an additional flight back east to the small airport in Newburgh.

I called Sabine and told her that I was coming. Next, I called Sabine's sister Danielle and asked her if I could leave my car at her house. She said yes and agreed to drive me to the airport.

I made an appointment with my obstetrician in Brussels for early the next morning; I needed an examination, and I did not know how long I would be gone.

Then, after sitting quietly for a few moments, I called my parents. In what I hoped was a calm voice, I told them only that the FBI had requested me to come to the States for two or three weeks. "Could you take care of Noélie and Gautier while I am gone?" I asked.

My mother said, "Of course."

My father asked, "What do they want from you?"

"I don't know," I hedged. "They just asked me to come as fast as possible." The lie made me feel extremely uncomfortable.

Papa was skeptical. He knew that the FBI would not call me to America on such short notice unless something very important was going on. In an attempt to get more information out of me, he questioned the expense of yet another transatlantic flight, when there appeared to be so little concrete information. But I did not take the bait; I argued that we could not risk losing the FBI's cooperation. (After the call, Papa told Maman, "I think this will be Patsy's last trip to the States.")

Walter and I packed the car that evening. We spoke late into the night about the best way to prepare Noélie and Gautier for the advent of their three older siblings, and decided that the babies were young enough to make the transition smoothly. The more troubling question was: How would Marina, Simon, and Moriah adjust? Walter counseled patience. From what Kogut had said, I might be in the U.S. with the children for several weeks. That would give us all time to prepare.

All night long, adrenaline pumped through me. I slept fitfully, for only two or three hours.

Thursday, May 6. I arose early and put on the same travel outfit I always wore on these long flights: a cotton shirt under demin overalls with decorative patches on them. Sabine often joked that she had never seen me arrive wearing anything else. But comfort, not fashion, was my priority, and this was the most comfortable outfit I owned.

I left home about 7:00 A.M. for the hour-long drive to Brussels. After I left Noélie and Gautier with my mother, I drove to the airport and checked in early. Anxiously I asked the ticket clerk if a Mr. Dooms was booked on the flight to Chicago. She looked at her records and said yes. I requested that I be seated next to him, although it was still too soon to know whether he would make the flight. Already I was exhausted, and I felt the effects of morning sickness.

My next stop was the obstetrician's office. The doctor examined me and assured me that everything was fine.

It took some time to get to the bank in the center of Brussels and then back out to Danielle's house. I knew that I was running late. When I realized that Danielle was not home, I panicked. Has she forgotten me? I wondered. What shall I do? I cannot leave my car at the airport for weeks. My watch told me that I had better hurry.

I jammed the car into gear and turned around to head for the airport. Suddenly I saw Danielle driving toward me. I made a U-turn and followed her back to her house. She had not forgotten but was simply running an errand.

As Danielle drove me to the airport, she was full of questions about my trip. I told her what I had told everyone else: "The FBI just asked me to come. I don't know why." But I could sense by the way Danielle looked at me that she knew this was not just another flight to America.

The gas gauge on Danielle's car was registering empty. We stopped at a service station, and the few extra minutes seemed like hours. Everyday occurrences took on monumental importance. It was getting more and more difficult to hide my excitement. I felt as though I were running in an endless marathon. I placed my right hand across my stomach, and a new concern arose. The doctor had said everything was fine, but now I worried that this new life that Walter and I had created might not be able to withstand the stress my body was under.

The flight crew was already boarding passengers when I reached the gate. Dooms was waiting for me. "Ah, you could make it," I said with relief.

At 1:00 P.M., the American Airlines flight took off for Chicago.

As the Boeing 767 began its ascent and commenced its nine-hour voyage westward, I closed my eyes. Several times I came to the brink of sleep and felt as if I were falling into a huge, dark hole. Then a small noise would cause my head to snap up and startle me away from that calm, dark place.

I vacillated between excitement and apprehension. Very soon I might be face to face with three small strangers who were my children. What had they been told about me? Would they remember me? They had been told so many lies about me. Could they trust me? Would they reject me? What could go wrong? How would they react to Noélie and Gautier? Would they accept Walter? How would they feel about the unborn child I was carrying—if, I thought darkly, it survives.

I tried to read but could not concentrate. I tried to watch the movie screen but it held no interest. The combination of nerves and my pregnancy sent me on repeated trips to the lavatory.

By the time we landed in Chicago, I was even more exhausted. We had to wait more than an hour for our connecting flight to Newburgh, and as I waited I began to feel seriously ill. My legs throbbed. My mood became sullen and angry.

Finally we boarded. Everyone seemed to be moving in slow motion. The flight attendants took their time stowing bags in the overhead compartments. The engines started grudgingly. A tractor pushed the plane from the gate at a snail's pace. Slowly, we taxied along the tarmac and took our place in an endless line of aircraft awaiting takeoff. The sickening odor of kerosene fumes seeped into the cabin. It was *so* hot.

Chicago's O'Hare Airport is the busiest in the U.S.—perhaps in the entire world—and a professional voice on the intercom informed us that there were more than twenty airplanes in front of us, with a two-minute interval between each takeoff. We would be on the ground for at least another forty minutes.

My face was flushed and bloated. I felt clammy and weak. I pushed the lever on my seat, causing the back to tilt.

Dooms glanced at me, and his face registered deep concern.

A flight attendant approached and ordered me to put my seat back into an upright position. Reluctantly, I complied. But soon I felt a sickening feeling return to my stomach, so I tilted the seat once again. A tug of war ensued. Every few minutes the flight attendant returned, insisting that I keep my seat in an upright position. The instant she left I tilted it again. Finally she snapped, "We're taking off in five minutes."

"Could you please leave me alone?" I retorted. "There are five minutes left for me to lie down. I'm pregnant. I don't feel well. For takeoff I will bring it up, that's it. Now you don't touch it or me anymore!" The attendant scurried away.

My outburst broke the tension, and I felt somewhat better. Dooms could not resist a grin. With raised eyebrows he silently conveyed the message: Ohhh, you better not mess with Patsy!

It was nearly 6:00 P.M. by the time we landed in Newburgh. Sabine waited for me at the gate, but Hilda Kogut and her boss, Newburgh FBI supervisor Ken Maxwell, were also there. I did not know to whom I belonged and, as we awaited our luggage, I vacillated between the FBI agents and Sabine. We all tried to make small talk.

The presence of the FBI agents was evidence to Sabine that this trip was very special.

Kogut said that she had booked two rooms for the night at a motel in Tarrytown, close to where the children were living. I don't believe this, I thought. Every time I took the train from Sabine's house, it stopped in Tarrytown. All that time I had been so close to them without knowing it!

Fear of the emotional unknown took hold of me, leaving me feeling confused. Sabine had assumed that I would be staying with her, and that was what I really wanted to do. Kogut saw my indecision and said, "First, we will go to the office, to talk a bit. Sabine can follow us there. Then we can decide about the night."

The FBI office was very close to the airport. By the time we arrived, Kogut had already convinced me that she needed me at the motel, close to where the children were, and I agreed. Sabine took this news with genuine excitement. "Keep in touch," she said, her voice cracking. "Let me know."

After Sabine left, we got down to business. Maxwell explained how they had located three children in the Kasho community, and that they believed the children were Marina, Simon, and Moriah. If I was able to provide positive identification, they would attempt to retrieve the children early the following morning. But he warned, "We never know. Something can go wrong. One of the kids might be away from the house."

I translated much of this for Dooms, and the activity helped me to concentrate.

Dooms leaned forward in his chair, rubbing his palms together in nervous anticipation. To his delight, he realized that Maxwell was fairly conversant in French. Kogut relaxed him further when she presented him with her FBI baseball cap.

Kogut explained that Samaritan had taken photographs of the children on Kasho Drive. She handed me three six-by-nine prints and asked, "Do you recognize these children?"

The force of my emotional response paralyzed me. The most recent photos I had seen were taken in front of the White House, four and a half years earlier. How much had they changed? Would I know them? For several moments, I could not look.

I counted to myself: *un . . . deux . . . trois . . .*

I stared at a photograph of a white-and-tan cement-block room, devoid of pictures or decoration of any kind. Two curtainless windows with torn screens flanked an old-fashioned radiator. Four long tables were visible, each covered with white plastic. Paper plates holding slices of cantaloupe and *chalukkah* (egg bread) waited. A girl stood behind the center table, wearing a checkered smock with long sleeves and a high collar. Her dark hair was pulled back. She appeared matronly for one so young. But she was smiling, and the beautiful, bright grin belonged to Marina. There was absolutely no question.

I took a long, hard look at the next photograph, taken outdoors. In the middle of a gray expanse of road, a young girl in a long-sleeved, ankle-length, blue-flowered dress with a collar that reached up to her chin, stared directly into the camera and grinned. She clutched a large book in both hands as she walked across the street. Protruding from beneath the dress were heavy black shoes and a glimpse of dark tights or stockings. "Yes, that's Moriah," I said.

It was the boy's picture that caused me to pause. He was standing in the same room in which Marina was photographed. Behind him were two long folding tables, their surfaces bare. His face appeared rounded, with the hint of a double chin. Beneath the yarmulke, his dark hair was almost shaved. Ringletlike *peiyot* dangled several inches below his ears, reaching to his shoulders. A flashbulb glare shone beneath the black-rimmed frames of his glasses. A blue-and-white long-sleeved plaid shirt was buttoned to the collar and tucked into a pair of dark trousers. He appeared soft, fleshy, and pale, as if sunshine were a distant memory. I began to shake. Be calm Patsy, I thought, but I feared I might lose control. Once more I counted to myself: *un . . . deux . . . trois . . . quatre . . . cinq . . .* I studied the photograph with special care. He had gained weight. The thick eyeglasses and the *peiyot* had changed his appearance dramatically.

The office was quiet. Two FBI agents and a Belgian detective stared at me and held their breath.

"Yes," I said finally. "It's Simon."

Maxwell then briefed us with a minute-by-minute description of the plan. Numbed, I listened.

At four-thirty the next morning, Dooms would meet at the Tarrytown office of the New York State Troopers with members of the FBI, a contingent of troopers, and the local police to coordinate their plans. The people who live in the Kasho community are early risers; children prepare for school, men rush off to work or study, women busy themselves with their daily tasks. The agents wanted to get into the community while it still slept. By five-thirty, Kasho Drive would be surrounded by cars. They expected no trouble, but no one could predict with certainty what would happen. Kogut noted, "People are angry and offended when you come into their homes at that time in the morning." They would operate on the theory that it is better to be overly cautious; thus, they would have many officers in place. They emphasized that their major concern would be for the children, who they realized must have been traumatized by six and a half years of being shuttled about.

The FBI had conducted aerial surveillance and determined that the street ended in a cul-de-sac. Police vehicles could easily block the only escape route. Maxwell would call the Jacobovich family from a car phone and inform them that they were in front of the house. If they did not answer the phone or if they resisted, the police would enter and take the children by force. As a Belgian police officer, Dooms could not participate in the raid; he would simply act as an observer. If everything went as planned, someone from the FBI—not Kogut—would meet me in the motel lobby. "You have to be there starting at six-thirty," Kogut said. "But it might be later. We don't know how long it will take."

Maxwell repeated, "We never know. Something can go wrong."

Someone from the New York Office of Health Services would be on hand to examine the children immediately. They would be taken to the FBI office in New Rochelle, where the Westchester County Department of Social Services would provide a nurse and three social workers—women for Marina and Moriah and a man for Simon—to care for the children. Legal experts, as well as Belgian officials, were prepared for the necessary court procedures that would follow. Hilda said that the process might take two or three weeks. She told Dooms that they had prepared a "safe house" for me and the children.

It all sounded unreal.

Waiting alone at the motel would be very difficult, but I knew it was the right thing to do. The raid would shock the children. They would need time to adjust. Let the professionals handle it, I thought.

After Maxwell dropped Dooms and me off at the motel, I wondered how my body could perform even the most mundane functions: to stand up, to sit down, to walk, to see, to hear, to wait.

58

Sarah's Story

My back was hurting me a lot, so I told Mrs. Jacobovich. She didn't believe me.

"Go to your bedroom!" she shouted. "I don't want to see you anymore until you come and say you're sorry."

I was confused. I didn't know what I had done wrong. So I just stayed in my room until it was time to eat. Mrs. Jacobovich kept being mad at me, but I wouldn't apologize.

"How long is it going to go on, this thing?" she asked.

"I won't apologize until you tell me what I did," I insisted.

"You know what you did."

"If you know what I did, just tell it to me, and I'll tell you I'm sorry."

"No, I won't."

I thought it was so stupid. I went back to my room and thought: I will stay here until die or get away from here.

I had a big test the next day, so I set my alarm for four-thirty to get up and study.

59

Friday, May 7. It was 1:00 in the morning before I fell into a fitful, light sleep.

By 2:00 A.M. I was wide awake. From the far side of the room, the motor of a small refrigerator buzzed softly. The roaring sounds of night traffic on the interstate rushed in through the open window.

I attempted to read but quickly tossed the book to the floor. It was impossible to concentrate.

I tried to sleep some more. I thrashed from side to side. My eyes darted from my watch to the clock—every second an hour, every minute an eternity.

My leg went numb. I got up and paced the room. A wave of nausea hit. I took a quick shower.

I slept. I woke. I slept.

4:30.–Okay, everything is starting, I thought.

4:45.–The meeting is in progress.

5:15.–They are getting close to the Jacobovich house, for sure. I began to pack my suitcase.

5:25.–The Jacobovich house is surrounded.

5:30.–The telephone is ringing at the Jacobovich house. Will somebody answer it? What will they say? What if the children are not at home? What if only one or two of them are there? What if they cry and refuse to come?

Stop it, Patsy, I commanded myself.

Un . . . deux . . . trois . . . quatre . . . cinq . . .

60

On Kasho Drive, Jean Dooms watched nervously from the backseat of a police cruiser. Hilda Kogut was walking to the front door of the house. A team of fifteen agents was in place, including several SWAT team members armed with shotguns, who guarded the periphery of the house. One agent held a battering ram, a long, heavy, cylindrical device, in case they had to force entry.

Various agents were ready for their special assignments. Several women agents had been designated to stay with Marina and Moriah. Two male agents would watch Simon; both had sons about the same age.

Precisely at 5:30 A.M., Special Agent Ken Maxwell used his car phone to dial the Jacoboviches' number. He allowed it to ring several times.

61

Sarah's Story

I was studying for my test with a small light. It was still dark outside. I heard noise. I peeked out the window and saw many police cars. I knew they were coming for us.

I thought: My dream is coming true.

I heard the telephone ring and didn't know what to do. I decided to answer it, but first I had to cover my legs. In a big hurry I struggled to pull on my tights, but I only got them halfway up. I ran for the stairs, but it was like I had a long tail behind me. My feet caught on the tights and I tumbled down the stairs. Dazed, I lay on the landing for a moment, happy that I was still alive!

The phone was still ringing. I picked myself up and waddled to it, but I fell again. I was on the carpet, but it hurt anyway.

"Hello?" I said.

A man asked to speak to Mr. Jacobovich, but I knew the rules. I may not wake him unless it is an emergency.

"Is it important?" I asked.

"I want to speak to your father," the voice insisted.

I didn't know what to do.

I set the phone down and went upstairs to wake Mr. Jacobovich. I told him to look out the window, and he saw all the police cars too. He rolled his eyes like something bad was happening and then he went downstairs. I ran back to my room, crawled into bed, and pretended to be sleeping, but I heard somebody knock on the front door.

62

The police activity was noticed immediately by everyone in the neighborhood. The grim-faced Hasidic men of Kasho Drive gathered in the streets, soon outnumbering the police. Dooms feared there might be trouble.

What's on the other side of the door? Kogut wondered. Her heart pounded in anticipation. Before resorting to the battering ram, she tried the simple tactic of knocking on the door. Within moments Hershel Jacobovich opened it slightly and peeped out. Kogut noticed other faces peering through the curtains of upstairs windows. She identified herself as a special agent of the FBI.

Jacobovich opened the door wide. He wore a white nightdress that bulged over his ample belly. Skinny legs protruded from beneath the hem. Curly reddish-brown *peiyot* dangled from beneath his nightcap.

Maxwell asked a carefully worded question: "Where are the Belgian children?"

"They are here," Jacobovich acknowledged. He stepped back, allowing the agents to enter. He invited Kogut and Maxwell into his study. The agents displayed the search warrant that allowed them to enter the house and seek the children. Offering no resistance, Jacobovich ushered them upstairs. He said he knew that, at some point, people would come for these children.

Waiting in a car outside, Jean Dooms checked his watch. The second hand swept slowly around the dial. It made a full circuit, and then another half. Beads of sweat formed on his forehead.

The police radio crackled with static. A voice said, "Okay, we have the kids."

Dooms wiped at tears in the corners of his eyes.

63

The Children's Stories

Rachel

I was still in my bed, sleeping, when I started to hear a lot of noises. It was dark outside, but I could see flashing lights and I knew it was police cars. I was nervous. I tried to stay very still, but I knew, deep inside, that whatever was happening was because of us. I knew that I was not the daughter of Mr. and Mrs. Jacobovich, and I knew that Sarah and Josef were my real brother and sister, even though we were not allowed to talk about it.

The door to my room opened and a woman I did not know came in. "Hello, little girl," she said. She told me I should get dressed and that we were going somewhere. She followed me everywhere, and it made me very uncomfortable.

The house was full of strangers. There were so many people that some of them had to stand outside. Mrs. Jacobovich didn't say anything. She just went to the kitchen and prepared some cake for us to take with us. The woman who was with me kept saying that everything was going to be all right and that we were going back to our mother. I was afraid. I wished she would quit following me everywhere.

Josef

I woke up when I heard a lot of people in the house. I woke up Yoely and asked him what the noise was. He didn't know anything. Then Mr. Jacobovich came into our room and said, "Josef, you have to get dressed. You're going to see your mother." I asked him if I was going to come back and he said yes.

I didn't want to go. I was very scared, because if my mother is not Jewish, things will be very bad. My head started to hurt and I needed to go to the bathroom every three minutes.

Sarah

I was scared. The newspaper said the FBI were very mean, bad people. I heard Mr. Jacobovich say that they wanted to disturb his life. I remembered how they pulled at me and laughed at me in my dreams.

All of a sudden there was a strange lady in my bedroom, and she told me I shouldn't be afraid of anything and that everything will be okay. But I was not so sure. She told me to get dressed, but I was not so comfortable. There were so many people in the house, and everywhere I went, someone followed me.

When Josef, Rachel, and I got into the car, they told us we would see our mother, and when we got to the FBI building, another lady kept telling us, "Oh, you have such a lovely mother. She has looked for you for such a long time."

64

I switched on the television. I switched it off. A bath, I thought. I'll take a long, relaxing, hot bath. Patsy, you're not supposed to take a hot bath when you are pregnant.

My eyes stared at the digital readout of the motel's clock-radio, until the numbers changed from 5:58 to 5:59—anything to make the time pass.

I slipped into the water, but five minutes later I was out, toweling myself dry. I simply could not sit still. I dressed quickly. I swallowed a pill, thinking that this was not the day to have morning sickness. Once more I attempted to read, but I couldn't.

At 6:15, fifteen minutes before I was supposed to be in the lobby, I decided to go to the coffee shop to eat breakfast. I had eaten nothing the night before. Despite my nervousness, I was starving. Walter always called me "Mrs. Fifteen Minutes Too Late," but for once in my life I would be early.

The coffee shop was closed. A sign on the door indicated that it would open at 7:00 A.M., and I found this ominously upsetting. If a simple thing like eating breakfast did not go as planned, then everything else would go wrong.

My watch told me that it was finally 6:30. Only now did the real wait begin. Kogut had warned me that they did not know how much time they would spend on Kasho Drive. I settled into an easy chair in the lobby and once again opened the cover of my book, but it was no use.

It will be a long time yet, a long time, I thought. Suddenly, through the glass doors of the lobby, I saw Kogut approaching. Oh, my God! It's bad news, I thought. Someone else was supposed to meet me, not her.

I stood up warily. My knees nearly gave way.

Kogut spotted me, and even before she came in through the glass doors, she flashed a huge smile and held up three victorious fingers.

Her first words to me were, "Everything is all right."

I did not know what to say, so I simply hugged her. I wanted to cry on her shoulder, but I stopped myself.

We went out to her car. Before we drove off, she asked a surprising question: "Do you mind if I buy breakfast?"

"No, I don't mind," I said. I was too shocked to be in a hurry and, in fact, I was extremely scared. I did not know if my children would accept me. I wanted extra time to prepare myself for the possibility that, as the French say, they would spit in my face. I wondered what Kogut thought of this. For six and a half years I had waited to see my children. And now I was not in a hurry? But I could see in her eyes that she understood.

Kogut drove to a nearby take-out, slipped out of the car, and returned with bagels and coffee. As we drove toward New Rochelle, I ate a bagel but I did not taste it. I hate bagels, I remembered. "I still cannot believe it!" I said to Kogut. "How did it go? Were there any problems? Did the kids resist?"

"Everything was fine," she said. "Everything is fine." She detailed her observations of their individual reactions. "Marina was very hyper, very nervous, and kind of scared, like a doe caught in the headlights of a car." Simon clung to Mr. Jacobovich, speaking to him in Hebrew; he did not want to leave. Finally, two of the male agents simply told him that he had to come with them, and he went. I smiled. Despite the complex emotions that I was experiencing, I was aware of a bit of wry humor. It was very much in character for Simon to protest verbally but to acquiesce physically. "Moriah was very interesting," Kogut said. "We went in and told her we were going to take her to see her mother, and she popped out of the bed like a piece of toast from a toaster. Her eyes lit up. She wasn't upset; she wasn't frightened. She was ready to leave."

I wondered if I was dreaming.

At the FBI headquarters in New Rochelle, a sea of familiar and unfamiliar faces floated in front of me. I recognized some of the state troopers who had searched the Catskills with me the previous August. Greetings and congratulations bounced back and forth. Jean Dooms gave me a jubilant hug.

But I did not see Marina, Simon, and Moriah.

I moved back and forth, from one side of the busy room to the other. Whom should I talk to? What should I say? What should I do?

Kogut told me that the children were sequestered in the supervisor's office, a large room on the other side of the building, where a specialist in child welfare was gently explaining their situation to them. Kogut said that I could see them soon. It would be a busy day, she said. Sometime in the afternoon we would go before a judge. There was a small chance that he would allow us all to return to Belgium quickly, but it was likely that we would have to remain in the U.S. for several weeks.

A nurse came to speak to me. She had examined the children for any signs of neglect, abuse, or illness. She reported that there had been no hysteria. "Basically your kids are fine," she said. "Moriah has an ingrown toenail and it's badly infected. She also says she's been taking antibiotics for a few weeks."

"Did a doctor prescribe them?" I asked.

"No. Mrs. Jacobovich gave them to her. It's something we should look into. Other than that, they are fine."

I asked about two of my long-held fears. Had the children been subjected to plastic surgery?

"No."

Did Simon have open-heart surgery?

"No."

Then a social worker approached. "The girls did not give us any opposition," she reported. Simon, on the other hand, still protested that he wanted to return to Mr. and Mrs. Jacobovich. She suggested that it was wise to move slowly. It would be one or two hours before I could see the children. The terrified part of me was glad for the extra time.

I tried to phone Walter at work but was unable to reach him, so I called Gautier's godfather, Eric, a good friend of ours, and asked him to find Walter and tell him the news. Dooms reported to his boss and to Nadia De Vroede.

I also wanted my parents to know, but I was afraid that the shock would be too much for my father. I knew that if I placed the call, I would blurt out the news with my characteristic bluntness. Dooms agreed to make the call for me, and he handled the task expertly. In a calm, slow voice, he said that the investigation was proceeding and that we had new hope. "Very shortly, we will find the children," he said. My father, of course, asked for more details. Dooms led him along in the conversation, and when he felt that my father was sufficiently prepared, he said, "Okay, we have them."

"I don't believe this," my father said. "Are you sure?"

"I am sure," Dooms said happily. "I just wanted to tell you slowly."

From across the ocean, the detective heard my father shout, "Mizou, we have them. We have them!"

Only then did I take the phone. "I'm coming," Papa said.

"No, no, Papa," I responded. "They say there is a small chance that we might come home right away. If you take the first plane, we just might pass each other across the Atlantic. Wait for news. If we are staying here for a while, you can come."

"Okay," he agreed.

I could hear his voice crack and I could almost feel the lump in his throat. It was the first time I had ever heard him cry.

Mother took the phone, sobbing. "I cannot believe it," she said. "I'm so happy! How are they?"

"I haven't seen them yet, but the nurse told me they are fine."

"When do you come back?"

"I don't know. We don't know what the judge will say. It might be two or three weeks."

Next, I called Sabine. She had been awake all night. The moment she answered, I blurted out, "We have them!"

"It's not true, it's not true," she cried.

"It's true!"

"How are they?"

"They are fine."

Sabine said she had been so distracted this morning that she sent her own children to school without lunch money. "When are you coming home?" she asked. "Are the kids coming to my place?"

"Oh, it would be impossible, for security reasons," I said. "We don't know what the Satmars will do. They could find your house."

Sabine was disappointed. But she asked again, "When will you come?"

"I don't know. I don't know. I'll keep in touch with you throughout the day."

The social worker asked, "Are you ready to see your children? We told them you were coming in."

I was suddenly more afraid than I had ever been in my life. Words caught in my throat. I had waited for this moment for so long, and now I was terrified. "Now?" I asked in a shaking voice.

She nodded.

Dooms and Kogut accompanied me as I followed the social worker and nurse down a long hallway until we reached the closed door that stood between me and my children. The social worker placed her hand on the doorknob and turned it. I froze in place. It had been years since I had allowed myself to cry. Now, silent tears slid down my cheeks. The Belgian detective and the American FBI agent stood quietly at my side.

I did not know exactly how they would look. I did not know if they would accept me. Would they even speak to me? What was I supposed to say: *Hey, I'm your mother!* I pulled back, wailing, "No, I cannot. I cannot." More tears formed at the edges of my eyes.

The social worker handed me a tissue and gave me a moment to compose myself. Then someone opened the door. I felt a hand on my back, gently edging me forward. It was the most difficult step I had ever taken.

Marina and Moriah were quietly playing a board game. Simon was staring out the window. I felt awkward and desperately wished I could disappear. I did not know what to do with myself. Through a fog I heard the social worker say quietly, "This is your mother, and she's searched so long for you."

Marina looked at me, not in an unfriendly manner, but with confusion in her eyes.

Moriah glanced up, smiled, and then returned to her game.

Simon remained expressionless and stared out the window, refusing to make eye contact with me.

"Simon," I asked, "do you speak English?"

"No."

"Do you want to speak to me?"

"No."

They looked like three little refugees in their old, shapeless clothing. The long, thick socks that both the girls wore had large holes in them. Afraid that someone might catch a glimpse of their legs, they constantly pulled at the socks, yanking them upward. Their shoes were ill-fitting and worn. Simon and Marina appeared overweight, as if their diets had consisted of too much starch and their activities had not included any exercise. Moriah had retained her lanky, wiry build.

Marina tried to explain the game she was playing. It was a Jewish game called *kugala*. Moriah offered me a piece of chocolate cake that Mrs. Jacobovich had packed for her. Simon continued to stare out the window.

"Do you have any pictures of the children from when they were little?" the social worker prompted.

I had not thought of this, but I searched through my purse and found two old photographs, taken long ago when we had all been together. One of them showed Simon and Marina dressed up for a wedding. Marina giggled. The photograph brought the first response from Simon. He said, "Oh, we look like a small king and queen."

This was enough for the moment, I thought. I whispered to the social worker to find an excuse for me to leave the room.

Outside there was a partylike atmosphere. The operation was a success, and everyone was celebrating. Dooms laughed and joked and practiced his English with Kogut. The Belgian detective's easygoing personality was an instant hit with the FBI personnel.

But I saw all of this through a thick veil of shock.

I returned to the children at intervals throughout the day, gradually lengthening the time of each encounter. I gently explained to them that I had a new husband, named Walter—there was no need at the moment to detail my delay in getting an official divorce from Chaim—and two additional children named Noélie and Gautier.

With each visit, Marina and Moriah smiled more. Little by little they warmed to me. They showed me pictures that they were drawing. We played *kugala*. Marina told me, with pride, that she had made the dress she was wearing and that she had saved money by making it herself. She constantly looked after her younger brother and sister, acting like a mother hen in a child's body.

Simon remained nervous. His English skills were indeed limited, and Marina translated for him. Tentatively, they asked about their religion. It was the only life they understood, and they wanted to know: "Are we going to be able to keep Shabbat? Are we going to be able to eat kosher?"

I reassured them that of course they could keep Shabbat and, yes, their food would be kosher. "I cannot promise that everything will be like it was at the Jacobovich house," I said, "but I will do my best."

The first chink in Simon's protective armor showed when he asked if I would buy him "Time Out."

"What is it?" I asked in response.

He explained that it was a handheld electronic game, and he really wanted it.

Okay, I thought, he is asking me to buy him something. He is beginning to accept me!

In Brussels, Maman, Papa, and Walter were already trying to prepare Noélie and Gautier. How do you explain something like this to a three-year-old girl and a toddling boy who is only beginning to speak?

Walter asembled some of the dozens of photos that decorated the house. Noélie and Gautier knew these three children by name, but they were only faces in pictures. Walter said, "Soon, Maman will come back. And she will have Marina—" his finger pointed to a photograph—"Simon, and Moriah with her."

Jozef Devos, vice-consul of the Consulate General of Belgium in New York, readied the documents we would need for court.

Kogut introduced me to Assistant U.S. Attorney Margaret Groban. Groban told me that she had three children of her own, and I liked her immediately. She said that I had to appear in court this same day to receive a judge's confirmation of my custody rights and his approval for me to take the children back to Belgium. We had no idea how long the process would take. The key was whether or not Satmar lawyers lodged a protest, perhaps claiming that the children had been mistakenly identified. Since the raid had occurred on a Friday, the approach of Shabbat would disrupt the community's ability to respond. But if they protested, the judge might order DNA testing, and we would live in the safe house until the case was resolved.

The precautions proved unnecessary. New York State Court Judge Elliott Wilk listened carefully to Kogut's account of the raid and of Maxwell's brief, doorstep conversation with Herschel Jacobovich. Kogut noted that Maxwell had purposely asked, "Where are the Belgian children?"

Jacobovich's immediate response, "They are here," proved to the judge that the children were Belgian and, therefore, mine. He granted permission for us to leave the country immediately, dismissing me with the words: "Good luck, be happy with your children. Have a good trip."

Devos had already booked passage for us. We would leave this very evening! Someone from the FBI had arranged for kosher meals to be served to the children on the plane. Kogut removed a gym bag from the trunk of her car, emptied it of her bullet-proof vest and other FBI paraphernalia, and lent it to me to use as carry-on luggage to pack the children's few belongings.

I was deeply distressed. By now it was late on Friday afternoon. Throughout the day I had promised the children that I would respect their traditions. How could I force them to make a transatlantic flight on Shabbat, when travel is forbidden? "How will they ever trust me?" I asked Kogut. "I'm promising them something and the first thing I do is break that promise?"

Kogut came to my rescue. "Your mother has nothing to do with this decision," she explained to the children. "It is illegal for you to be in the United States and you have to leave right now. For your own security, you must leave tonight."

I had the presence of mind to phone Sabine. "I will not be coming to your house," I explained. "They are taking us back to Belgium tonight."

"It's not true, it's not true," Sabine said. "I have made a party for you. The house is filled with balloons. People are coming over. I really want to see the kids. I cannot believe that we are so close and I can't see them. I have waited four years for this day to finally happen. I bought so many balloons."

"Just send them by mail," I joked.

I knew from her laugh that the disappointment was only momentary. She truly was happy for me. I said, "They are really in a hurry. I have to go. But you will see the kids when you come to Belgium."

Sabine promised, "I will come."

We drove to JFK International Airport in a motorcade of police cars and were allowed to wait in an office of the New York Port Authority Police. While FBI agents escorted the children into the terminal to purchase a few small trinkets for the trip, Dooms, Devos, and I held a hastily arranged press conference. "I had my Mother's Day today," I told a reporter from the *New York Post*. "It's the most beautiful day in my life. We have to start a new life together. We don't know each other anymore . . . But whatever happened, whatever they've been through, they're still my children."

We were driven onto the tarmac straight to the waiting plane, bypassing the standard boarding procedures. Marina, Simon and Moriah felt very special, like heads of state.

Everything was happening so fast, and suddenly it was time to say good-bye. I kissed the nurse on both cheeks, in the French manner. Kogut hugged me and I kissed her too, thanking her for lending me the travel bag.

"It's okay," she said, "but when you send it back, put Jean Dooms inside."

At the door of the plane, the flight attendants offered us their congratulations. They escorted the children and me, along with Dooms and Devos, to the upper level, then blocked off the stairway to the lower cabin, creating a private oasis for us. Despite their trepidation, I could sense that the children found the attention exciting and temporarily forgot about the restrictions of Shabbat. Their wide, questioning eyes told me that they were in shock.

I was careful not to move too fast. I did not want to force

myself on the children. I sat in the same row but across the aisle from them, allowing them space. They spoke to one another in Yiddish.

As the giant aircraft rumbled down the runway, Simon lowered the shade on his window, afraid to look.

Shortly after we were airborne, flight attendants presented Dooms, Devos, and me with flutes of champagne; I sipped only a tiny amount, aware that mixing alcohol with my new pregnancy, lack of sleep, and raw nerves was not a good idea.

The children read for a bit. When a light dinner was served, they looked anxiously for the small piece of paper bearing the rebbe's signature, which certified the food as kosher. Simon kept the paper as proof.

Dooms could not contain his relief and delight. He showered hugs and kisses on everyone. We snapped some photographs, including one of us sipping champagne in celebration.

After dinner, the pilot invited the children into the cockpit, where they were transfixed by the computer screens and bright controls of a modern jetliner. After a time, they walked about the lower level of the huge aircraft, accepting the good wishes of other passengers.

Later, a movie appeared on the screen. Observing Shabbat, the children refused the headphones, but they occasionally glanced up at the film.

Slowly the long, emotional day took its toll. I flipped up arm rests so that each of them could stretch out across three seats. I arranged pillows to make them comfortable. Simon and Moriah fell asleep quickly. I pulled blankets from an overhead storage compartment and tucked them around my babies. Then Marina got up and checked to make sure that her brother and sister were comfortable.

I studied my firstborn as she sat back in her seat, across the aisle from me. I realized that, for the past six and a half years, *she* had been the mother, the one responsible for her younger siblings. Take care, Patsy, I thought. Don't take all the responsibility away from her or she will not feel useful. Let her understand slowly that it is all right for her to be a sister and a teenager, not a mother. Slowly, slowly. Landing in Belgium, I realized, would not be the end but the beginning.

Now, some forty-thousand feet above the Atlantic Ocean, Marina suddenly looked very lost, very confused. Poor kids, I thought. It's happening to them again. Once more they have been pulled away from what they thought was home.

I stood up, moved across the aisle, and sat in the seat next to her. I wanted to reach out to her but was nervous and terrified of rejection. Gingerly, I took her hand, half expecting her to pull away.

She said nothing.

After only a moment, still trying not to rush, I started to pull my hand away. But with the tiniest hint of a squeeze, Marina indicated that she wanted her moist, warm hand to remain in mine.

Epilogue

We remained in Brussels until Sunday evening, and at times things were quite difficult. Marina, Simon, and Moriah had to adjust to their new surroundings and to a strange society. They even had to readjust to their names. Language was a barrier, for they had forgotten their French. Moriah could remember the lyrics of "Frère Jacques," but she did not understand the words. Walter's fluency in Dutch was helpful, for the language is similar to Yiddish.

For their part, Noélie and Gautier had to cope with the sudden appearance of three new siblings in their lives.

We were all in shock.

The phone disturbed us constantly as well-meaning friends and relatives called to express their good wishes.

During a quiet moment I confessed to Walter: "I don't dare touch them. This feels like a fragile soap bubble. I'm afraid that if I touch it, everything might disappear."

Walter did not scold or coax. He waited for the right moment, when all of us were together, and gently teased, "Look what your silly mother is doing. She doesn't dare to touch you!" The children looked at me expectantly, grinning at the challenge. Now that it was out in the open, I had to do it. I embraced them, kissing them for the first time in six and a half years.

On Monday, our first day at home, I glanced out the window to see Marina sitting in the garden, playing idly with a pile of stones, a trancelike expression on her face. I went out to her. "Marina," I said, "you have to know that today is the worst day of your life. You will see that starting tomorrow it will be better, but today is the worst. We are all lost. We have to get used to one another. Tomorrow we will start again."

I knew that the children had to have structure in their lives. I planned out the days, cramming them with activities.

Not surprisingly, most of our initial problems were related to their religious concerns. The children had left the United States with only the clothes they had on their backs. Shopping seemed as if it would be a good diversion, but it proved to be very difficult. To follow their religious principles, the girls had to keep themselves covered at all times, including during the night. Somehow, in May, we had to find long nightgowns that fully covered their legs and also buttoned all the way up to their chins. For a time, they slept with their leggings on.

Simon took it upon himself to become the kitchen police, constantly supervising my cooking techniques as I struggled to keep the food as kosher as possible. We made it clear that we would try to respect their wishes, but everyone in the family would eat the same food.

Simon caught a glimpse of Noélie and Gautier scampering bare-bottomed down the hallway for their evening bath. "Ah, disgusting!" he said, a look of total revulsion on his face.

I took him aside and explained, "This is the way we live here in Belgium, Simon. You don't have to become that way, but you may not stop us from behaving naturally. We will not shock you on purpose, but we will live the way we live. We will respect you, but you must also respect us. That is the way it has to go."

Friends and neighbors rallied around, inviting the children to play. Moriah had never been in a situation where boys and girls played together. Now, they played tag, and when one of the little boys tagged Moriah, I saw her push him away, a look of panic on her face. She burst into tears and ran to her room. "It's bad!" she wailed, "we're not allowed. What's going to happen to me?" She was terrified that God would punish her.

"Look around you, Moriah," I said. "All the boys and girls are playing together. They are normal children. Nothing bad is happening to them. God doesn't send them punishment twice a day."

Although he is not a religious person, Walter knows a great deal about the Bible. This knowledge, combined with his language ability, enabled him to discuss with the children the philosophical basis of the rules that so dominated their lives. Gradually, he was able to persuade them that Biblical passages are open to a variety of interpretations, and that God expects one to use one's own judgment, rather than to rely upon rigid doctrines.

One day as we were out shopping, I suggested lunch at Quick's. When I saw Marina, Simon, and Moriah wolf down a decidedly nonkosher meal of fish sandwiches and French fries, I knew that we had crossed an important boundary.

"How are you, Mrs. Heymans? I'm happy you have the children back." The smooth voice on the telephone belonged to Simon Friedman, the prosperous diamond merchant from Antwerp. I was immediately on guard. After a bit of small talk, Friedman asked, "And what do you want to do for their religion?"

"It's up to them to choose," I replied.

"Why don't you come and live in Antwerp?" he suggested.

"Yes," I growled. My voice was laced with sarcasm. "Sure, why not? And put them in a Hasidic school?"

Friedman resented my anger. He said, "After all I did for you, you should listen to me."

"You didn't do anything for me," I responded. "Can you tell me a single thing that you did for me? Just tell me now."

He stammered an incoherent phrase.

"See," I interrupted, "you cannot tell me what you did for me. What you did for me was to make me lose hope and time—that's what you did for me. But it didn't come to anything. And you knew exactly where the children were, from the beginning."

He did not acknowledge this. His voice regained its composure and then took on a more ominous tone as he warned, "If you keep on speaking like that, Mrs. Heymans, you will just bring more problems. And it can lead to somebody taking back the children."

"Okay, good-bye!" I said, slamming down the receiver.

Friedman also had the audacity to contact my father. First, he congratulated him on finding his grandchildren and then he reminded him of our "gentlemen's agreement" to continue educating the children in the Hasidic tradition. My father pointed out that the Hasids had not relinquished the children voluntarily. Friedman then proceeded to scold him for allowing the children to travel on Shabbat. "The FBI required it," my father said.

Friedman warned my father that if the children were not provided with the proper religious education, they might possibly be kidnapped once again.

Refusing to speak further, Papa referred him to Nadia De Vroede and Jean Dooms. Friedman contacted both of them with the same threatening message and also complained that now that I had the children back, I was unwilling to speak to him. He warned the police that my life might be in danger.

I knew that this was an idle threat; if it was real, Friedman would never have said it to the police. But I had my phone number changed to a private listing.

Many in the Jewish community were shocked to learn how Friedman worked behind the scenes in an attempt to quell unfavorable publicity—as well as to delay us—even as he supported Chaim. Today they say that such trickery is against the principles of a good Jew. Belgian authorities are investigating the man and may bring charges against him.

Herschel and Rachel Jacobovich were not arrested, because U.S. prosecutors believed there was insufficient evidence to charge that they knew the children had been kidnapped. Belgian authorities, however, have considered placing charges against them and asking for their extradition, as a means of pressuring the Satmar community to prevent further troubles.

* * *

Chaim sent a letter from prison, asking to see the children. Marina and Moriah were willing, but Simon refused to go. I insisted that several conditions be followed: They had to speak French, the visit would last no more than twenty minutes, religion would not be discussed, and two witnesses would be present—one representing my interests and one representing Chaim's.

My witness was Jean Dooms. On the day of the visit, he drove us to the prison in Leuven, where Chaim was now housed. I waited nervously in an outside reception area as Dooms took the girls to see their father. Chaim's witness was a representative from the Hasidic community.

The result was predictable. Chaim tried to tell Marina and Moriah what a bad mother I was. They tried to be respectful, but they disagreed. Defiantly, he spoke English instead of French.

After the short visit with the girls, Chaim wanted to speak with me. Confident that I now had the position of power over him, I agreed.

Chaim's Hasidic observer watched as he replayed his old themes: my father had forced me to do all this; I was a bad wife, a bad mother, a bad person. "Give me your phone number," he demanded. "I want to be able to speak with the children."

"No."

"Give me your phone number."

"No."

"Yes."

"No."

"It's private," I said. "I don't want people to have my phone number."

Chaim grinned. "Ah, it's private," he said. "Okay, don't worry. I won't give it to anybody. You can trust—"

The Hasidic witness interrupted—"You don't understand," he said to Chaim. "It's for you that it's private."

During a September 1993 trip to the U.S., Jean Dooms visited one of the Satmar elders, who admitted that he had never bothered to check the veracity of Chaim's claims that I had converted to Judaism, that the children were Jews, and that they had been abused. "Sorry," the elder said, "we made a mistake."

On December 19, 1993, Olivier joined our blended family. A healthy and happy infant, he is so well-behaved that I call him "Superbaby." Sabine did us the honor of serving as his godmother. Simon was especially pleased, because Olivier's arrival balanced the ratio of men to women in the family.

Chaim asked to see Nadia De Vroede. He said to her, "You told me that you would set me free once the children are back."

"Sorry," the prosecutor replied. "If you had helped, yes. But you didn't."

His most recent sentence for the continuing offense was supposed to run until August 1994, but an amnesty shortened the term. He was released from prison on February 7, 1994, and expelled from Belgium for the next ten years.

In February 1994, Rebbe Aryeh Zaks brought Shai Fhima to a New York courtroom as a condition of a plea-bargaining agreement that would drop kidnapping charges against Monsey Rebbe Shlomo Helbrans. In a controversial decision, Family Court Judge Bernard Stanger awarded custody of Shai to Rebbe Zaks, in order to ensure that the boy would continue to receive a religious upbringing. However, when Shai disappeared again, the kidnapping charges were refiled.

In August, Shai was detained at a Paris airport while attempting to travel on a false passport. He mysteriously disappeared from custody but soon resurfaced and was called to testify against Rebbe Helbrans.

In October, the FBI brought Simon from Belgium to appear as a prosecution witness in the trial. I accompanied him to court and was very proud as he testified with composure, despite the fact that the courtroom was filled with hostile Satmar observers; one of them was a son of Herschel and Rachel Jacobovich. Simon testified that he had seen Shai Fhima in the Kasho Drive community, in the company of one of Rebbe Helbrans's associates.

On November 9, 1994, Rebbe Helbrans was convicted of the kidnapping.

Marina, Simon, and Moriah are now flourishing. Their French and English language skills are good, they are doing well in school, and they have made new friends. They gradually gave up the Satmar traditions. Today, they are normal, happy Belgian kids.

They do not want to live with the Satmars—or their father—ever again. With his characteristic false bravado, Simon growls, "I will beat him up!"

Simon, like nearly everyone, was captivated by the warm and lively personality of Jean Dooms. Now, the same little boy who once thought that he would grow up to be a rebbe has a different ambition. He declares: "Maybe I'll be a policeman."

Acknowledgments

Thanks to all my family—my mother Mizou, my father, Jacques, my brothers, Eric, Géry, and Michel. Without your love and total support, there would be no happy ending.

Walter—you who have endured my moods, my cries of hope and despair, my fears, my silences, my doubts, my frequent and lengthy absences from home—I will never be able to love you enough.

To all those who, anonymously or not, have assisted me during the seemingly endless years of turmoil and travail—your moral and material help enabled us to hold on throughout the entire six-and-a-half-year ordeal.

Hilda Kogut, Nadia De Vroede, Jean Dooms—one of the positive aspects of this story was being able to meet and get to know you. Without you, only God knows if we would ever have found Marina, Simon, and Moriah. Forever, please accept my friendship and gratitude.

Sabine, the sister I never had, and Paul—without you this nightmare would have been so much harder to survive. The depth of my gratitude is difficult to express.

Echo and Samaritan: although your identities remain hidden, my appreciation to you does not. Thank you.

P.H.

*   *   *

Many people have contributed unselfishly to the production of this book, and several must be singled out for special mention.

Thanks are due to Bernard Fixot, Antoine Audouard, and Susanna Lea of Editions Fixot for their unwavering support, and to our agent Mel Berger of the William Morris Agency for his always professional and welcome efforts on our behalf.

We are also extremely appreciative of the time and effort Sam and Caroline Frye gave to the successful completion of this project. Their careful comments were extremely valuable to us. Thank you.

W.H./M.H.